To

Bill, Mary and Jim Rogers,
who I feel are also
"my children."

Printed in the United States of America
First Edition
Library of Congress Catalog Card Number: 61-13153

The Will Rogers Book

compiled by

PAULA MCSPADDEN LOVE

Curator, WILL ROGERS MEMORIAL

Claremore, Oklahoma

THE BOBBS-MERRILL COMPANY, INC.
A SUBSIDIARY OF HOWARD W. SAMS & CO., INC.
Publishers • INDIANAPOLIS • NEW YORK

THE WILL ROGERS BOOK

“想い”と“頭脳”で稼ぐ
社会起業・実戦ガイド

「20円」で世界をつなぐ仕事

TABLE FOR TWO
International 事務局長
小暮真久

日本能率協会マネジメントセンター

「20円」で世界をつなぐ仕事

おや おや

こりゃ 立派な
おなかだ

そうか

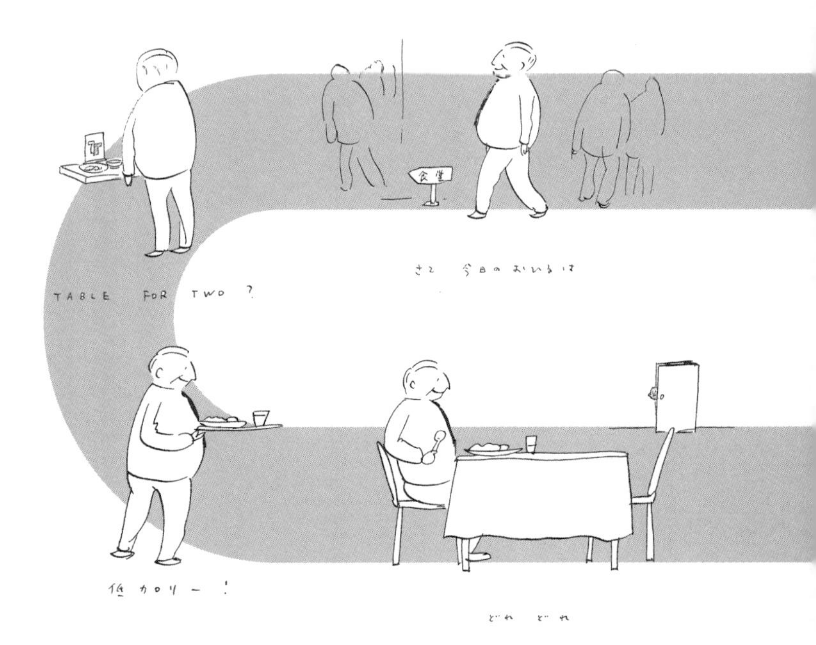
食堂
さて 今日のおひるは
TABLE FOR TWO ?
低カロリー！
どれ どれ

TABLE FOR TWO
2人の食卓

はじめに

社会起業家という仕事

仕事って何だろう？
モノやサービスをつくったり売ったりして利益を上げる、あるいは、そういうことを行っている企業に所属して自分の力を役立たせること。
おそらく、ほとんどの人は、そんなふうに考えているのではないでしょうか。
資本主義の経済では、利益追求の競争によって社会が発展していくという前提があるので、どうしても「仕事は会社の利益を上げるためにする」という考え方が主流になります。
だから、僕のやっているような、「社会事業」というもの、そして「社会起業家」と呼ばれる人々のやっていることが一般の人から仕事として理解されにくいのは、当然のことだと言っていいでしょう。

でも、社会事業というものは、利益を追求しないわけではないのです。主に社会事業を担っている団体の総称が「非営利団体」だというのも、誤解を受ける一因なのですが、「利益を上げなければ事業活動が継続できない」という点は、一般の事業も社会事業も同じです。

違うのは上げた利益の使い道です。一般の事業では、利益は主に出資した株主に還元されます。対して社会事業では、利益は再び社会を変えるための活動に使われるのです。

現在、世界の政治や経済のシステムは、残念ながら完璧とはほど遠い状態にあります。そうでなければ、地球温暖化、貧困や格差、紛争やテロなどの地球規模の課題がこれだけ起こっている理由を説明できません。そして、完璧ではないからこそ、誰かがその矛盾や歪みを正していく役割を引き受けなければならないのです。

もちろん、それは国や政治家の仕事でもあります。けれども、グローバル化が進み、国境を越えて資本や情報が行き来する現代においては、多くの社会問題はもはや国単位の取り組みでは意味をなさず、国や政府といった既存の枠組みを超えて解決を図らなければ、どうにもならないところまできているのです。

また、今こうしている間にも、救いの手を必要とする人がいるという現実を前にして、いずれ為政者がなんとかするだろう、などと悠長なことを言っている余裕はありません。

そんな社会が抱えている問題に光を当て、解決策を模索し、人類全体が幸せになる方向に国や人々を導く。僕がやっているのはそういうことであり、それが社会起業家という人たちなのだと思います。

「就職先」としての社会事業

日本では、社会事業というと、正義感の強い人が集まって手弁当で行う善意のボランティアや左翼系の思想活動のように思われがちですが、それは正しくありません。確かにそういった団体や活動があるのも事実でしょう。でも、僕のやっている社会事業は、あくまでビジネス＝仕事なのです。

仕事である以上、厳しく結果を求められるし、その結果に対する責任も生じます。利益を上げ続けるためには緻密な戦略も練らなければなりません。営業やマーケティング、ファイナンスなどの知識やスキルも要求されます。

そう見ていくと、目指すゴールがちょっと違うだけで、やっていることは一般の事業と

たいして差はないのです。また、そこで働く人は、定時に出勤し、営業に出るときはスーツを着てネクタイを締め、月末には給料を受け取るという点も、一般的なビジネスパーソンと変わりないと言えます。

社会事業を仕事にしているからといって、清貧の暮らしを強いられるとか、既にビジネスで成功した人だけにしかやる資格がない、というのも誤解です。

今どき、「会社のために生活のすべてを犠牲にする」という人がいないように、「人生を捧げなければ社会事業なんてできない」と考えるのはまったくのナンセンスです。

ただ、日本では社会事業は歴史が浅い上に、それがどういうものかという説明もこれまで十分されてこなかったので、正しく理解されていないのは仕方がない面もあります。正直に言えば、僕自身も以前から社会事業に関心はありましたが、それが仕事として成り立つという実感が持てるようになったのは、実際に自分がそこに飛び込んで、さらにしばらく経ってからのことでした。

もちろん、これまでも本業に加えて社会貢献に熱心に取り組む企業はたくさんありました。でも、今起こっている変化は、「社会事業そのもの」をビジネスとする企業や団体がどんどん増え、そこを働く場とする人もどんどん増えている、という事実なのです。

僕はこの本を通じて、一般の企業で働くことも、社会事業を行なう団体で働くことも、単なる職種の違いでしかないということを、ちゃんと説明していきたいと思います。

就職先や転職先の選択肢として社会事業もある、ということはもっと広く認知されていいはずです。今、この新しい分野の仕事はどんどん増えているのです。「社会を変えたい」という想いとチャレンジ精神のある人にとって、社会の歪みを改め、よりよくしていく、というこの分野の仕事は、とてもやりがいのあるものに感じられるはずです。

誰もが、お金をたくさん稼げばそれだけ幸せだと感じるわけではないでしょう。中には人を笑顔にしたり、感謝の言葉をかけてもらったりすることを、お金をたくさん稼ぐよりも価値がある、と感じる人もいることでしょう。

そういう人たちが、そんな自分の想いを実現できる仕事があるって、素晴らしいことだと思いませんか?

テーブル・フォー・ツーって？

NPO法人「TABLE FOR TWO International（テーブル・フォー・ツー＝TFT）」の事務局長、というのが、現在の僕の肩書きです。
全世界にいる六十七億人のうち十億人が、食事や栄養を十分に摂ることのできない貧困状態に置かれています。その一方で、日本を含む先進国では、ほぼ同じだけの数の人が、食べ過ぎによる肥満や生活習慣病に悩んでいるのです。
TFTはこの「食の不均衡」を解消し、先進国と開発途上国の人々をともに健康にすることを目指し、二〇〇七年二月に発足しました。

TFTがやっていることを簡単に説明しましょう。
社員食堂を持つ企業や団体と提携して、通常より低カロリーで栄養バランスのとれた特別メニューを提供してもらいます。そして、そのメニューの価格は二十円を上乗せして設定します。その二十円は寄付金としてTFTを通じてアフリカに送られ、現地の子どもたちの給食費にあてられます。つまりは、「食糧が余っている先進国」と「食糧が足りない

開発途上国」の、世界的な食糧の不均衡を解決する、というしくみなのです。
「二十円」という値段には大きな意味があります。
二十円は、ＴＦＴが支援しているアフリカの子どもたちが学校で食べる給食一食分の値段なのです。つまり、ＴＦＴのヘルシーメニューを選ぶと、その人は自動的にアフリカの子どもに給食を一食寄付したことになる、という寸法です。

普通にランチを食べることがそのまま社会貢献になるので、面と向かって寄付だ募金だ、と言われると思わず構えてしまう人も、抵抗なく参加することができます。いいことをしながら自分自身も健康になれるので、これまでのボランティア活動にありがちだった義務感や心理的強制といった重苦しさがないところも、ＴＦＴの活動が多くの人に支持される理由になっています。ＴＦＴを導入した企業側が、ＣＳＲ（企業の社会的責任）活動として対外的にアピールできることもポイントです。

ＴＦＴは創設されてからまだ二年。動き出したばかりなので、もちろん不十分な点もたくさんあります。でも、まだそんな段階にあるにもかかわらず、既に約百もの企業・団体がＴＦＴに参加してくださり、六十万食の給食をルワンダ、ウガンダ、マラウィの三ヵ国

の子どもたちに送ることができました。六十万食の給食というのは、延べ六十万人の人がＴＦＴに参加してヘルシーメニューを食べてくれた、ということであり、二千七百人のアフリカの子どもたちが一年間給食を食べられる、ということでもあります。ＴＦＴを導入する企業・団体は、日本を代表する大手企業をはじめとして、参議院食堂やほぼすべての中央省庁、そして全国の大学などに広がっています。活動の輪は海を越えた広がりも見せ、インドやアメリカの社員食堂や世界の政界、財界の要人が集まった国際会議のランチ会場などでもＴＦＴプログラムが実施されました。この実績は、僕たちの理念や方向性が決して間違っていない、という自信につながっています。それだけ多くの人がＴＦＴの活動に期待してくれていることの証左なのだと思っています。

事実、立ち上げからこれまでに数多くのメディアの方が取材に来てくださいました。また、政治家や閣僚、アーティストといった人の中にも、ＴＦＴに関心を持つ人は多く、イベントに足を運んでくださったり、寄付をしてくださったりする人もどんどん増えています。第一線で活躍するビジネスパーソンや経営者の中には「中途半端な社会貢献なんて意味がない」「自分には関係ないし、忙しくて時間もない」と言う人もいます。けれども、そういう人たちがメディアで取り上げられたＴＦＴを知り、僕たちのビジネスや戦略を理

解して、「これは今までの社会貢献とは違うから、仕事として協力したい」と言ってくれるのです。そして実際に、時間を割いて彼らの経験や知識や商材を提供してくれています。
僕が出演したラジオをたまたま聴いていた人が寄付金を送ってくれたり、「自分の故郷に関心を持ってくれてありがとう」とウガンダの方が突然事務所にやってきたり、そういったうれしい驚きも日々あります。そして、そのたびにこの事業への期待の大きさと、責任の重さを感じるのです。

「ワクワクしながら働く」ということ

「天職」というものがあるとしたら、僕は三十代半ばにしてようやくそれに出会えた、と実感しています。
しかし、「天職に出会う」ということは、その仕事をしていればつらいことが一つもないとか、毎日が楽しくてたまらないとかいう意味ではありません。むしろ、この社会事業という仕事は、これまでにやってきたどの仕事よりも苦労が多いような気がします。
なぜかと言えば、まずは社会事業に対する世間の見方が挙げられるでしょう。特に日本

の場合は、「社会事業なんて仕事じゃない」「善意のある人が無償でやるべきこと」と考える人が多く、そういう人からの言葉で落ち込むこともあります。

あるいは、一般的なビジネスとの違いからくるものもあります。

たとえば、提携をお願いしている企業の方から「資料を至急百部送って」という依頼を受けたとします。普通のビジネスであれば、ごく当たり前の要求でしょうが、できたてのNPOである僕たちはギリギリの人員と予算で活動をしているので、そうした依頼にも「一部お送りするので、あとはそちらでコピーしてください」といった対応になってしまいます。ただ、それだけでは気分を害される方もいるでしょうから、「今、スタッフ二人だけでやっており、予算もギリギリなのでどうかご容赦願います」と言って、その都度僕たちの状況を説明しています。このように日々の事務的なやりとりだけでかなりの神経を使う、というのもちょっとつらいところです。

それから、スタッフの報酬の問題もあります。

アメリカなど社会事業が仕事として根付いている社会では、大規模なNPOで働くスタッフは一般の企業に勤める人と遜色ない収入を得ているのが普通です。そうでなければ

優秀な人材から見向きもされない、という現実があるからです。しかし、残念ながら、日本のＮＰＯにはまだそれだけのステイタスがなく、財務的な基盤も脆弱です。

僕もＴＦＴが事業として成長するまで、自分を含めたスタッフが薄給なのは仕方がないことだと思っています。ところが、わずかであっても給料を取ること自体がよくない、と言う人もいるのです。「社会事業をやるならボランティア＝無給でやれ」と言われると、「僕たちにも生活があるので」という話をさせてもらいますが、そういうことが何度もあると、ちょっとげんなりするのも事実です。

そんなもろもろのことがありつつも、僕が今の仕事を天職だと思うのは、どんなにつらい思いをしても、これは「僕がやるべきことなんだ」という確信があるからです。

これまでは、どんなに成果を出し、たくさん給料をもらっても、「もっと他にやるべきことがあるのではないのか」という、どこか居心地の悪い感覚が頭の片隅から去ることはありませんでした。今はそういう迷いのようなものが、まったくと言っていいほどないのです。

これは、「やりたかったことをやっている」という、単なる自己満足とは少し違います。

これまで、日本が国際社会に貢献することといえば、ＯＤＡを通じてお金を出すことしかない、と思われていました。その日本と日本人が、地球から貧困を追放するしくみを考え、それを世界中に広めようとしているのです。そして、それが現実のものとなる確かな手ごたえを、今の仕事からは感じるのです。

これまで、「仕事というのはつらいものであり、意に染まないこともやらなければならない」とされてきました。小さいころ抱いていた夢や希望も会社に入ったら最後、自分の中に閉じ込めなければならない、多くの人がそう思って働いてきたのではないでしょうか。

でも、それは本当でしょうか？　小さいころの夢や希望は、その人の一生を方向付ける「想い」の根幹を成すものであるはずです。この想いを素直にいかせる仕事こそ、その人にとっての天職であるはずです。

僕自身、いくつかの仕事といろいろな悩みを経て、ＴＦＴの仕事に出会いました。そして今、想いをいかして働くことがいかに自分にとって自然で楽しいことか、それを心から味わっています。

人は何のために仕事をするのでしょうか？

これが正しい、と思われてきた価値観が一瞬で壊れる今の時代にあって、もはや自分だけが幸せになるための働き方や生き方といったものはあり得ない、ということに多くの人が気付きはじめています。

想いを実現すること、そしてその想いとは、自分だけではなく、他人を思いやる気持ちであること。自分だけではなく、他人を幸せに、そして社会をよいものにすること。これが、社会事業に限らず、これからの時代の「働く意味」なのだと思うのです。

今はまだ微力ですが、日本ではじまったＴＦＴがやがて各国に広がり、一大ムーブメントを引き起こす。そして世界中の人たちがＴＦＴに参加したとき、この地球上から貧困が消える。

そのときのことを想像すると、僕は胸の高まりを抑えることができず、思わず叫び出したい気持ちにすらなります。日々こんな気持ちでのぞめる仕事が他にあるなら、教えて欲しいくらいです。

僕は、自分を特別だとか特殊な能力や才能にあふれている、とか思ったことは一度もありません。どこをとってもどこにでもいる普通の人間でしょう。けれども、そんな僕でも、

自分の想いが充足される満足感と、この仕事は自分がやるべきなんだ、という使命感を感じ、社会とつながる実感を持って、毎日ワクワクしながら働くことができるのです。

どうすればそうなれるのか。僕にも答えそのものはわかりません。

その代わりに、僕がこれまで何を考えてどう生きてきたか、そして今、何をしているのか。そのことについて、この本でご紹介できればと思っています。

そんな僕のこれまでが何らかのヒントになって、天職に出会える人が出てくるなら、こんなに嬉しいことはありません。

二〇〇九年　二月　小暮真久

目次

「20円」で世界をつなぐ仕事

はじめに

第1章 TFTのビジネスモデルと苦難の創業期

第2章 世界最高峰のコンサル会社からNPOへの転身

僕が自分の「想い」を見付けるまで……84

社会起業にビジネススキルをいかす

Profit【利益・成果】——収益を上げ続け、最適な投資をする……156

終章

「しくみ」と「想い」が大きなつながりをつくる

おわりに

第1章

TFTのビジネスモデルと苦難の創業期

テーブル・フォー・ツーの誕生と出会い

企業の社員食堂にカロリーを抑えたヘルシーメニューを加えてもらい、その代金のうちの二十円が開発途上国の子どもたちの給食一食分として寄付される。そのことで、貧困とメタボリック・シンドローム（メタボ）という二つの社会課題を同時に解決することを目指す。

これがテーブル・フォー・ツー（TFT）のコンセプトです。

このコンセプトができあがったのは、二〇〇六年の夏、カナダ・バンクーバーで行われた「ヤング・グローバル・リーダーズ会議」の席上でした。

世界中のトップリーダーが一堂に会するダボス会議の主催者でもある「世界経済フォーラム」。ここでは、さまざまな分野で実績を上げ、さらに将来にわたって活躍が期待できる四十歳以下の若手を「ヤング・グローバル・リーダー」として認定しています。

世界中から毎年二百～三百人が選出されるこのリーダーに、二〇〇五年には現在TFTの代表理事を務める近藤正晃ジェームスら数人の日本人が選ばれました。

会議のテーマは「世界の飢餓と飽食」。それまでは、社会問題というと欧米人の意識が高く、日本人は会議でも聞き役に回ることが多かったのですが、このときは近藤たちが「世界をうならせる国際貢献のアイデアを日本人が出そう」と意気に燃えていました。必死で知恵を絞り、その結果生まれたのがＴＦＴのコンセプトだったのです。

残念ながら、僕はその誕生の瞬間には立ち会っていません。僕がＴＦＴのことをはじめて知ったのは、ちょうどその会議の開かれた一年後。前職の先輩として出会った近藤から教えてもらったのです。

それでも、説明を聞いたときすぐに、これはすごいシステムだと感じました。感動すら覚えたのです。当時、社会事業に関心を持ちはじめていた僕にとって、彼の口から出てくるＴＦＴの構想は衝撃的なものでした。

従来の社会貢献というのは、「持てる人から持たざる人への、善意に基づいた施し」という考え方で行われるものがほとんどでした。僕自身、社会事業というのはそういうものだと、無意識のうちに思い込んでいました。

ところが、ＴＦＴは、寄付をする方が飽食ゆえに抱える肥満・メタボという問題も一緒

に解決してしまおう、という画期的なものだったのです。

寄付にあてる二十円という金額にも無理がありません。しかも、それはランチの価格に含まれているので、新たに財布を開かなくて済むというのがいい。何より僕が感心したのは、「二十円が開発途上国の給食一食分になる」と明確に示して、寄付する人に食糧問題にコミットしている意識を持ってもらう、というしかけが施されていた点です。

当時、既にＴＦＴのプログラムを試験的に導入している企業もあり、これが広まるのにそう時間はかからないだろうと思いました。

しかし、引き続き話を聞いているうちに、そう簡単なものではない、ということもわかってきました。コンセプトは完璧であるにもかかわらず、ＴＦＴの展開は決して順風満帆ではなかったのです。

最大の問題は「人」でした。ＴＦＴのコンセプトを考えた中心メンバーはみな本業を持つ超が付くほど多忙な人たちで、ＴＦＴの仕事に十分な時間が割くことができない状況でした。結果としてＴＦＴの導入を検討する企業へも満足のいく対応ができず、当初の見込みよりも展開に時間がかかってしまっていたのです。

図1

「食の不均衡」が引き起こす深刻な健康問題

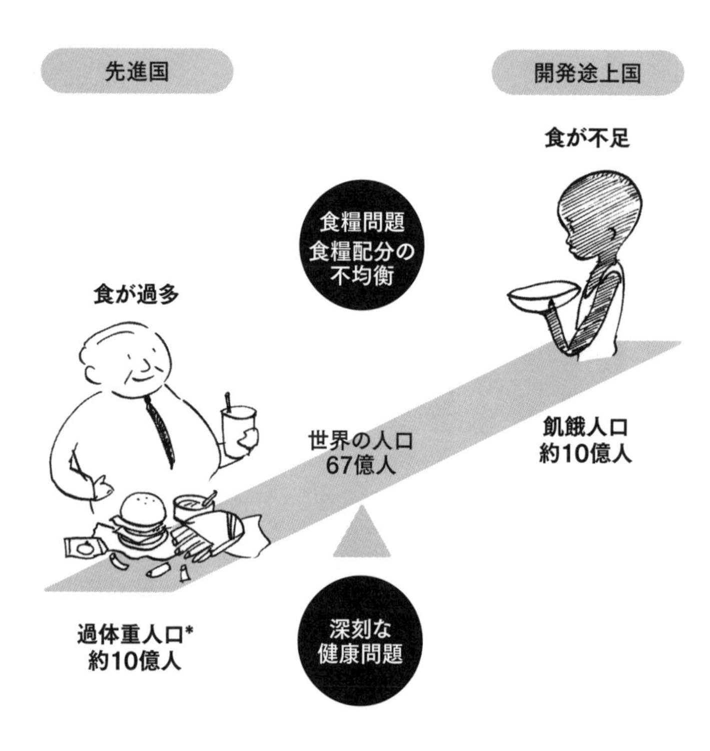

*WHOの定義では、BMI値30以上の人が「肥満」、BMI値が25-30の人は「過体重」となる。またWHOによれば、BMI値が21を超えると、生活習慣病のリスクが急激に高まることが実証されている。現在、肥満人口は約3億人と推計

「ＴＦＴの事業で起業してみないか？　専任で実務の指揮をとって欲しい」
そう近藤から頼まれたことを縁にして、僕はＴＦＴの事務局長となったのです。

フレームワークで「しくみ」を考える

ＴＦＴに参加してわかったのは、そのコンセプトは素晴らしいものの、それを実際に展開して継続させていくだけのしくみができていない、ということです。
たとえば、寄付金の二十円にしても、それを負担するのは食事をする人なのか、食事を用意する食堂側なのか、そして開発途上国に給食を提供すること自体にどの程度関わっていくのか、そうした重要なことが、まったくと言っていいほど決まっていなかったのです。

そこで僕は立ち上げメンバーと話し合いながら、しっかりしたビジネスモデルをつくり、事業計画に落とし込むことからはじめました。
事業計画と言うと、まずは数値目標というのが頭に浮かびます。
最初は僕も「○年までに給食を○食提供する」とか「○円の経費が必要だから寄付は○

円集める」といった目標から入ろうとしたのですが、途中で「これはちょっと違う」ということに気付きました。

もちろん、数値を意識すること自体は、社会事業においても重要なことです。けれども、このTFTの活動の一番の目的は「食糧問題に関する啓蒙をして、多くの人の意識を変える」ということにあります。人の意識が変わらなければ、結局のところ地球規模の社会課題は決して解決しないのです。でも、この「意識改革」という目標は、数値に落とし込むには難しい面があります。そう考えていくにつれ、数値だけをもとにして事業を考えることに、ますます違和感が募り、むしろこの違和感を大事にしよう、と思いました。

そこで、最初の段階では数値目標はざっくりしたものにしておいて、「TFTはこの社会においていかなる存在なのか」ということを、僕らなりの形で整理することにしました。

僕は前職が戦略コンサルタントだったので、どうしてもフレームワーク的にものごとを考えるクセができています。ここでも「5P」というフレームワークで整理し、それをもとにしくみをつくることにしました。

❶Purpose（目的・達成目標）

テーブル・フォー・ツーのミッションは何か。

❷Partnering（提携）

どんな組織や団体とどのような形態で連携していくか。

❸People（組織・人事）

どんな人たちを巻き込んでいくか。また、組織づくりに必要なのはどういう人か。

❹Promotion（宣伝・広報）

ミッションや活動内容を、どんな媒体や手段でどのように伝えていくか。

❺Profit（利益・成果）

どうやって事業収益を上げて目的を達成するか。

ビジネスモデル、組織、運営プロセスなどを細かく設計していくとき、必ず判断に迷う局面が出てきます。迷った際、判断の基準となるのがこの5Pです。そして、これは立ち上げ期だけでなく、今後事業活動をしていく中で僕やメンバーが判断に迷った際に、立ち返って判断の基準にするものでもあるのです。「世界の食の不均衡を解消し、深刻な健康問題を解決する」という既にあるコンセプトを大本にして、そこに「スピード」「期待成

果の大きさ」「拡張性」「独自性」「透明性」といった視点を加え、5Pのそれぞれの内容を落とし込んでいきました。

その結果は、次のようになりました。

People

［組織・人事］

組織設計と運動に携わる人たち

- 理事・事務局・相談役・支援者など、運動に関わるすべての人が同じ目線で事業に取り組む
- 日本を国際展開の本部とし、世界に支部をつくり事業を展開する。本部で主要な戦略策定を行い、各国の採用は基本的に現地に任せる
- 「目的」に共感して、かつ組織が必要とするスキルや経験を持つ人材を、事業拡大にあわせ採用する
- 専従スタッフに妥当な水準の給与を支払えるよう、資金調達と環境整備をする

Promotion

［宣伝・広報］

マスメディア・自主メディアでの情報発信

- 運動の目的がぶれないよう、核となるメッセージの発信方法を考え抜く
- 情報の透明性を大切にする。寄付や募金の使途もできる限り具体的に説明する
- 戦略を立て、少ないリソースで効果的なプロモーションができるようにする

Profit

［利益・成果］

社会的インパクトと事業収支

- 定量的な成果だけでなく、定性的な成果も追求する。すなわち、寄付金額や提携企業数だけでなく、意識改革や感動・共感を生み出すことにも重点を置く
- 社員食堂事業は、創設後3-4年で1,000団体の参加を目指し、事業収入により運営費をまかなうことを目指す

図2
TFTとは：「5P」で考える

［目的・達成目標］

取り組む社会的課題

- 「日本のカロリーOFFを、開発途上国のカロリーONへ」（先進国の食事で抑えたカロリー分を、開発途上国で栄養豊富な食事にすることで、食糧配分の不均衡を解消する）
- 先進国と開発途上国と双方の人々の健康を食・食事を通して推進する。両方の目的を同時に達成することを目指す
- 「一方が他方へ与える」という従来型の寄付集め事業とは一線を画し、「お互いをわかりあい、分かち合う」という精神を大切にする
- 上記の目的が達成されるまで取り組みを継続する

P artnering

［提携］

民間企業、公的機関、NPOなどとの協力関係

- 各分野を得意とする団体、個人と積極的に連携し、既存のしくみやノウハウを最大限活用する
- 政治・ビジネス・大学など分野の壁を越えて協力する
- 国や文化の壁を越えて日本発の社会運動を世界に発信する
- 事業企画や進行管理・調整といったプロジェクト・マネジメント機能に特化することで、価値を発揮する

「勝てるところ」を探して一番になる

次に考えたのは、他の団体とどう差別化を図るかです。「社会事業なのだから競争とは無縁」と思っている人も多いかもしれません。でも、それは違うのです。社会事業であっても、活動を継続するためには利益を上げ続けることが必要、ということは前にも述べたとおりですが、社会事業の場合には、収入＝ほぼ寄付、というケースが多い。寄付というのはその組織が生み出す価値への対価です。収入を確保するためには同業者よりも価値を発揮しなければ生き残れない、という面があるのはどこの世界も一緒です。

ただし、僕は「他の団体と戦って勝つ」という競争の部分よりも、「他の団体がやっていないことを探す」「他の団体にはない活動の特徴を出す」といった差別化の部分が大切だと思っています。

地球規模の社会的な課題が無数にある中で、やるべきこともたくさんあります。他の人が既に着手していることをやっても、先行者の方が有利に決まっています。それならば、どんなに小さくてニッチなテーマでも、自分たちの強みがいかせる、自分たちだけにしか

できないことをやろう。そういった、マーケティング用語で言うところの「ポジショニング」的な発想はとても大切です。

僕たちは、世界から食の不均衡を根絶する、という使命感を持ってTFTをはじめました。そして、それができるのは僕たちだけだ、という自負があります。TFTにお金を託せばそのお金が有効に使われる。活動に参加する人や寄付してくれる人にそう思ってもらわなければなりません。だからこそ、他の組織や団体とは違った特徴付けをして、寄付をした人から「TFTはオンリーワンの存在である」と感じてもらえるよう、いろいろな工夫をしているのです。

僕は、前職の戦略系コンサルティング会社で、そうしたビジネスの考え方を叩き込まれてきました。そういう厳しい姿勢で臨まなければ成功なんてできない、そうした考えは社会事業をするようになっても、変わることなく持っています。

そう、社会事業の世界であっても、生き残るためには戦略が必要です。

TFTの戦略を立てるにあたっても、コンサルティング会社でやってきた手順をそのまま応用してみました。すなわち、同じようなテーマを扱うNPOなどの他団体をリスト

アップし、活動内容やできている点・できていない点を研究したのです。

たとえば、ある団体では、食品メーカーが流通に乗せられなかった商品や、外食産業の余剰品などを集めて、それをホームレスの人に配る「フードバンク」という活動をやっています。食品関連の企業からすると、廃棄コストを減らせて、かつ企業のCSR活動としてアピールしやすいというメリットがあるため、寄付や募金も集めやすくなります。TFTもそれをやったらどうか、という意見が出ました。

でも、僕はそれを却下しました。その活動に社会的意義があることは間違いないでしょうが、そのためのノウハウの蓄積や知名度などの点では、先行する団体が有利なことは火を見るよりも明らかです。企業側にしても、支援するのであれば実績のある方を選ぶでしょう。同じ資金と人手を投入するのであれば、自分たちが確実に価値を発揮できる市場を見付けなければならないのです。

食糧問題という僕たちのビジネス領域には、国際的に知名度が高い団体がいくつかあります。僕はそうした団体の事業報告書や収支決算書などを手に入れて、その事業内容を研究することもしました。

この作業はとても有意義なものでした。収支決算書からは他団体のビジネスモデルの変遷なども見えてきます。また、そうした団体の支援者の方へヒアリングをしたところ、「寄付したお金が具体的にどう使われているかが見えにくい」という声がありました。こうした他団体の活動を研究することから、TFTのビジネスモデルなど、しくみづくりのヒントを数多くもらったのです。

他団体以外にも、いろいろな人から話を聞きました。たとえば、TFTの「ヘルシーメニュー」に関する規定をつくるときには、実際に食事をつくることになる給食会社の人に話を聞きました。

社会事業では、「いいことをやっているんだから」という気持ちが強くなり過ぎると、独善や独りよがりに陥る危険があります。こうしたとき、「ビジネスとして最善の方法をとる」ということに意識を集中すれば、常に外部の意見に耳をそばだて、よりよいパートナーとの提携を探るなど、合理的な判断ができるようになるのです。

電話・印鑑・口座…ないない尽くしのスタート

僕が正式にＴＦＴの事務局長になったのは二〇〇七年の八月。

それ以前に、ＴＦＴは伊藤忠商事の社員食堂を皮切りに活動をスタートしており、その後もファミリーマート、日本アイ・ビー・エム、日本航空、日本電気（ＮＥＣ）、横浜市などで試験的に導入が進んでいました。

なので、僕としては、人手が足りなくても、きちんとしたしくみに則って運営されているとばかり思っていたのです。

ですが、そうではなかったのです。

僕がＴＦＴに加わってすぐ、参加企業の担当者から、「寄付金がたまっているのですが、どこに振り込めばいいのですか？」という問い合わせがありました。立ち上げメンバーに確認すると、なんとＴＦＴ名義の口座がまだない、というのです。

「口座がなくたって、お金が集まったら誰かが受け取りにいけばいいんじゃないの？」、そんなのん気な発想もちらりと浮かびましたが、常識的に考えたら、振込口座もないよう

な団体と企業が長期的に提携してくれるはずがありません。
そこで、何はともあれ銀行に口座を開くことにしました。ところが、今度は代表印も事務所の電話番号もない、ということがわかったのです。
TFTの設立メンバーは皆理想を高く持ち、戦略やコンセプト立案には非常に秀でてはいたものの、この時点では日々の業務を滞りなく行なうための実務面はまったくといっていいほど整備されていませんでした。
何よりも僕が驚き慌てたのは、TFTがまだNPO法人の認証申請すらしていない、という事実がわかったときです。株式会社として社会事業を行なう、という選択肢もなくはなかったのですが、企業や団体と連携するTFTの事業内容を考えたときには、NPOの方が何かと有利になるだろう、と考えていました。その肝心のNPOの認証がないというのでは、いくら高邁な理想を掲げても社会から信用を得るのは至難の業です。
そこで、大急ぎでNPO法人の認証申請をすることにしました。
申請には、定款、設立趣旨書、二年分の事業計画書と収支予算書などの所定の書類を書式に則って作成して、内閣府に提出しなければなりません。これは実際やってみると手間

のかかる大変な作業でした。

書式を埋めようとすると、どうしてもすんなり書けないところが出てきます。二十円の出所や、給食費になるまでの道筋、活動資金の集め方などは、この時点では完全に固まっていませんでした。だからといって「未定」や「空欄」では審査を通りません。うまく書けないところが出てくると、僕と立ち上げメンバーが話し合って細部を詰める、という作業を書類が完成するまで延々と続けました。

とはいえ、この作業のお陰で、TFTのビジネスモデルや事業計画であいまいなままにされていたところがずいぶんクリアになりました。

たとえば、最初の構想段階では、「開発途上国に給食室をつくって実際に食事を提供する」ところまでやろうと考えていたのですが、細かくコストを計算してみると、どう考えてもお金がかかり過ぎる。それで、その分に関しては既に給食を配るしくみを持っている現地の団体と組む、という現実的な選択をしました。

ともすれば夢や理想に走りがちだったTFTの構想を、地に足の着いたビジネスモデル

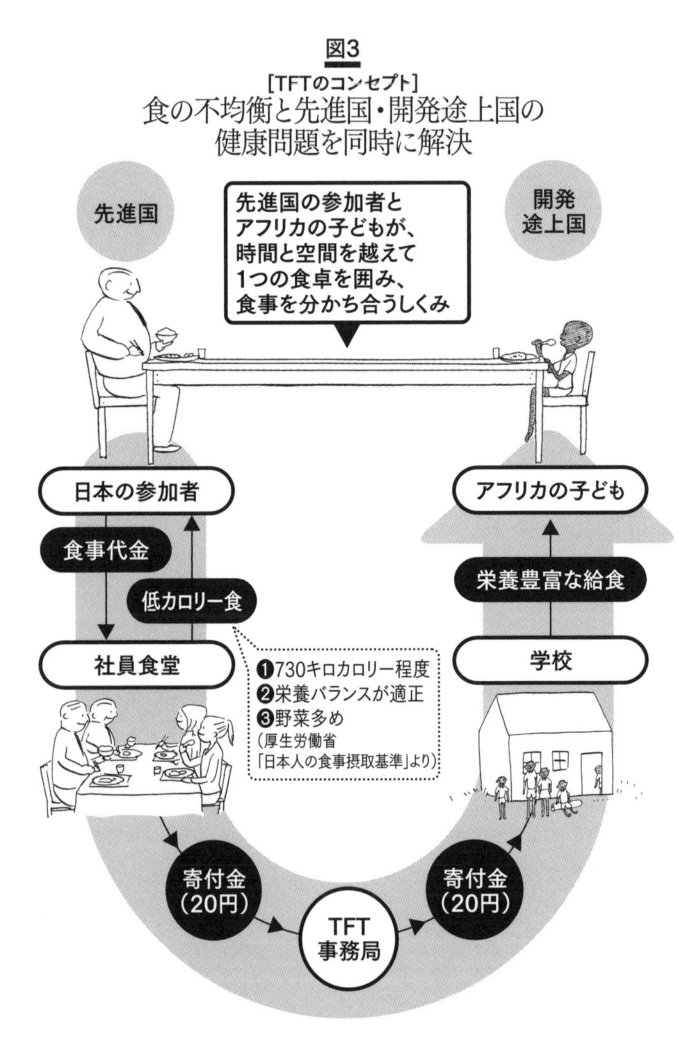
図3
[TFTのコンセプト]
食の不均衡と先進国・開発途上国の
健康問題を同時に解決
先進国
開発
途上国
先進国の参加者と
アフリカの子どもが、
時間と空間を越えて
1つの食卓を囲み、
食事を分かち合うしくみ
日本の参加者
食事代金
低カロリー食
社員食堂
❶730キロカロリー程度
❷栄養バランスが適正
❸野菜多め
(厚生労働省
「日本人の食事摂取基準」より)
アフリカの子ども
栄養豊富な給食
学校
寄付金
(20円)
TFT
事務局
寄付金
(20円)

と事業計画に落とし込むことができたという意味でも、ＮＰＯ法人の申請作業をしたことは大きかったと思います。

何もないけど、営業からはじめよう

ＮＰＯ法人の認証申請と前後して、僕はそれまで勤めていた会社に辞表を出し、晴れてＴＦＴの理事兼事務局長になりました。ここまでビジネスモデルをつくったり、ＮＰＯ法人の申請書類を書いたりしていたときは、まだ会社員の身分だったのです。それゆえ、昼間は出社して通常の業務をこなし、夜や週末にＴＦＴの仕事をする、という関わり方しかできず、どうしても時間が足りなくて満足のいく活動ができませんでした。ＮＰＯ法人の申請書類の作成が遅々として進まなかったのには、そういう理由もありました。

会社を辞め、これからは思う存分ＴＦＴの活動ができる、二足のわらじの中途半端さから解放されて、心からやりたいと思うことに専念できる。そう思うと本当に嬉しかった。でも、もちろん不安もありました。最大の懸念要素は収入面です。

僕の最初の勤務先は外資系戦略コンサルティング会社、次の勤務先は日系のエンターテインメント会社で、どちらでもそれなりの収入を得ていました。

以前、友人から、「アメリカでは大手ＮＰＯのマネジャークラスになると平均三千万円くらいの年収をもらっている」という話を聞かされて驚いたことがありましたが、それはあくまで社会事業がビジネスの一形態として認知されているアメリカだからであって、日本のＮＰＯでそんな話は聞いたことがありません。ましてや、ＴＦＴはその時点ではまだＮＰＯ法人の認証も下りていない有様でした。

ただ、そうはいっても活動資金がまったくゼロというわけではないし、僕自身の貯えも多少はあるので、まあなんとかなるだろう、と思っていました。

しかし、現実は想像以上に厳しかった。

収入は減ったどころではありません。なにしろ、それまでの三分の一以下になってしまったのです。さすがにこれでは生活もままならず、しばらくは講師業などのアルバイトをして足りない生活資金を補っていました。

ただ、社会事業に限らず、起業にはこうした試練が付きものです。これくらいのことは想定の範囲内と、自分としてはわりあい平然と受け止めていました。それに、「善行をし

ているのだから清貧で生きよう」というつもりはなく、「この困難は一時的なもので、TFTが事業として軌道にのったらそれなりの収入も得られるだろう」とも考えていました。とはいえ、はじめての経験にプレッシャーも大きく、家族に言わせると、このころの僕にはかなりの悲壮感が漂っていたそうです。

お金もそうですが、はじめて経験する社会事業の仕事自体にも厳しいものがありました。収入減は想定できても、こちらはまったくの想定外。日本で「社会起業家」を名乗って仕事をすることが、こんなに大変だとは思っていなかったのです。

「怪しい団体？」目線との戦い

NPOの認証には思ったよりも時間がかかりました。といっても書類の不備や、事業内容に問題があったというわけではなく、日本においてはどのNPOも、申請から認証までには、最大で四カ月間の審査期間を経なければならないのです。それまでは事務局長といっても、実際は単なる任意団体の代表に過ぎません。

とはいえ、今こうしている間にも、世界には貧困で苦しんでいる人や、飢餓で命を落と

す子どもがいるのです。一方で、先進国は飽食ゆえの肥満とメタボという悩みをかかえたまま。NPOの認証を待って、四ヵ月も何もしないというわけにはいきません。

とにかく今できることをやろう、そう思いました。

「では何から?」と考え、そこで出した答えは「営業」でした。

TFTを取り入れてくれそうな企業を回ることで、そうした企業と担当者のニーズを知ることができます。このニーズを体感することが、今後の活動の計画を立てるときに役立つだろう、そう思ったのです。

事務局には僕ともう一人、女性のスタッフがいるだけでした。彼女に協力してもらって企業をリストアップし、電話をかけ、担当者を紹介してもらって説明に出向く、という地道な活動をはじめました。

新規開拓はラクな仕事ではありません。誰もが好意的に話を聞いてくれるわけではないし、無視されたり手ひどく断られたりするのも日常茶飯事。僕自身、コンサルタント時代に営業関連のプロジェクトを手掛けていたこともあったので、そのくらいのことは承知しているつもりでした。

でも、ここでも現実は想像を超えたものがありました。大変だったのは、活動自体の説明に加えて、無名の団体が相手の信頼を得ることです。自分が所属する団体が「何か怪しいんじゃないの？」という目で見られることは生まれてはじめての経験だったので、これに慣れ、説得するためのノウハウを身につけるまでは本当に苦労しました。

社会事業に従事する人間は、企業などから対等のビジネスパーソンとしては見てもらえない場合が多々あります。

——自分たちは毎日額に汗してモノやサービスをつくり、市場経済の熾烈な競争を戦っているのに、そういうことと無縁の場所にいて、「地球から貧困をなくそう」なんて浮世離れしたことを言っていられるのだから、気楽なもんだよな——

あからさまには言われないものの、多くの場所でそうした目で見られ、応対をされます。おまけにまだ認証を受けたＮＰＯですらないわけですから、団体としての信用も何もあったものではありません。知名度だってゼロに等しく、いくら名刺交換をしたって〝怪しい団体〟であることに変わりはありません。

やっている事業についても、それが善意のボランティア活動ではなくビジネスなのだ、

ということを理解してもらうのが大変でした。たとえば、寄付金の一部がTFTの運営費やスタッフの給料になる、という点に納得してくれない人もいました。寄付金を集めるのも、集めた寄付金を必要な人のところに届けるのも、それから活動を広げていくのも、人手を含めたコストはかかるので、という話をしてもなかなか聞いてもらえないのです。

日本は他国に比べて社会事業の歴史が浅いので、NPOなどに対する偏見や認識不足があるのは仕方のないことです。詐欺や脱税をはたらくような、〝怪しい団体〟という見方をされることもあります。自分たちの活動を理解してもらうためには、忍耐強く説明し、実績を重ねるしかないのです。

ただ、僕も今でこそそう思えますが、当時はそうした意識がなく、訪問先から追い払われるような扱いをされるたびに傷ついていました。いっときはあまりにそうしたことが続いたもので、名刺を出すことにためらいを感じるようになってしまいました。

さらに、活動をはじめた当初は気負いもありました。

「社会事業をやっている人はビジネスマインドが低い」と思われるのがどうしても嫌だったのです。それまで勤めていた企業と同等か、それ以上にきちんとした対応をしてみせる、

と意気込んでいました。それで、人数も予算もぎりぎりのところでやっているのに、何とか相手の要望に応えようと必死にもがいていたのです。

「この資料をあと百部持ってきて」と言われても予算的に難しく、「明日契約の覚書を持ってきて」と言われても、行ける人間は僕しかいないのでとっさには対応できない。でも、「できません」と素直に言えなくて、悔しい思いばかりが募っていました。

今では、「できるだけたくさんのお金を開発途上国に送りたいので、資料は一社一部とさせてもらっています」「人手が少ないので順番に対応させていただいています。ご理解ください」とこちらの状況を包み隠さずお話しすることに抵抗がなくなりました。当時は背伸びをして何とか相手に認めてもらおうと無理をしていたのです。

誠意を持って率直に話せば誰でもわかってくれる。そのことをたくさんの経験の中から学んできました。

NPO認証と活動戦略の練り直し

二〇〇七年十月、内閣府から待ちに待ったNPOの認証決定通知が届きました。さっそ

く登記を済ませ、翌十一月、ＮＰＯ法人「ＴＡＢＬＥ ＦＯＲ ＴＷＯ Ｉｎｔｅｒｎａｔｉｏｎａｌ」がついに設立したのです。

インターナショナル、という言葉を入れたのは、ＴＦＴの活動は国際的な展開を目指すものであり、その本部となるのがこの日本なのだ、という想いがあったからです。

「テーブル・フォー・ツー」（二人のための食卓）という名前には、「一つの食卓を囲み、先進国の参加者と、開発途上国の子どもが、時間と空間を越えて一緒に食事をしている」という意味を込めました。アルファベットの「Ｔ」をかたどったロゴも赤と白の二色に分け、二人の分かち合いの意を示しています。

ＮＰＯ法人となったことで、ようやく肩の荷が少し下りました。名刺に「ＮＰＯ法人」と刷り込めるし、銀行口座も開けます。

そして、これを機会に、活動開始からこれまでの苦しかった期間の棚卸しをして、活動戦略を練り直すことにしました。

まず、営業についてです。これまでは企業の担当者と会って一社一社開拓していく方法と、協力してくれた企業トップの方から別の会社のトップを紹介してもらう方法、という

二本立てで行っていました。
　成約率だけをみれば、後者の方が断然いいに決まっています。しかし、ここはやはり地道に開拓に励む、という前者の方法を中心にすべきだと考えました。というのも、トップの一存で導入を決めても活動が長続きしないということが、この頃までにははっきりとした傾向値として出てきたからです。

　トップダウンでTFTを導入しても、実際に社員食堂にヘルシーメニューを加えて、社員に告知して、という一連の活動を担うのは、総務・人事・CSRといった部門の社員の方です。そうした現場の方たちが、「トップダウンだから仕方ない」とやらされ仕事になってしまっては盛り上がりに欠けるし、長期的に活動を続けることも難しくなる。
　TFTのプログラムは、一度参加してもらえばいい、というものではありません。ヘルシーメニューは、飽きられないように随時手を加えていく必要がありますし、TFTそのものの意義を社内の人たちに説明することも大切です。最終的には多くの人が世界の食糧問題に目を向けるよう意識改革を図ることが目的なのですから、どうしても企業担当者の方の当事者意識が大切になるのです。
　そのためには、トップダウンという空中戦よりも、時間はかかっても、総務・人事・C

SR、そして労働組合などの関係者を一人ひとり説得して回る、という泥臭い営業方法が合っていると考えました。

当初の営業活動では大企業を中心に回ることにしました。それも、各業界のトップクラスの企業に導入してもらうことを戦略の核に据えました。大企業は人や予算のリソースが豊富でかつ社員食堂を持っている可能性が高く、新しい情報への感度もいいので、初期の参加企業として適している、と考えたのです。それに、トップ企業ほど「業界で最初に導入した」というフレーズを重視する、というのも理由の一つです。

もちろん、誰もが知っているような有名企業がTFTプログラムを導入してくれれば、それがそのままTFT自体の信用拡大につながる、という計算もありました。NPOの法人格があっても信用獲得までは長い時間がかかるという現実の中、「大手企業が採用」というフレーズは、ぜひとも利用させてもらいたいものでした。

他者の「色」が付かないよう細心の注意

この時期に悩んだのは、「特定の会社にスポンサーになってもらう」という選択をどう

考えるか、という問題でした。大手企業のスポンサードを受ければ、資金をはじめとした多くの資源を提供してもらうことができるので、運営は格段にラクになります。その代わり、その企業の広報的役回りを担うことやＴＦＴの経営に対する意見を受け入れることはある程度避けられないでしょうし、スポンサーと競合関係にある企業はＴＦＴを導入してくれなくなることも予想されます。

実際にこんなことがありました。

ある大手銀行に営業に行ったところ、とんとん拍子で話が進み、すぐにでも参加したい、ということになりました。しかも、個人の寄付金二十円に加え、企業からも四十円を上乗せしてくれるという、願ってもいない好条件です。さらには寄付金振り込み用に手数料無料の口座をつくり、イベントを開催するときには本社のホールを無料で提供する、とまさに至れり尽くせりの申し出をして頂きました。

ただし、そこには一つ条件がありました。

それは寄付する先を開発途上国ではなく日本にする、ということ。その銀行は日本国内での企業ブランドの向上を望んでおり、国内問題に寄付金を使って欲しい、というのです。

確かに、日本にも貧困層に属する人たちはいます。ですが、地球規模で見ると、開発途上国の貧困と日本のそれとでは深刻さのレベルが違います。もちろん、日本の貧困はたいしたことがないから援助など要らない、というつもりはありません。同じ日本人として放っておけない社会課題であるとは思います。

けれども、そうした課題については、それを解決しようと取り組んでいる人や団体が既に存在します。なので、その領域は彼らに委ねるべきだと思いました。僕たちがやっても、そういう人たちよりもうまくはできないでしょうし、限られた資源の有効活用にもならないでしょう。

それで、先の銀行に「寄付先を日本に変更するのは無理です」という話をすると、「では別の団体と組んで展開したらどうか」という提案を頂きました。しかし、紹介された団体ともミッションが合わないことは明白だったため、結局その話はまとまりませんでした。好条件の提携だったので惜しくはありましたが、この経験から、自分たちが絶対に守らなくてはならないラインというものについて、改めて考えることができました。

僕たちのやるべきことはあくまで、「世界の食糧の不均衡を根絶する」ということです。

一社の要求に応えるために、自分たちのやるべきことから外れたことをするのはやめよう。主な収入源が寄付である以上、常に難しい選択を迫られる部分ではあります。
でも、意思決定に迷ったとき、立ち返れるＰｕｒｐｏｓｅ（目的・達成目標）を持っておくこと。そして、無所属中立であること。これから自分たちの活動を広めていくために、この二つは欠かせないはず。この経験から、そうしたことを学んだのです。

第2章

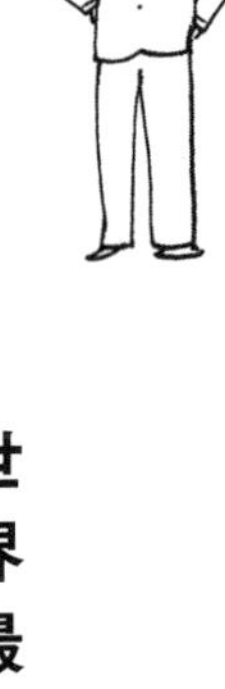

世界最高峰のコンサル会社からNPOへの転身

戦略コンサルタント時代に学んだ究極の問題解決法

僕の居場所はどこにある?

僕が社会人になったのは二十六歳、ちょっと遅めのスタートでした。大学では人工心臓の研究をしており、さらにオーストラリアへ四年間留学し、工学修士号を取得しました。

さすがにそろそろ働こうかと考え、さて、何をやろうかとあれこれ探していたとき、最初に頭に浮かんだのは、「医療機器メーカーに就職して人工心臓の研究を続ける」という選択肢でした。それで、その手の企業をいくつか訪問して話を聞いてみたのですが、どうも「ここで働きたい」という気にならないのです。学生として出席させてもらった学会でも、医療機関とエンジニア、あるいは医者同士など立場が違う人たちが各々自分たちの主

張を声高に言い合うばかりで、相手を心から理解しようという気持ちが見えないことに幻滅しました。

こういう状況の中でメーカーの研究室に入っても、きっと満足感を得られないだろう、そうした感触がずっと頭から離れませんでした。

学会で意見がまとまらないのは、異なる組織に所属する人たちを一つの旗の下に集め、同じ方角に顔を向けさせることができる「プロデューサー」がいないからだとも思いました。そう考えると、日本には、あらゆる分野でプロデューサー感覚を持った人が不足しているのです。一方で、僕自身は一つのことを極める職人のような生き方より、人と人をつないだり束ねたりすることに喜びを感じるので、ならば自分はプロデューサーのような役割を仕事にした方がいいのではないか、と思ったのです。グローバルな視野をあわせ持っているプロデューサーというのも、自分らしくていいかもしれない、と。

そこで、ある大手メーカーの門を叩いてみました。そこは日本の会社ながら世界に進出していたので、社員もみなグローバルな人たちばかりに違いない、勝手にそう判断したのです。

ところが、面接にあたって修士論文を持参したところ、面接官に「こんなもの読めるわけがない」といきなり突き返されてしまいました。なぜなら、その論文が英語で書かれていたからです。「これが日本のグローバル企業の実態なのか」とがっかりしました。オーストラリアでの四年に渡る留学生活のあとだっただけに、この国に僕の居場所はないのかもしれない、そう考えて暗澹たる気持ちになりました。

猛烈に面白かったマッキンゼーの面接

なかなかやりたい仕事が見つからず、落ち込み気味だったある日、僕の話を聞いた友人が、「ここならお前に合うかもしれない」といって紹介してくれたのが戦略コンサルティング会社、マッキンゼー・アンド・カンパニーでした。

耳慣れない社名でしたが、あらゆる分野の問題解決を手掛けるのが仕事、というところに興味が湧き、とりあえず面接を受けることにしました。

その面接が猛烈に面白かったのです。

僕がそれまでやってきた研究について、人工心臓のモデルを見せながら説明すると、

「それはこういうことだよね」と、門外漢のはずの面接官がするすると理解してくれるのです。さらに「これをこうしたらどうなの？」と次々に改良のアイデアまで出てくるので、こっちも話をしていて楽しくてたまりません。こんなに優秀な人がたくさんいる会社ならばぜひ働きたい、そういう気持ちが募りました。

何回かこうした刺激的な面接が繰り返され、最後に「うちに来る？」と聞かれたときは、「お願いします」と答えていました。

「アップ・オア・アウト」のコンサル時代

今でこそ日本でも有名になったマッキンゼーですが、僕が入社した一九九九年には、名前を言ってもわかる人はほとんどいませんでした。

しかし、本国のアメリカでは、民間企業から政府系の組織まで「困ったときに最後に助けを求めるのはマッキンゼー」というくらい、その名は鳴り響いていたのです。

入社すると、最初の一カ月間は、研修で課題分析や仮説の立て方といったマッキンゼー

流の問題解決法を叩き込まれます。具体的には「ロジックツリー」「イシューアナリシス」「ピラミッドストラクチャー」などの思考のためのツールと、「マーケティングの4P」「分析の3C」などのフレームワークと呼ばれるものを教わり、その後、さまざまなケースに沿った問題解決に実践さながらに取り組むのです。

そして、研修が終わると、いきなりプロジェクトに放り込まれます。あとは自分でサバイバルしろ、というわけです。実際、一定期間内に成果を上げる実力を付けないと自分のところに仕事が回ってこなくなるので、会社にいられなくなります。「アップ・オア・アウト」（昇進か退職か）という過酷なルールもあって、評価が規定に達していない場合にはイエローカードが出され、これが二枚たまったら実質的な退職勧告。サッカー並みの厳しい世界でまったく気が抜けません。

ただ、そういう厳しい環境の中で生き残っている人たちというのは、みんなものすごく優秀で、なおかつマッキンゼーの一員であることに強烈なプライドを持って働いています。言い方を換えると、そんな「マッキンゼーカラー」に染まれば染まるほど、ここでは仕事ができるようになるのです。

僕はこうした強烈な個性を持つ社風に惹かれつつも、どことなく違和感もありました。もともと人に合わせるのが嫌いなマイペース型人間だということに加え、入社したときには既に二十六歳になっており、国内外でいろいろな経験を積んでいたので、一つの価値観に身を委ねられるほど素直ではなかった、ということもありました。

マッキンゼーでは定期的に、さまざまな国の社員を一同に集めて研修を行います。そういう研修に参加するときも、僕は研修そのものよりも、そこに来ているちょっと毛色の変わった人たちと交流することに魅力を感じていました。

フロリダでの研修中のことです。

仲間を誘って毎晩のように遅くまで飲み歩き、空が白むころ帰ってきて、ひと眠りだけして翌日の研修に参加する、という日々。寝過して遅刻することもしばしばです。それがあまりにも続いたので、この期間中には、朝の研修に出てこないことを、僕の名前の「マサヒサ」をもじって「マサイング」と呼ぶようになりました。「そろそろ時間だけど、彼はまだ来てないね」と誰かが言うと、「ああ、昨日はかなり飲んでいたみたいだから、午前中は〝マサイング〟だろ」と答える、といったように使うわけです。

研修に集まる仲間は、入社した年が近いだけで、あとは国籍も経歴もてんでバラバラのメンバーです。でも、飲みながら話をしてみると、皆同じようなところで悩み、苦しみつつ、日々格闘しているのです。そうしたことを話し合って人と共感し合うことが、僕にとっては研修そのものよりもよっぽど楽しく感じたのです。

そんなマイペースな僕が途中でドロップアウトすることもなく、ビジネスアナリストからアソシエート、マネジャー職と、わりあい順調にキャリアパスの階段を上がることができたのは、周囲の人たちの力によるところが大きかったと思います。

同じチームのメンバーやクライアントから信頼されているのがわかると、「期待に応えよう」「もっと喜んでもらいたい」という気持ちが湧いてきて、実力以上の力が出てしまうのです。逆に、そういう人間臭さがあまり感じられないプロジェクトは、どこか力が入らず、当然結果も振るいません。上司からはいつも「プロジェクトによって成果に差があり過ぎる」と注意されていました。

僕が得意だったのは営業関連のプロジェクトです。クライアント企業の営業担当者は、情熱や想いというものを大切にしている人が多く、自然と馬が合いました。そうした人た

ちの想いに応えつつ、自分の問題解決力をその人たちのためにいかす仕事は、とてもやりがいがあったのです。

マッキンゼーで叩き込まれた究極の問題解決法は、どこの場においても応用できる非常に優れたものでした。僕もこれを身に付けて実践してきたお陰で、「どこにいってもやっていける」という自信を持つことができました。

これは余談ですが、あるとき、友人たちと「彼女とうまくいかない理由をロジックツリーにしてみよう」とマッキンゼー流で問題を整理してみたのですが、こんなところにもかなり使えることがわかりました。

その一方で、マッキンゼーにいた七年間ずっと、どこか違和感が拭えなかったことも事実です。マッキンゼーの価値観は「論理がすべて」というもの。「その人ならではの感性や直感」といったものは、ほとんど評価されません。

論理や数値といった「左脳的なもの」、感性や直感といった「右脳的なもの」

僕はこの二つのバランス・融合にこそ価値があると思っていたので、どうもこの「左脳絶対」の価値観に染まり切ることができなかったのです。

「あなたにはわからない」限界を突きつける一言

マッキンゼーでは、大企業の組織変革から映画館の立て直しまで、さまざまなプロジェクトにかかわりましたが、数として一番多かったのは、大学までに学んだ専門性が直接いかせる医療機器や製薬といったヘルスケア関連の仕事です。

マッキンゼーに勤めて五年経ったとき、僕はニューヨークに一年間駐在することになりました。ここで関わった日本の製薬会社のプロジェクトが、僕にとっての大きな転機となりました。

そのクライアントはアメリカに進出したものの、現地で採用した社員の定着率が悪く、生産性が上がらない、という状態にありました。組織・業務を改革して仕事の効率を上げることが、僕らに与えられたミッションでした。

僕はマネジャー役としてこのプロジェクトに参加し、苦労しながらも最後には、ほぼ完璧と思われる業務システムをつくりあげることに成功したのです。その会社の現地法人の日本人社長もたいへん喜んでくれました。

プロジェクトが終了したあと、その社長に一対一での会食に招かれました。社長は僕の労をねぎらってくださったあと、「でもね、君は民間企業に勤めたことがないでしょう。だから、私たちの気持ちの本当のところはわからないよ」と言葉を継いだのです。

三カ月間、それこそ身を粉にしてその会社のために働き、これだけの成果を上げたのだから、当然その社長からも全幅の信頼を得ているものだとばかり思っていました。それなのに、当の相手はそうは思っていなかったのです。これはショックなんてものではありませんでした。

このとき、あらためてコンサルタントという仕事の限界というものを感じました。マッキンゼー流のやり方は確かに効率的ですし、問題解決には抜群の効力を発揮します。でも、そればかりやっていると頭でっかちになって、企業経営の現場が見えなくなってしまう。現場で揉まれない限り、決して出せない人間としての幅や厚み、そうしたものが僕には欠けている。その社長はきっとそういうことを言いたかったのでしょう。

僕自身もニューヨークに来てみて、結局ここでの仕事も東京でやっていたのとたいして変わらないと気付いてから、そろそろ「マッキンゼー後」を考えるべきタイミングなのかな、という気持ちが、少しずつ芽生えはじめてきました。ニューヨーク駐在を終えて東京

に戻ると、さらにこの思いは強まりました。

次は「実業」をやっている会社で働いてみよう。そう決心するまで、それほど時間はかかりませんでした。

「一緒に働きたい」で転職を決意

マッキンゼーに辞意を伝えたものの、転職のあてがあるわけではありません。日本に帰国してヘッドハンターに相談したところ、外資系のファンドをいくつか紹介されました。ヘッドハンターは「これからは金融が時代の花形だ」と言うのですが、そう言われてもどうもしっくりこない。僕はマッキンゼー時代から、金融やITにはまるで興味が湧かなかったのです。そして、心底好きにならないことには、さっぱりパフォーマンスが上がらない、という自分の特性もよくわかっていました。

僕がやりたいことっていったい何だろう?

落ち着いて考えてみると、自分でも意外でしたが、そのときに心惹かれたのがエンター

テインメント業界でした。感性やクリエイティビティという右脳的要素が強い業界に魅力を感じていたのです。

それで、ヘッドハンターに「エンターテインメント関連」で「実業をやっている企業」という自分の希望を伝えました。すると、数日して映画会社・松竹の資料が届けられたのです。松竹と言えば、『男はつらいよ』

僕の父親は土日休みの仕事ではなかったので、幼い頃は一緒に遊んでもらった記憶があまりないのですが、なぜか『男はつらいよ』のシリーズだけはよく父親と映画館に観にいったことを覚えていましたので、松竹という社名には、不思議な縁のようなものを感じました。また、社長が交代したばかりで、これから社内改革を進めるところだという点も、安定よりも変化が好きな僕にとっては願ったり叶ったりでした。

映画業界のことはあまり知りませんでしたが、何はともあれ面接を受けてみることにしました。

そして、その面接がこれまた強烈なものでした。

会社での面接は形ばかりで、そのあとにインターネットや歌舞伎関連の新規事業の担当部長である井上貴弘さんに飲みに連れていかれたのです。気が付いたら朝の五時になって

いました。時間を忘れるくらいこの井上さん、話がめちゃくちゃ面白いのです。
その日別れてから、仕事の説明をまるで受けていない、ということに気付きました。それで、「この前は仕事の内容を伺うのを忘れてしまったので、もう一度時間をください」と井上さんに連絡すると、今度は蕎麦屋に呼ばれてまた朝まで飲み明かしです。そして、またもや仕事の話はまったくないのです。
知り合ったばかりの人間と、二日間も仕事の話抜きで語り明かせてしまう井上さんに、僕はすっかりしびれてしまいました。そして、こういう人がいる会社で働いてみたい、という気持ちになったのは言うまでもありません。
結局、僕はいつでも、事業の内容や仕事の中身よりも、誰と一緒に働くのかという、人とのつながりの部分を一番大切にしているようです。

誰かのためになっていないと力が出ない

松竹入社後は経営企画部に配属されました。希望は井上さんのいる新規事業部だったのですが、社長は会社の経営全般を見て欲しいと考えていたらしいのです。でも、経営の手

伝いをするのだったら、わざわざマッキンゼーを辞めた意味がありません。

それで、「一番業績の悪いところでいいから現場に出して欲しい」としつこくお願いし、最終的に、経営企画の仕事をしながらという条件付きで、ビデオ事業部に配属されることになりました。現場の業務を改善する、というのが僕の役回りです。

配属後には、五十人ほどいる部署のメンバー一人ひとりにインタビューし、その結果をチャートにまとめ、そこから問題点を抽出する、という作業をやりました。ここでも、これまでの僕なりのやり方を踏襲して、コワモテの古株社員たちと毎日飲み歩き、時間をかけて本音を言い合える関係をつくっていきました。問題点を探り、改善策を考え、半年ほどそうした作業に明け暮れて、さあいよいよ改革に着手しよう、というところで何と僕は配置転換になってしまったのです。「あとは別の人間にやらせるから」というのです。

その後も、業績の悪い子会社の経営改善案をつくったり、マッキンゼー時代のコネクションを利用して有力海外メディアとのM&Aを提案したりしましたが、どうも僕が経営企画以外の仕事をすることはあまり歓迎されていないようでした。たいていは「それは君の仕事じゃないでしょう」と言われてしまいます。何か新しいことをしようとしても「仕事が増えるんだよ」と迷惑がられることもありました。

しかし、経営企画の仕事だけやっていればいいと言われても、そこにそれほど仕事があるわけではありません。マッキンゼー時代には時間がいくらあっても足りず、いつも追い詰められているような状態で働いていましたが、だからこそ、やり遂げたときの達成感や満足感は格別だったし、自分の能力が格段に伸びていく感触がありました。

ところが、ここでは能力を伸ばすどころか、力を使い切らないまま一日が終わってしまう感じなのです。仕事をしたいのにできないというのがこんなに苦しいとは、それまでは思ってもみませんでした。でも、僕以外の社員はみんな、それなりに納得して働いているように見えます。僕だけがこの空気に順応できないまま悶々としているのです。

社会問題をテーマにした映画をプロデュースしようか、とも考えましたが、その企画を通すには、会社にこれだけの利益をもたらすという提案書をつくって承認されなければなりません。営利企業にいるのですから当たり前の話なのですが、そのときはなぜかその現実を素直に受け入れる気になれませんでした。

地球温暖化や南北問題、中東の紛争など世界中には解決しなければならない課題が山のようにあって、苦しんでいる人もたくさんいるというのに、自分は会社が利益を上げるこ

とだけに注力しなければならない。

だけど、これって自分が本当にやりたかったことじゃない気がする。僕は、もっと直接世の中のためになる仕事がしたい。

三年は頑張るつもりで入った会社でしたが、そうした想いは日に日に募っていきます。しかし、そうはいっても、いったいどういう仕事であれば自分の気持ちを満足させてくれるのか、当時はよくわかりませんでした。

模造紙一枚に「自分の想い」を書き出す

迷った挙句、これは「自分をもう一度見つめ直さないと答えが出ない」という結論に達しました。

そこで大きな模造紙を買ってきて、物心ついたときから今日までを振り返り、どんなときに心の底から楽しかったか、何をつらいと感じたかといったことを、とにかく思い出せる限り、雑多にそこに書き出してみました。「これは一気にやらないといけないな」と思ったので、部屋に閉じこもり、半日ほどひたすら書き続けたのです。

その大きな模造紙にはこんな言葉が並びました。

「感情・共感・共鳴を大切にしたい」
「クリエーションが原動力」
「高い目標に、仲間と、チームで向かっていく」……

この作業をしてみて、三つのことがはっきりしました。
まずは、常に新しいことを生み出せる環境に身を置いていたい。そして、その価値観を共有する仲間と一緒に働きたい。さらには、誰かのためになっている実感を持てる仕事でないと力が出ない、ということでした。

「ソーシャル・セクター」の存在を思い出す

この作業から思い出したのが、マッキンゼーのニューヨーク時代のエピソードです。
当時、同じチームで働いていた仲間が、「このプロジェクトが終わったら、あるＮＰＯの経営メンバーに加わるんだ」と話すのを聞いて、非常に驚いたことがありました。当時

の僕はNPOというのはボランティアや慈善団体のようなものだと思っていたので、そんなところに行って食べていけるのだろうか、と思いました。ところがそのアメリカ人の同僚は「いや、給料は今より上がるんだよ」とあっさり言うではありませんか。

「どういうことなんだろう？」と思っていろいろ調べてみたところ、アメリカではNPO、財団などの社会事業分野＝ソーシャル・セクターの団体が一般の企業と同じように社会的に認知されていることがわかりました。そういえば、マッキンゼーと仕事のつながりのあったところにも、ビル＆メリンダ・ゲイツ財団やクリントン・グローバル・イニシアティブといった団体がいくつもあったことを思い出しました。

また、HIV撲滅のための世界最大の基金であるグローバルファンドの理事をマッキンゼーの元代表ラジャ・グプタが務めている、というように、戦略コンサルタントからソーシャル・セクターへというのが、一つのキャリアパスとして成立しているということもわかりました。

当時はこれだけ調べて「ふーん、すごいな」と思っていただけだったのですが、仕事に行き詰まって人生の棚卸しをしていたとき、この記憶がふっと頭に浮かんできたのです。

「僕の居場所はもしかしたら社会事業の分野にあるのかもしれない」、そういう思いが湧いてきました。

しかし、そうしたキャリアパスは、当時の日本ではまるでリアリティがありませんでした。大企業から社会事業団体に転職したという人は、少なくとも僕の周囲には一人もいませんでした。

それなら、もう一度そういう人たちがいるところに行って、とにかく話を聞かせてもらおう。

思い立ったら行動せずにはいられない僕は、会社の休みを使って再度ニューヨークに飛びました。そして、前職のマッキンゼー時代の知人のところに押しかけ、アメリカのNPOなどで活躍している人たちを、半ば強引に紹介してもらったのです。

そうしていくうちに、「ソーシャル・セクターで働いているのはどこか変わった人が多いのだろう」という僕の中にわずかに残っていた偏見は、ものの見事に打ち砕かれました。そのとき会った人たちは、変わり者どころか誰もがしっかりした考えを持ち、とてつもなく優秀だったのです。そうした超優秀な人たちが、社会の課題と向き合い、解決することに真剣に取り組んでいたのです。

僕がやりたかったのは、まさにこういうことだ。日本の会社で不完全燃焼の日々を送っている場合ではない。ようやく自分の未来に希望の灯が見えたような気がしました。

「一気に串を刺すように」問題を解決する

自分の進む道は社会事業分野しかないと思った僕は、帰国してすぐに日本のＮＰＯや財団を調べまくりました。ですが、ここでもすぐ壁にぶちあたりました。「ぜひともここで働きたい」と思うところがないのです。

僕が探していたのは、「社会貢献に対するしっかりした理念と戦略があり」「世界に開かれていて」「志を同じくする人で構成されている少数精鋭の組織」でした。しかし、そうした条件に当てはまるところはなかなか見付かりません。

そんなふうに悶々としていたころに出会ったのが、前にお話ししたマッキンゼーの先輩であり、現在ＴＦＴの理事も務めている近藤正晃ジェームスだったのです。

そのときのことは今でも鮮明に覚えています。

「とりあえず食事でも」ということだったのに、あれこれ話しているうちに気が付けば

あっという間に三時間がたっていました。興味を持ちはじめたとはいっても、このときまで、僕は社会事業が何たるかということをきちんとは知らなかったのです。そんな素人同然の僕に、彼は社会事業の何たるかを一から丁寧に説明してくれました。

話の中で印象に残ったのは、社会の課題を地球規模で考えるという点です。通信や移動、輸送手段の発達によって、今や世界は網の目のようにつながり、依存し合っています。そうした現状を踏まえれば、一国や一つの地域の取り組みで解決する課題というのは少なく、大半は地球を俯瞰的に見て、「一気に串を刺すような方法」をとらないと、根本的な解決に至らない。そうした考え方には深く共感しました。

たとえば、環境問題においては、割り箸やレジ袋の使用を制限することにも意味はあるでしょうが、それよりも二酸化炭素の排出を抑えることで世界中の人がメリットを享受できるようなしくみを考えた方が、きっと早く問題の解決につながることでしょう。

また、社会問題に対する意識が高くても、日本の外に出たことがなければ、グローバルな視点を持ちにくい。だから、海外経験が豊富でコンサルタント的な問題解決のスキルを持った人間は社会事業分野にこそ必要なのだ、という考え方にも共感するものがあ

りました。

そして、このときの最大の収穫が、ＴＦＴの構想を知ったことです。「今これに取り掛かっているんだけど」とはじまった近藤の説明を聞いているうちに、僕は自分が興奮してくるのがわかりました。このしくみならば、誰もが無理なく参加できて、しかも貧困と飽食の二つの課題を同時に解決できる。それまで僕が聞いてきた日本における社会事業とは、まるで次元が違っていたのです。

さらにこれが「日本発のしくみである」というところにも価値があると思いました。日本人は能力も技術力もある。世界を変えるくらいインパクトのある社会事業が日本から起こってもおかしくないのに、現状はそうなっていない。この新しい市場である社会事業分野でそうしたビジネスモデルをつくりあげ、日本から世界に通用するような社会起業家を輩出しよう。そうした話は震えがくるほど刺激的でした。ＴＦＴがそうした存在の第一号になることができるはず。強くそう思ったのです。

世界的経済学者との二十分が「ダメ押し」

「TFTを事業化する仕事をやらないか」

近藤からそう誘われ、大いに心が動いたものの、TFTはこの時点ではまったくの構想段階でした。松竹での仕事と並行してTFTの立ち上げ準備も手伝うようになったものの、完全に社会事業の世界に飛び込むことにはまだ不安がありました。それは、ここが日本だからです。

これがニューヨークであれば、社会起業家といえば社会から認知された存在であり、社会事業だけで食べていくこともできるでしょう。実際、そういう人にこれまで何人も会いました。しかし、同じことが東京でもできるだろうかというと、身近に成功している人がいないのです。

そんな僕の迷いを見透かしたのか、ある日近藤は「近々ニューヨークでジェフリー・サックス教授と会うのだけれど、よかったら一緒に来ない?」と僕を誘ってくれました。世界でも有数の国際経済学者で、貧困や環境問題の第一人者である彼の名前は、当時の僕

でも知っていました。

興味はあったものの、そのときは、「会社の仕事もあるので考えてみます」としか答えられませんでした。帰り道に本屋でジェフリー・サックス教授の著書『貧困の終焉』（早川書房）を買い求めて読んでみました。全世界から貧困をなくすための具体的な方策を提案したこの本は実に衝撃的な内容で、一気に読み終えたときには「絶対にこの人に会いたい話を聞きたい」、という気持ちになっていたのです。

数日後、休みをとり、またまたニューヨークに向かいました。

実際にサックス教授に会えたのは正味二十分程度でしたが、そのわずかな時間でも、彼の考え方を知るには十分でした。彼は「私たちは、人類史上はじめて世界の貧困問題を解決できる可能性を手にした世代である」と考えており、先進国がＧＮＰのわずか一％を拠出するだけで、全世界で貧困にあえぐ十億人を救うことができる、と主張しています。

その言葉を彼の口から直接聞いたときには、社会事業に専念することへの迷いは消し飛び、そのために力を使いたいという想いを抑えることができませんでした。

その後、まもなくして僕は会社に辞表を出しました。それが三十五歳の夏でした。

僕が自分の「想い」を見付けるまで

「世界平和に役立つ」という名前

「想い」というものはどこから来るのだろう?
二つめの仕事に行き詰まり、悩んで自分のこれまでを整理していたときには、就職する前、それこそ生まれたときからの出来事を思い出したり、家族に聞いたりもしました。
僕の「真久」という名前は、信心深い母が当時日本一の尼僧と呼び声の高かった梶山智孝上人という方にお願いして授けてもらったものです。僕が生まれようとしていたとき、経を唱えていた上人の頭に、ふいに真と久の二文字が浮かんだということでした。「世界平和に役立つ人間になってほしい」という願いが込められている、と聞きました。

まさに現在の自分の仕事を暗示するような名前の由来ですが、本当は「真」の方は異字体だったらしく、人名用漢字になかったので「真」で間に合わせた、と聞いたときには、「僕の考え方がどこか世間一般とずれているのはそのためか」と妙に納得してしまいました。

母はその名にふさわしい人間に僕を育てようとしたのでしょう。挨拶をはじめ、しつけはかなり厳しかったと記憶しています。その甲斐あってか二歳のころには、毎朝家の仏壇にごはんとお茶、水をお供えし、線香をあげて手を合わせるのが日課の子どもになっていました。

幼稚園時代には、なぜか「乱暴者の問題児といじめられっ子の両方から好かれる」という僕の特異なキャラクターが注目され、母は先生から「いったいどういう育て方をすればこういう子どもになるのか」とたびたび質問されたそうです。

小学校では東京から地方に移りました。

転校して環境が変わったこともあって、徐々にいい子から、自分が納得しないことには従わない、という今に通じる僕の性格が姿を現しはじめます。

転校先の小学校では〝あてっこ〟という遊びが流行っていました。ボールを当てられた

人が鬼になり、次に誰かにぶつけると鬼が入れ替わる、という単純な遊びです。ドッジボールのように枠がなく、どこに逃げてもいいので、遠くに行かれてしまうと鬼はお手上げです。いったん鬼になるとなかなかそこから抜け出せない、というちょっと過酷なゲームなのです。

子どもは残酷なところがありますから、全員で示し合わせて一人を鬼に追い込むようなことをします。転校生である僕は格好の餌食でした。ここで存在感を見せなければいつまで経ってもここで受け入れてもらえない。そう思った僕は鬼になると、「こいつにぶつける」と決めた相手を徹底的に追いかけました。中には学校の外まで逃げていく子もいましたが、そんなときも追及の手を緩めません。昼休みが終わって掃除の時間になってもおかまいなしです。

そのしつこさのおかげで仲間内から一目置かれるようになったのはよかったのですが、いくら今より大らかな時代とはいえ、毎日掃除の時間を無視して走りまわっている子どもを先生が見逃すはずはありません。しかし、いくら注意されてもどこ吹く風で一向に態度を改めようとしないのですから、ほとほと手を焼いたと思います。

こんなこともありました。その学校は廊下の中央に白線が引いてあって、児童は左側を

整然と歩かなければいけない、という決まりになっていたのですが、例によって、どうしてそんなことをしなければならないのかを理解できない僕は、わざと反対側や白線の上を歩くようにしていたのです。当然、いろいろな先生から注意されたり叱られたりします。けれども反省しない。それどころか、「これはルールが間違っている、だって……」と先生を言い負かそうとする始末。態度は悪いけれど弁は立ったのです。

そんな生意気な僕のことを、先生たちもよほど腹に据えかねたのでしょう。卒業文集には「いたずらやルール破りが多く、注意されても屁理屈をいって正当化しようとする」という、僕に対する評価がしっかりと書かれています。

型にはめられるのは我慢ならない

中学になるとまた東京に戻りました。

しかし、学校は面白くなかった。小学校時代はサッカーに夢中になっていたので中学校もサッカー部に入ったのですが、小学校にはなかった上下関係や、守らなければならない決まりなどがたくさんあって、僕にはそれが押し付けにしか思えず、嫌でたまらなかった

のです。しまいにはあれほど好きだったサッカーに対する情熱すら薄れてしまいました。
学校は嫌いでしたが、その分は塾に救われました。塾で別の中学の生徒たちと学校とは違う話題で盛り上がり、勉強よりもその時間の楽しさのために塾に通っていたといってもいいぐらいです。塾が終わると仲間と雑居ビルに入り込んで、警備員の目を盗んで屋上に出るのも好きでした。屋上に立つとなんだかそのビルを制覇した気分になって気持ちがいいのです。街中のビルを制覇するぞ、と盛り上がっていました。

型にはめられるのが苦手で、未知のものへの好奇心を満足させることにこの上ない喜びを感じる僕にとって、進学先に早稲田大学高等学院という大学の付属校を選んだことは大正解でした。
自由な校風のせいか、そこに集まってくる生徒のタイプも千差万別で、中学のころ塾で味わったような時間を学校で過ごすことができました。先生は大学で教鞭をとっている人が多く、大学受験と無縁でいられる付属校の授業では自分の得意分野に思い切り偏向した授業をやっており、これが実に面白いのです。
縄文時代だけを三年間教え続ける日本史の先生がいたり、古文の授業なのにいつも投資や株のしくみの解説しかしない先生がいたり、他の学校ではちょっと考えられない、そう

いう変わった授業が僕は大好きでした。全国大会出場を決めたラグビー部の友人が、練習が忙しくて勉強する時間がなく、地理のテストに「僕の知識はこれしかありません」と断って、中央線の東京から八王子までの全駅名を書いて提出したところ、満点に近い点数が付いて戻ってきたこともありました。

そんな雰囲気の中で、僕はバレーボール部に所属して練習に打ち込む傍ら、映画を観たり本を読んだり友だちと語らったりしているうちに、三年間はあっという間に過ぎていきました。自由を謳歌できるってなんて素晴らしいんだろう。そのことに改めて気付かされた時間でした。

退屈な大学生活を救ってくれた海外旅行

付属高校だったので大学もそのまま進学することができました。高校三年になると進学先の学部を決めなければなりません。それまで好きなように過ごしてきた僕も、ようやく自分は大学で何を勉強したいのだろうと考えはじめました。そして選んだのは理工学部の機械工学科。これは積極的に希望して、というよりも消去法からでした。

まず、政治や法律や経済にはまるで興味がなく、文学青年でもないので、文系の学部はどれも候補から外れました。学校の勉強もどちらかといえば理系の成績がよかったということもあり、理系の学部から選ぶことにしました。

とはいえ、特に研究したいテーマがあるわけではなく、どうしたものかと悩んでいたところ、友人から「機械工学は扱う範囲が広いから、迷っているのならとりあえずそこにしておけば」と言われ、それで理工学部の機械工学科に決めたのです。

ところが、大学に入ってみてすぐに後悔しました。講義は退屈だし、そこに集まってきている学生たちは、その退屈な講義にじっと耳を傾けて黙々とノートをとるような、僕がもっとも苦手とするまじめタイプばかりだったのです。

同級生の大半は、一所懸命勉強して、「いい会社」に就職することを目標にしていました。機械を専門とする彼らにとって、当時の「いい会社」はイコール大手の自動車会社です。だけど、僕は車のエンジニアになんかなりたくなかったし、そんな敷かれたレールの上を進んでいくような人生のよさを理解できませんでした。でも、そんなふうに思うのは僕だけで、他のみんなはそれを当然という顔で受け入れているのです。

高校時代を個性的な友人たちと過ごしてきた僕には、この空気は耐え難いものでした。サークル活動にはけ口を求めようとしても、体育会系的な上下関係が幅を利かせていて、高校のときのような開放感を味わえそうなところはありませんでした。

「もう大学に期待するのはやめよう」と思っていたとき、高校時代の友人からアメリカに行かないか、と誘われました。

サンフランシスコ、ロサンゼルス、サンディエゴから国境を越えてメキシコのティファナと西海岸を南下し、それから東に移動してフロリダ半島のマイアミまで、安宿に泊まりながらの一カ月にわたる旅行が、それまでの鬱々とした日々を抜け出す転機となりました。大学がつまらないなら、キャンパスを飛び出せばよかったんだ。だって、世界には刺激と驚きがあふれているのです。ようやくそのことに思い至りました。

帰国すると、すぐに「今度は別の国に行ってみたい」という気持ちが湧き上がってきました。でも、その前に英語力を付けなければ、と思いました。マイアミで泊まる予定だったホテルがハリケーンに破壊され、急きょ別の宿を探さなければならなくなったとき、英語が通じずにものすごく苦労した経験をしたからです。

「とにかく実践で使える英語を身に付けよう」と、自宅に近い座間の米軍キャンプで英語の勉強をはじめました。それから、次の旅行資金のためにアルバイトに励み、お金が貯まるとふらりと海外に行くというのが、僕の大学生活の基本スタイルとなったのです。

シンガポール、マレーシア、タイ、韓国、オーストラリア、ヨーロッパ……、世界中を放浪し、そこで出会った人たちを通してさまざまな文化や価値観に触れるのがとにかく面白くて、もう大学生活の退屈さは気にならなくなりました。

大学在学中には、イアエステ（ＩＡＥＳＴＥ／社団法人日本国際学生技術研修協会）の国際インターンシップ・プログラムを使ってスロバキアに二カ月間住んだこともあります。そのプログラムは世界中の理工農薬系学生を対象としており、国籍や宗教の異なる人たちと寮で共同生活をしたのは、実に貴重な体験でした。

ルームメイトが朝から床でお祈りをしていたり、野菜以外は口にしないベジタリアンと食事を一緒につくったり、「正義とは何か」を議論するうちにそれぞれが自分の国を代表しているような気になって夜通し意見を闘わせたり、そんな毎日は刺激に満ちていました。

それから、地元のスロバキアの学生が、異国から来た学生がホームシックにならないようパーティーを開いてくれたり、週末に旅行に連れてくれていったり、いろいろと気を

遣ってくれるのもありがたいことでした。日本人でも東欧人でも思いやりの気持ちは同じなんだ、ということが身に染みました。

肝心の勉強はと言えば、英語で授業が行われるものだと思っていたら、担当教授がスロバキア語とドイツ語しか話せないということがわかり、初日から暗礁に乗り上げました。教授の専門はエンジニアリング・デザインなので、「毎日何か一つデッサンして提出すればいい」ということにしてもらい、毎日街に出ては絵を描いていました。

せっかくスロバキアまで来たのだから、と最初のうちこそまじめにこの課題に取り組んでいたのですが、スロバキアというのはテニスが盛んで、市内のいたるところで女子学生がテニスをしているのです。しかも、東欧の女性は、みんなめちゃくちゃにかわいいときている。テニスコートを見付けるとつい吸い寄せられて、ボールを追う彼女たちの姿を見つめてしまうので、デッサンにかける時間は日に日に短くなり、最後の方ではほとんど描かなくなってしまいました。

つまり、ここでも勉強はほとんどしなかった、ということです。

人工心臓の研究との出会い

大学時代、僕はモヒカン刈りにピアスという格好で通していました。自分としては気に入っていたのですが、やはりまじめに勉強する気があるようには見えなかったのでしょう。四年生になって入った研究室の先生は、明らかに僕を避けていました。とはいえ、僕の方も車のエンジンや流体力学というその研究室のテーマにはまったく興味がなく、入った動機は「新設なので入りやすいから」というどうしようもないものでしたから、文句は言えません。

「大学でやりたいことなんて何もない」、梅津光生教授と出会わなければ、僕はそう思ったまま卒業していたでしょう。梅津先生は、僕の研究室の隣にある研究室の責任者で、人工心臓の研究が専門でした。

梅津研究室は開放的で、隣の研究室に所属する僕にもやっていることが自然と耳に入ってきます。どうやら人工心臓を研究しているらしいということがわかってくると、それがどういうものか気になりはじめ、ときどき隣にも顔を出すようになりました。そうしたら、

自分のやっている自動車のエンジンの研究よりも断然面白そうなのです。
そこで、あるとき梅津先生をつかまえて「人工心臓にものすごく魅力を感じるので、そちらの研究室で何かやらせてもらえませんか」とお願いしてみました。もちろん普通であれば断られるに決まっています。加えて、僕のモヒカン・ピアスという風貌であればなおさらでしょう。ところが、梅津先生は懐の深い方で、「なんとかしてあげるよ」と了解してくださったのです。そして、研究室を途中で変わることはできないので、元の研究室に所属したまま梅津研究室に参加させてもらえることになりました。
梅津先生の開発した人工心臓は「スパイラルモデル」と言って、ポンプの入口と出口を結ぶ管をらせん状にしたものです。血液は少しでも流れが悪くなるとすぐに血栓ができ、その破片が脳の血管を詰まらせて脳梗塞を引き起こしたりします。なので、人工心臓において血液の流れをよくして血栓ができないようにするというのは、とても重要なことなのです。僕は梅津研究室でその血液の流れを見る実験を任されました。
実験には人間の代わりに牛の血液を使います。品川の食肉処理場で採取した新鮮な血を冷凍保存して研究室まで運んでくる、というのも僕の役目でした。
あるとき駅のホームで職務質問を受け、アイスボックスの中身を見せろというので、フ

タを開けたところ、氷で冷やされた血液の容器がわんさか出てきたものだから、大騒ぎになりました。いくら「牛の血です」と言っても聞き届けられず、一も二もなく警察に連行されてしまいました。時期も悪かったのです。ちょうどある宗教団体が世間を騒がせているところで、おまけに履いているジーパンには採取の際に飛び散った牛の血がこびりついている。その上頭はモヒカンですから、「こいつは何か悪いことをやっているに違いない」と疑われるのも、まあ無理はありません。

食肉処理場では、忘れられない光景も目にしました。

これから殺される牛たちが並んで順番を待っています。その牛たちは自分の運命を知っているのでしょうか？　目にいっぱいの涙を浮かべているのです。泣いている牛がずらりと並ぶその光景は、とても衝撃的なものでした。

僕が食べものを残さないよう、かなり気を付けるようになったのは、このときからです。

楽しかったオーストラリアの研究時代

大学を卒業しても、すぐに就職するつもりはありませんでした。希望は海外で人工心臓

の研究を続けることでした。

当時、人工心臓ではアメリカ、シンガポール、オーストラリアのそれぞれの大学に有名な研究室がありました。僕が海外で勉強したいと言うと、梅津先生はそのすべての大学に僕を連れていってくださったのです。

この中から僕はオーストラリアを選びました。大学の特性もありましたが、住む国として最も心惹かれたことが決め手となりました。

オーストラリアは人工心臓の移植手術が盛んな上に、病院にお願いすれば簡単に学生にも手術を見学させてくれるなど、自由が大好きな僕にとってはとても研究がしやすい環境でした。僕は当初二年間だった留学予定を大幅に延長し、四年近くかけて修士論文を書き上げました。研究に没頭していたらあっという間に時間が経ってしまった、というわけではなく、例によって異国の人たちとの交流が楽しくて、そちらをエンジョイしていたせいで、なかなか論文が書けなかったのです。

「自分の生きる軸＝想い」を見付けた

今から振り返れば、この学生生活のときまでに、自分の生きていく上での「軸」のようなものがおおよそ固まっていたように思います。

一つには、「国や組織の壁を超えて物事に取り組みたい」ということ。各国を旅した経験から違う文化の人たちとコミュニケーションをとることの楽しさを知り、オーストラリアでは現地の医師の方と立場や国籍を超えて研究をすることがとても楽しかったのです。

二つには、「社会に役立つことをしたい」ということ。人工心臓の研究をしていても、僕が感動するのは、新しい発見をしたり成果を上げたりしたときではなく、患者さんに感謝されたときなのです。こうした感動を得るために仕事をしたい、と思いました。

三つには、「日本を舞台にしたい」ということ。オーストラリアでは研究と並行して日本語講師のアルバイトもしていたのですが、ここで日本への興味や期待を強く感じる機会

がありました。外から見てはじめてわかる日本の価値に触れ、日本人に生まれた以上は自分の生まれた国の価値を上げることに関わりたい、そう考えるようになりました。

この三つが、いつしか僕の「想い」となって、その後の仕事と人生を形づくるベースとなってきたように思うのです。

第3章

社会起業にビジネススキルをいかす

社会起業にこそ必要なビジネススキル

「自分たちの主義や主張を声高に語るばかりで、ビジネスの常識を持ち合わせていない」、社会事業をやっていると言うと、こんなふうに見られることがよくあります。

実際、会社勤めを嫌って駆け込み寺のような感覚で、ＮＰＯに居場所を求めて逃げ込んで来る、というケースもあるのでしょう。

では、社会事業には、本当にそのような人たちしかいないのでしょうか？

そんなことはありません。

それほど多くの同業者と交流があるわけではないので、社会起業家や社会事業に従事している人たちのことを何から何まで正確に把握している、とは言えませんが、それでも、既に多くの優秀な社会起業家やスタッフに会ってきました。それに、僕たちのように、一般の企業と提携してビジネスを行なうＮＰＯでは、ビジネスマインドや社会常識を持っている人でなければやっていけません。

また、内閣府の認証を受けたＮＰＯであれば、毎期の決算書類を所轄庁に提出すること

が義務付けられているので、財務会計の知識が必要になります。人事面でも広告宣伝面でも、「限られたリソースを最大限有効に使っていかなければ生き残れない」というのは、営利を追求する一般企業と何ら変わりはないのです。

つまり、社会事業であっても、「志は善、しかしビジネススキルがない」という人では、うまくやっていくことはできません。

それでは、社会事業で働く人は、具体的にどんな仕事をしているのか。また、特にどんな能力を必要とされるのか。それをＴＦＴのこれまでをモデルにしてまとめていきたいと思います。

これらは、前にご紹介したＴＦＴの「５Ｐ」と密接に関わってきます。

❶Purpose（目的・達成目標）＝ＴＦＴのミッションは何か。
❷Partnering（提携）＝どんな組織や団体とどのような形態で連携していくか。
❸People（組織・人事）＝どんな人たちを巻き込んでいくか。また、組織づくりに必要なのはどういう人か。

❹Promotion（宣伝・広報）＝ミッションや活動内容をどんな媒体や手段でどのように伝えていくか。

❺Profit（利益・成果）＝どうやって事業収益を上げて目的を達成するのか。

Purposeに基づき、そのほかのPartnering、People、Promotion、Profitという各要素を考えていく必要がありました。きっと、これはどんな社会事業の団体でも必要になるものだと思います。

Purpose［目的・達成目標］
――何のための事業なのか、徹底的に考え抜く

「自分たちにしかできないこと」は何か

世界の食の不均衡を是正し、先進国の肥満と開発途上国の飢餓、この二つの問題を同時

に解決する。

ＴＦＴの事業内容を考えるということは、このコンセプトを実際にどう展開していくのかを考えることでした。数値目標だけを追うのではなく、意識改革にも重点を置く、ということが見えてくると、その後は「そこで僕たちの出せる付加価値は何だろう」と考えていきました。

「二つの問題を同時に解決する」

僕がすごいと思ったこの驚きのポイントをどう具体化するか。二つの問題が同時に解決することをどうやってわかりやすく見せるか。寄付金は誰に出してもらい、どういうしくみで支援先まで届けるのか。

活動場所についても、先進国と開発途上国というだけでは、該当する国は星の数ほどあります。その中で活動を展開する国と事業領域を合理的に決めなければならない。

僕は、ここでもコンサル時代の思考法を活用しました。

論理思考や問題解決の基本とされるロジックツリーを描き、活動地域、活動内容、展開の方法、考えられる課題などについて、考えられる要素をすべて列挙、整理したのです。

そしてその中で、自分たちができること、やるべきことを考え抜いていきました。

●インパクト（効果）が大きいものはどれか
●自分たちのビジネスモデルやスキルで実行できるのか
●現況はどうか（既にその手段を着手している先行プレーヤーはいないか）

といった点から検討を加えていきました。「ここところがやるべきこと」「ここもやりたいが優先順位は低い」「こちらは他の団体にまかせるべき」という仮説を立てながら、TFTのPurposeを精査していきました。

ニューヨークで経済学者のジェフリー・サックス教授と会ったときのことです。

彼の切れ味鋭い思考に圧倒されつつも、彼の思考回路もロジックツリーを描き、課題を分解していく、僕がマッキンゼーで叩き込まれた手法と同じであることを感じました。ただ、彼の場合は、ロジックツリーの一番上に来る大命題が「世界の貧困をなくす」という、とてつもなく大きな課題であるわけです。でも、そのくらい大きな課題にも、この手法が使える。そのことを実感してとても心強く思いました。

一見、解決することなど到底できないと思われるような難題であっても、課題を細かく

要素分解して整理することで、解決可能と思われるレベルまで落とし込むことができる。それがこのロジックツリーという武器の強みです。そして、このロジックツリーは地球規模の課題に対してもその強みを発揮することを、サックス教授が示してくれたのです。多くの人が解決可能と信じることで、多くの協力者を募ることができる、それが大きなうねりを生み出し、変革の原動力になる。そのことを強く感じました。

農業（農家）の活性化

20年内で農業の就業人口は4％強減少。担い手の減少
1980年に7003人→2000年3903人

外国産食糧（原料）減らす

食べ過ぎを減らす

- 一食当たりの量
- 食事の回数

食べ過ぎが原因のメタボ・生活習慣病が深刻化。
20000人がメタボ予備軍

食べ残し（廃棄）を減らす

輸入した食料の40％にあたる量が捨てられている。
金額に換算すると約11兆円分

農業生産性を上げる

- 農業指導
- 肥料・種
- 機械

海外に出て行く食糧を減らす

食糧を実際に入手する

食糧を購入する資金を得る

図4
世界の食糧配分の不均衡を解決するには

現状課題…………●世界で生産される食糧の熱量を換算、世界人口で割ると1日1人あたり2,700キロカロリーの食料摂取が可能。これは成人の必要摂取量を上回る

●ところが、国連人口基金の調査では、開発途上国105ヵ国中、約40ヵ国が深刻な食糧不足に直面。これらの国では約10億人が飢え、約20億人が栄養不足に苦しむ

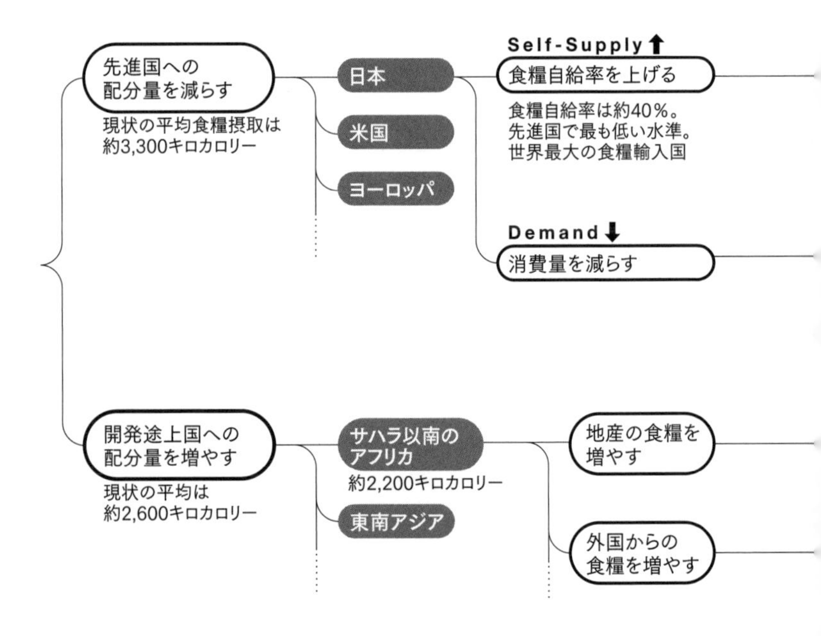

Partnering［提携］
相手を見極め、長く続くよい関係を築く

営業する先をどう決めるか

先進国と開発途上国と双方の人々の健康を食・食事を通して推進する、というＴＦＴのＰｕｒｐｏｓｅ（目的・達成目標）のためには、ＴＦＴの食堂プログラムを採用してくれる企業・団体を一箇所でも増やすことが第一歩です。

ＴＦＴのメニューを提供する場所は社員食堂であり、主な営業先となるのは企業をはじめ、学校、官公庁などになります。

営業の対象となる企業や団体は、

- 社員食堂があり、一定数以上の利用者がいる

●社員が参加できる社会貢献やＣＳＲに力を入れている
●社員の健康管理に積極的に取り組んでいる

といった条件から探し出し、直接訪問してＴＦＴの趣旨やしくみを説明して導入を打診します。このあたりは一般企業の営業担当者が自社の商品やサービスを売り込むときと同じです。訪問前にはアポイントメントをとり、訪問の目的を告げ、訪問時はスーツにネクタイを締める点なども変わりないでしょう。

訪問前に相手のことをできる限り調べてから出掛ける、というのも営業担当者であれば誰しもしていることだと思います。

業界でのポジションはどういったものか、どんな事業に力を入れているのか、工場や拠点はどのくらいあるのか、そしてどんなＣＳＲ活動を行なっているのか。さらには、相手とよい関係を築くために僕たちの持っている人的ネットワークをいかせる部分はないか。そうした基本情報をおさえてから出向くことは、営業の成功確率を高めるために大切な準備作業です。

対等なビジネスパートナーになるために

基本は一般企業の営業と同じだとは言っても、僕たちがＮＰＯだということで、相手に何らかの偏見を持たれたり、対等に扱ってもらえないこともままあります。僕たちは趣味や道楽ではなく、きちんとした使命を持ってビジネスとして活動しているわけなので、企業と対等のビジネスパートナーになり得ると思っているのですが、はじめてお会いするときにはそうは見てもらえないこともあります。ＴＦＴ導入を検討してもらう際にも、「こちらはやってあげているのだから」という態度をとる方がたまにいることも事実です。

僕たちが目指すのは、企業の方も僕たちと一緒に、社会の課題に対して当事者意識を持って課題解決に向けてパートナーシップを組んでいく、という姿です。ＴＦＴの活動は「やってあげる」ものでもなければ、「やらされる」ものでもなく、「寄付する人」が「される人」よりも偉いということもない、と考えています。

ＴＦＴのビジネスモデルは、提携する企業や団体なしには成り立ちません。だからこそ、提携先の相手とは同じ目線で「どうすればもっとよい活動ができるのか」という相談をし

ながら、強いパートナーシップを築いていかなければと思っています。

企業で働く人たちも、社会や人に対する何らかの「想い」を持っているはずです。でも、その想いが仕事の中では発揮できず、内に秘めざるを得ない場合も多く見かけます。僕たちの社会事業というビジネスは、そうした想いを解き放つ場として有効なのです。

つまり、僕たちが挑もうとしている社会課題や目指す変革について説明し、そうした人たちの想いに訴えることができれば、彼らはＴＦＴの活動に深い思い入れを持って賛同してくれ、自分の仕事として主体的に関わってくれるようになります。そうした状況をつくることが、本当の意味でパートナーシップを築くということなのだと思います。

僕たちの仕事というのは、ありとあらゆる情報やデータを駆使して相手の左脳に論理を説くのと同時に、熱意と情熱をぶつけて右脳に訴えることでもあります。それによって、ふだんの仕事で埋もれていた想いに寄り添い、対等なパートナーシップをつくりあげるのです。

そして、あらゆる手を尽くしても、いつまでもこちらを「御用聞き」として見るだけで、パートナーシップを築いて頂けない場合は長く関係を保つべきではない。ときにはそうい

う見極めも必要になります。

相手の想いに寄り添うことができたら、次はその方が所属する組織でＴＦＴのプログラムをスムーズに導入できるように、僕たちにどんなサポートができるのかを考えます。

ＴＦＴの一番のセールスポイントは「社会貢献と社員の健康増進を同時にできる」ということですが、売りになるのはそれだけではありません。「日本発のビジネスモデル」や「誰でも参加できる」といった点もポイントですし、場合によってはこちらを強調することもあります。

ボトルネックになっているのはどこか

たとえば、相手が伝統ある企業であれば「これは日本人によって発案され、日本ではじまった社会貢献活動です」という説明が有効ですし、社員を公平かつ平等に扱うことを重視している企業であれば「誰もが無理なく参加できるしくみです」という説明が効果的になる、といった具合です。

企業がＴＦＴの導入を決める際は、さまざまな立場の人が意思決定に参加します。実際、担当者の方は好意的であっても採用にまで至らない、ということもよくあります。つまり、僕たちからは見えない意思決定者に、「よし、やろう」と言ってもらえるかどうか、最後に大事になるのはこの部分です。

そのために、担当者の方とは膝を付き合わせて話し合い、部内会議や役員会議で指摘されそうなポイントについて詳細な情報提供をします。僕たちが意思決定の場に同席することは稀ですから、最終的には提案して頂く担当者の方にすべてを託すことになります。担当者の方が持つ懸念点を徹底的に洗い出し、一緒に問題解決を行いながら、自信を持って発表してもらえるように手を尽くします。場合によっては、既にＴＦＴを導入している企業を見学してもらい、自社が導入したときのイメージを膨らませてもらうこともあります。

こうして周到に準備を重ねた末、担当者の方から「無事通りましたよ！」と連絡をもらったときの感激はひとしおです。きっと一般企業の営業の方が商談をまとめたときも同じような気持ちになるのでしょう。

担当が複数の部門にまたがる企業では、社内のさまざまな部門、部署との調整も考える

必要があります。

通常、ＴＦＴ導入の担当となるのは、人事・総務・ＣＳＲなどの部門です。さらに企業によっては社員の福利厚生の面から労働組合が関わってくる場合もあります。ＣＳＲ部が窓口であっても、その部門のニーズに応えるだけでなく、人事部や総務部にも説明しやすい情報を提供することが、導入の成功率を高めるカギになるのです。導入に二の足を踏ませているのはどの部門なのか、そして彼らの懸念点はどこにあるのかといったことを探る洞察力や、参考になる情報を引き出す力が求められるわけです。

僕たちが多くの企業を訪問する中で学んだ「気にするポイントの部門別の傾向」をまとめてみましょう。

部門別「傾向と対策」マニュアル

ＣＳＲ部門の場合は、担当者の方が最も懸念するのは、「どれだけ多くの社員が社会貢献活動に参加してくれるのか」という点です。ＴＦＴのプログラムを導入したのはいいけれど、社員の士気が上がらずに寄付金も集まらないとなれば、旗振り役としての自部門の

立場がなくなってしまいます。

この懸念に対しては、社員の方が負担する寄付金は一食二十円であり大きな負担にはならない点、またランチで抑えるカロリーも通常の一、二割減程度と無理のない範囲である点を丁寧に説明します。また、忙しくて通常では社会貢献活動に参加できない社員の方であっても、社員食堂が活動の場であれば参加しやすいことを伝えます。その上で他社の参加率を紹介することで納得してもらえる可能性が高まります。

人事部の場合は、「メタボ対策」というＴＦＴのセールスポイントをアピールします。メタボ予防と対策を企業に義務付けた「特定保健指導（メタボ健診）」の開始に伴い、メタボ社員を減らすことを経営課題の一つに掲げる会社が増えています。この課題の担当になるのはたいてい人事部ですが、この降って湧いた仕事への対応に頭を悩ませているケースが多く見られます。忙しい社員に対する有効なメタボ予防策がないことが人事部を困らせる要因です。これに対してＴＦＴのプログラムは、多くの社員が毎日利用する社員食堂で食事のカロリーセーブができる点をアピールします。忙しくて過食になりがちな社員の方ほど社員食堂を利用している点も付け加えます。ＴＦＴのヘルシーランチを食べ続けて、半年で十キログラム近くの減量に成功した方の事例などを紹介すると、がぜん興味を持っ

てもらえます。

総務部門の場合は、気を付けているのが食堂の運営を行う給食会社との関係です。総務部の方は給食会社と価格交渉などでシビアな議論をしていることがあり、ＴＦＴプログラムの導入で新たに給食会社に負担をかけることを躊躇されることが多いのです。そうした場合には、給食会社との交渉や栄養士とのメニューの相談などは僕たちがやることをご説明して懸念を払拭するようにしています。

労働組合の場合は、「寄付金の二十円を組合員である社員が負担する」ということに難色を示されることがあります。ここでは、それは強制的な負担ではなく、「貧困のために満足に食事がとれない子どもたちに給食を提供する」という趣旨に賛同した人だけが自由意思で行う寄付であり、自分自身の健康のための投資にもなる、という話をすることで理解してもらえます。

「業種」によっても攻め方は異なる

一般企業でも自治体でも、社員食堂があるところはすべてＴＦＴの営業対象となります。
また、相手によってプログラムの中身が変わることはありません。
だからといって、どこに対しても同じアプローチをすればいいか、といったらそれは違います。「ここが決め手になる」というポイントは企業や組織によって異なるからです。
先ほどは部門ごとにアピールポイントを変えるお話をしましたが、そもそも相手の業種や組織の性質によっても、こちらの対応を変える必要があります。

理念やしくみは気に入ってもらったのに、なかなか採用に至らない、という他のＮＰＯの話を耳にしますが、それは相手の落とし所を押さえ、攻め方を変える、といった営業上の工夫をしていないからではないでしょうか。

「いい商品なら黙っていても売れるはず」というのが理想論であるように、「素晴らしい社会貢献のしくみだから、普通に説明すればみんな協力してくれる」というのも、また幻

想でしかありません。ＮＰＯの営業にも、緻密な戦略や理に適った営業スキルは必要なのです。相手の業種・職種別に、僕たちがとっている営業方法も少しご紹介してみます。

企業の「もう一つの想い」

一般企業の場合には、二十円という少ない額の寄付金で、どれほど意味のあることができるのか、という「社会事業としてのインパクト」に関する部分に関心が寄せられます。常日頃から、投資対効果について考えている一般企業であれば当然のことでしょう。

また、どこの企業も、多かれ少なかれ、同業他社の動向が気になるようです。ただし、他社情報をどう受け取るのかという点はさまざまです。ある企業では「○○業界では、御社が初の導入企業です」ということが決め手となりますが、反対に「同じ業界の○○社さんでも試験的に導入頂いていています」ということが安心材料となって話が進む場合もあります。そのあたりの業界・会社ごとの考え方や傾向は事前に調べておかないと、ちょっとした一言が思わぬ結果を招くことになりかねません。

それから、一般企業を相手にする場合は「相手のスピードに合わせられるかどうか」と

いうことも営業の成功率を高める重要なポイントです。特に大企業はＮＰＯに対しても、ふだんやりとりをしている協力会社と同じように迅速で行き届いた対応をしてくれるものと思っていることがあり、午前に受けたメールの返信を夕方にしたら「どうなっているんだ」とお叱りを受けたこともあります。

ＴＦＴの場合は人的資源が十分でないので、相手を完璧に満足させるだけの対応をするのは大変な面もあるのですが、だからといって「御社と同じ速度では走れません」と開き直ってもよい展開には結び付きません。

僕は、かつて一般の企業で働いていたので、会社の中でどのような手順で物事が処理されているかを理解しているつもりです。だから、多少の無理をしてでも相手の求めるスピードや内容で対応しようと努力しています。それでも、どうしてもできないときは、できない理由を説明します。「すみません、事務局のスタッフが二人しかいない上に今週は立て込んでしまって」と伝えると「えっ、そうなんですか！　何十人とスタッフの方がいるのかと思っていました。それならこの作業はこちらでやっておきますよ」と親切に対応してくださる方もいました。

こうして創業間もないＮＰＯ法人の現実をお伝えすることも、パートナーシップを築く上で大切なことだと思っています。

また、食の不均衡を解決するという想いを企業の方と共有することは、一緒に事業をする上での大前提ですが、企業の場合には、「自社の社会貢献活動を認知してもらう」というもう一つの想いがあります。株主、顧客、取引先といった、企業にとってのステークホルダーに社会貢献への取り組みを知ってもらうことは、事業や企業イメージのプラスになるためです。

僕たちもできる限り、こうした企業の「もう一つの想い」に応えられるようにしています。たとえば、導入企業はウェブサイトに企業ロゴとともに紹介していますし、メディアの取材を受ける際にはなるべく具体的に企業の名前や導入例を説明して、企業が取り上げてもらえるよう努力をしています。

そうしたメディアの露出や報道内容はまとめて担当者にフィードバックします。こうすることで担当者がＴＦＴプログラムを実施することのメリットを社内にアピールしやすくなるからです。

こうした小さな配慮を積み重ねることが、さらなる企業との連携強化につながるのだと思っています。

図5

TFT導入企業の増加

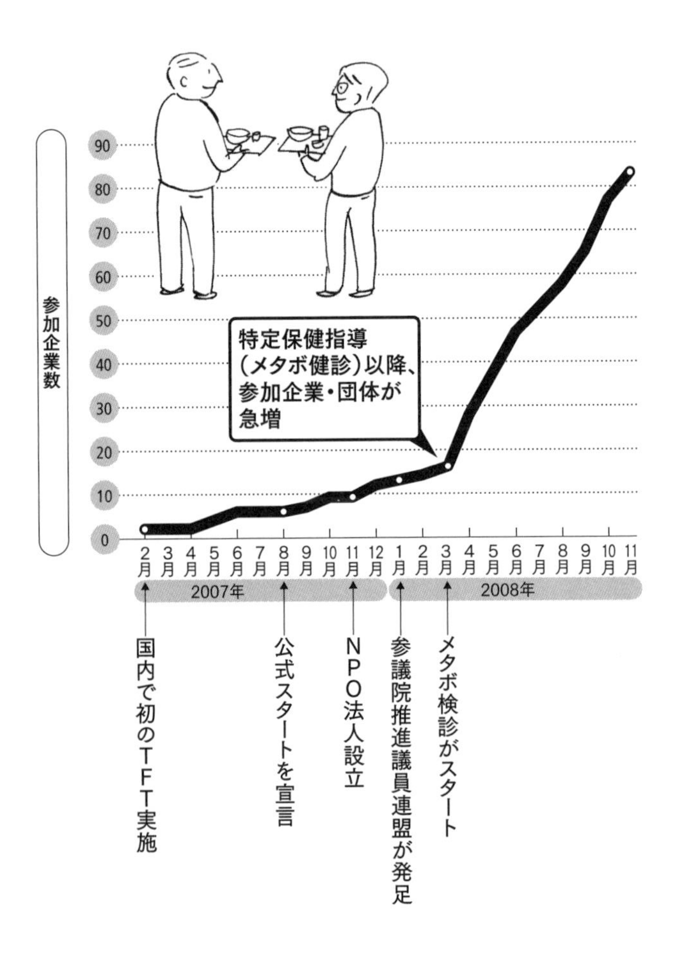
参加企業数
90
80
70
60
50
40
30
20
10
0
特定保健指導（メタボ健診）以降、参加企業・団体が急増
2月
3月
4月
5月
6月
7月
8月
9月
10月
11月
12月
1月
2月
3月
4月
5月
6月
7月
8月
9月
10月
11月
2007年
2008年
国内で初のTFT実施
公式スタートを宣言
NPO法人設立
参議院推進議員連盟が発足
メタボ検診がスタート

自治体・学校・議員の「決め手」

次に、相手方が自治体である場合には、寄付金の使い道に関する細かな情報開示が必須となります。寄付金のうち、開発途上国の給食費にあてる額と運営費の比率はどうなのか、運営費の中でも交通費や広告宣伝費はそれぞれどのくらいなのか、そういった細かな部分まで説明が求められることもあります。

自治体の場合、職員食堂の運営費も税金から賄われているわけですから、提携先である僕たちの財務内容を厳しく見極めるのは、ある意味当然のことでしょう。でも、「業者からボールペンを仕入れるときは原価やその内訳まで教えろとは言わないだろうにNPOにはずいぶん厳しいよなあ」、正直そう思うこともあります。

とはいえ、そこで反論しても仕方がないので、できる限りの情報開示をするようにします。さらに自治体は意思決定に時間がかかることも多いので、あらかじめその点を汲んだスケジュールを立てておきます。

また、自治体の場合は、提出書類のフォーマットや項目などにも細心の注意を払う方が多いようです。こうした相手の要求にその都度きちんと対応することが、信頼される

いい関係を築く第一歩になります。ＴＦＴの申込書や連絡用のフォームなどはいろいろな方からのヒアリングや改善要望を盛り込んで、何度も修正を重ねた自信作です。バージョンアップを重ねた結果、今では書類記入に際して問い合わせを受けることはほとんどなくなりました。一見、小さなことに見えますが、こうしたところにまで気を配ることが、相手の信頼を勝ち取り、最終的に「よし、やろう」と言わせるための大きな分岐点になるのです。

最近では、ＴＦＴの食堂プログラム導入先は大学を中心とした学校にも広がっています。学校の先生方に対しては、寄付金の使い道やインパクトなどの話よりも、僕たちの情熱やひたむきさが大切になります。学校の現場には、「世界から貧困をなくそう」「飢餓で苦しむ子どもたちに給食を提供しよう」というストレートなメッセージにきちんと耳を傾けてくれる方が多いので、そうした活動に真摯に取り組んでいる僕たちの姿を見てもらうことで、共感を持って導入してくださることが多いのです。

社会事業をやっていく上では、国会や地方議会の議員の方々とよい関係を保つことも重要です。お互いに程よい距離感を保つことは重要ですが、全国レベルでの活動告知や大が

かりな連携、官公庁や自治体でのＴＦＴ導入などの面においては、議員の方々との情報交換や協力依頼は欠かせないものです。こうした方々との信頼関係を築くためには、相手の価値観を知ることが必要になります。

僕がこれまで学んだのは、政治の世界にいる方は「人のために汗をかく」ことを大切にする、ということです。

ＴＦＴでイベントを実施したときのことです。

国会議員の方々にも参加して頂けないかと思い、かねてからＴＦＴを熱心に応援してくださっていた議員の方を訪ねました。その議員の方から、「議員に参加して欲しいのであれば議員会館のすべての部屋を回って、一人ひとりに案内状を手渡しするといいよ」とアドバイスされたのです。「わざわざ足を運んだ」というところを意気に感じて、何人かは会場に足を運んでくれるだろう、というわけです。

「えー、面倒くさいな。メールかファクスで送っちゃダメなの？」、一瞬そう思ったのですが、「それぞれの場に適した対応があるのだろう」と思い直してアドバイスに従い、議員会館を上から下まで駆け回って頭を下げました。

このように議員の方々は「直接顔を合わせる」ことを重視し、小さなことでも、「ちょっ

これもメールや電話で済まそうとしてはダメなのです。こうした要望にきちんと応え続けていくと、「じゃあ、あいつのためにやってやろう」と協力してくれる、そうやって貴重な応援を受けたことが何度もありました。

ビジネスパートナーの考え方

どんなに高い志を持ち、献身的に努力をしたとしても、個人や一つの団体ができることには限界があります。目的が「いいことをしたい」という気持ちを満たすためのボランティア活動であるならばそれでもいいかもしれませんが、事業・ビジネスとして行うのであれば、最適な相手と組んで結果を出すことを目的に活動するのは当然です。

ＴＦＴは、「地球上の飢餓と飽食という食の不均衡と、それによって生じるさまざまな社会課題を解決する」という目的を掲げています。しかし、大切なのは目的を唱えているだけではなく、それに基づいて実際に行動し、社会を変革していくことです。

できる限り早く変化を起こすために、ＴＦＴ創設時から、事業を自分たちだけで完結しようという気はありませんでした。不得意な分野までカバーしようとして失敗したり、時

間を浪費したりするくらいなら、その分野の先達や専門家の手を借りる方がいい。その方が僕たちの理念を早く確実に現実化できるはずだと考えたのです。

ＴＦＴの食堂プログラムを導入してくれる企業や団体はもちろん提携先になりますし、この他にも、新規事業やプロジェクトの設計や運営面でも多くの企業・団体と提携をしながらやっています。

たとえば、事業をはじめた当初から、開発途上国の学校給食をつくる段階については、「ミレニアム・プロミス」と「国連開発計画（ＵＮＤＰ）」という他団体と提携して展開しています。自前のスタッフが現地で給食を配ったり、独自に食堂をつくったりするには、現状では財政的にも人的にも資源が足りませんし、時間もないからです。

今、提携している団体には、支援するアフリカの小さな村の学校で給食をつくる施設と、調理を担当する村人とのネットワークがあります。それなら、そうしたところと提携するのが一番効率的だと判断しています。また、そうすることで、自分たちが一番必要とされ、得意とするエリアに資源を注力でき、集まる寄付金を効果的に活用することができるはずなのです。

コンビニとの提携をはじめる

さらに、最近ではより幅広い提携もはじまりました。
ＴＦＴの食堂プログラムは、提携先となる相手の企業や団体が社員食堂を持っていることが前提となります。社員食堂がない企業や個人の方の場合、活動の趣旨に賛同してくれたとしても参加してもらえる場がないのです。このことは、活動をはじめた当初から大きな課題だと思っていました。

その解決策の一つとしてはじめた新規プロジェクトが、コンビニエンスストアのスリーエフと、有名シェフでＴＦＴのアドバイザーでもある三國清三氏とのコラボレーションです。

これは、三國氏監修によるヘルシーメニューをスリーエフの商品企画の方たちと一緒に開発し、ＴＦＴの商品として店舗で販売する、というものです。コンビニ利用者から人気の高いお弁当、パスタ、ドリア、サラダ、デザートという五つの商品を開発しました。もちろん、これらの商品の売り上げの一部はアフリカの学校給食費になります。さらに、二

図6

コンビニ商品で活動を広げる

〇〇九年の横浜開港一五〇周年に合わせた期間限定メニューにして話題性を喚起することも狙っています。

コンビニという一般の方の多くが利用するところで、商品を介してTFTの活動に参加できるようになると、これまでの社員食堂に限定した活動から、さらに一歩、大きな広がりが出るはずです。これまでの一〇倍、一〇〇倍の規模で活動が広がるはず、とワクワクしています。

People［組織・人事］
――適切な評価と報酬、そして採用の考え方

組織づくりをどう考えるか

どんな団体でもそうでしょうが、組織をどうつくり、人をどう育てるか、ということは大きな問題です。

ＴＦＴの場合、組織は正会員・理事会・事務局で構成されており、このうち僕が事務局長を務める事務局が実務の部分を担当しています。理事のメンバーは営業、組織運営、新規事業開発などのあらゆる面で協力してくれますが、日々の運営は事務局の専従メンバーで対応しなければなりません。

現在、事務局の専従スタッフは僕を含めて二名だけなので、あらゆる仕事を兼務している状態です。少ないスタッフでギリギリのところでやっているので、スピーディで効率的な運営をしていく必要があります。

初期のころは、営業に行ったあとは必ずもう一人のメンバーと反省会をして、その日の訪問でよかったところ、悪かったところを振り返るようにしてきました。これまでにお話しした、部門や業種別の営業方法もこうした反省会を経てまとまってきたものです。

また、意欲ある学生にはインターン生として定期的に来てもらい、業務を担ってもらっています。学生には学校の勉強もあるので、入れ替わり立ち替わり何人ものインターン生に来てもらっていた時期もありました。そうした人たちが滞りなく仕事ができるよう運営業務の詳細をマニュアルにしておき、誰もがすぐに仕事に取り掛かれるようにしています。

こうしてどんどん仕事を任せていると、学生であっても驚くほどの仕事をこなしてくれます。入って数ヵ月のインターン生がテレビの取材に応対し、TFTの取り組みについて堂々と語ってくれたこともありました。

現状は、こうしてなんとか業務を回している状態ですが、将来を考えたときには、事業の拡大に応じて専従スタッフを増やし、機能別の組織にしていきたいと思っています。

具体的には管理部門と事業部門に分け、前者は総務、経理、人事、IT、後者は食堂事業の拡大と管理、新規事業開発、広報などに分けるようなイメージを描いています。

細かく部門を分けたいと思うのは、スタッフに専門性を十分発揮して欲しいと思っているからです。高い専門スキルを持ったスタッフがそれぞれの持ち場でその能力をいかんなく発揮する、というのが僕の描く理想の組織です。

実際にアメリカの大手NPOでは、マーケティング、ファイナンス、営業、広報、事業開発など、各分野の専門家が集団となって事業を展開しているのです。

大きな問題、報酬について

ＮＰＯ法人で働いているというと、「素晴らしいですね」という言葉のあとに、「ところで本業では何をされているのですか?」と聞かれることがあります。「ＮＰＯの活動はボランティアだからスタッフは無給で働いている」と思われているのです。学生からも「社会事業分野で就職したいのですが、実際のところ食べていけるんでしょうか?」という質問をよく受けます。

ＮＰＯなど社会事業団体の仕事は、社会問題の解決のために集めた寄付金や会費をできる限り有効活用することです。でも、だからといって労働に応じた報酬まで放棄しているわけではありません。

もし、スタッフに報酬を支払わない、あるいは支払えないＮＰＯがあるとすれば、それは社会事業をビジネスとして行なっていることにはならないはずです。海外の例を見ても、一定の評価を得ているＮＰＯではスタッフにきちんと報酬を支払い、役員クラスともなれば、一般企業と同等もしくはそれ以上の収入を得ている人もいます。

いくら「よいことをしている」という自負があっても、労働に見合った報酬がなければ、

仕事に本当の意味でのプライドを持てず、責任を持って最後まで仕事をまっとうしよう、という気持ちにはなれないのではないでしょうか。また、正当な報酬が得られなければ、社会事業に優秀な人材を惹きつけることもできません。

一般企業に比べ、人的資源の充実していない組織が大きな成果を上げることなどできません。だからこそ、僕は自分を含めたスタッフに正当な報酬を支払い、この事業はビジネスとして成り立つ、ということを示したいと強く思うのです。

お寺のお坊さんを見てください。意地悪な見方をすれば、彼らは新しいモノやサービスを生み出しているわけではなく、主な収入源はお布施＝寄付です。けれども宗教家という仕事に意義を感じない、という人は少ないでしょうし、「お坊さんは貧乏で当然だ。給料なんてなくていい」とも思わないでしょう。

ＮＰＯだって同じです。いい仕事をして、なおかつ経営能力があって、財政的にも成り立っている団体であれば、一般企業と遜色ない給料をスタッフに支払っていたところでまったく問題はないはずです。

そして、正当な報酬を払うためには、正当な評価システムが不可欠です。

ＴＦＴはまだ評価システムをきちんと整える段階には至っていませんが、組織が大きくなれば必要となるのは間違いないので現在研究中、というところです。

ちょっと難しいな、と思っているのは評価のはかり方です。

一般の企業でも、売上や利益目標に対する達成度をはかる定量評価とそれ以外の部分をはかる定性評価のバランスに頭を悩ませていることでしょう。加えて、社会事業の場合は、目標自体が「社会のため」といった雲をつかむような定量化しにくいものなので、これを数値化して評価するのはとても難しいのです。でも、この活動をきちんとしたビジネスとして続けるのであれば、ここはきちんと考えていかなければならない部分だと思っています。

社会事業で活躍したいという人たちが、ＮＰＯでは食べていけない、ＮＰＯでは快適に仕事ができないと言って、仕方なく一般企業に就職している。そういう現実を何とかしたい。一般企業も社会事業も、就職先の選択肢としては等価でなければおかしいのです。

そうなるためにはＮＰＯも利益を上げることをもっともっと真剣に考えるべきだし、働く側も働きと利益に応じた報酬を、胸を張って受け取ればいいのです。

とはいえ、お金を稼ぐこと自体にやりがいを感じる、という人はやっぱり一般の企業に行った方がいいでしょう。社会事業にはそこでなければ得られない満足感や自己実現の形があります。そういうものを大事にしたい人が収入の心配をせずにこの世界に入ってこられる、それが健全な姿なのだと思います。

どんな人が社会事業に向いているのか？

どのような人が社会起業家や社会事業で働くことに向いているのでしょうか？

社会問題に関心があり、なおかつ問題をそのままにしておきたくはない、自分の手で少しでもいい方向に変革してみせる、という気概を持っている人であることは大前提です。

「会社勤めよりラクそうだから」「ＮＰＯで働いているのは優しい人だろう」「毎日を楽しく送れるに違いない」という気持ちからＴＦＴに入ってきたら、目の回るような大量の業務と厳しく成果を追求する姿勢に驚かれると思います。

「ＴＦＴに転職したい」と言って大企業にお勤めの方がいらしたこともありました。でも、その人の最初の言葉は、「何をすればいいのですか？」だったのです。ＴＦＴに限らず、

社会事業というのは発展途上の部分だらけです。「こうすればうまくいく」というマニュアルがあるわけではありません。自分で問題を発見し、解決方法を考えていかねばなりません。「指示がないと動けない」という人は、残念ながら社会事業にはあまり向いていないと思います。

僕が一緒に働く仲間に欲しいと思う資質は「豊かな感受性」です。ＴＦＴのプログラムのように、目に見えず、さらに特徴が多いがゆえにそのよさを伝えることが難しいものを売るのですから、相手と話をしながら「この人はどこに興味を持ってくれたのか」「どの部分に不安を感じているのか」といったことを素早く感知し、話を組み立てたり、資料を用意したりする能力が必要です。それには、相手の気持ちを汲み取る感受性が欠かせないのです。また、社会事業に従事する人として、社会で起きていることに敏感になり、かつ自分のフィルターを通して、課題を自分なりに抽出し、設定できることも大切です。

そういった社会や自分を取り巻く環境に対して鋭い感受性がある人なら、仕事としての社会事業を楽しめるはずだと思います。

採用の理想と現実、そして「これから」

今は小さな組織のＴＦＴですが、今後は高い専門性を持った仲間にぜひ加わって欲しい。マーケティングや財務などの専門家が活躍するための土壌がたくさんあると思います。その一方で、ビジネス経験のない学生の方が「ＴＦＴに就職したい」と言ってくれることもあります。正直、こうした新卒の学生を積極的に採用していくかどうかについては、僕自身迷っている部分があります。

今の学生は、僕の世代が持っていた「なんとなく就職するか」といった意識はなく、真剣に自分の適性や能力を見極め、成長できる就職先を慎重に選ぼうとしているように思えます。また、自分たちの両親世代がリストラで苦い経験をしたり、先輩が仕事に満足していない姿を見たりしているためか、「自分の市場価値を上げなければ」と、成長への焦りさえにじませる人が多い。

大企業の倒産、バブルの崩壊、ベンチャー経営者の失墜などの社会情勢を目のあたりにして、「信じられるのは自分だけ」という気持ちもあるのでしょう。学生時代から将来やり

たいことを考え抜き、インターンやアルバイトなどを経験して自分を磨いている彼ら、彼女らは、とてもしっかりしていて能力も高い人が多いと思います。そして、そういった優秀な学生の中に、社会事業に従事することを希望する人たちが増えていることも感じます。

こうした状況の中で、ＴＦＴでも求める人物像、期待する能力・スキルを明確にして、優秀な人材を採用していきたいと考えています。僕自身の経験からも、最初の就職先はその後の価値観や仕事に対する美学・哲学を大きく左右する大切な場だと思います。また、インターンの学生たちと一緒に仕事をする中で、この年齢の人はスポンジのように何でも吸収していく、ということも実感しているところです。ＴＦＴのすべてを吸収して、将来組織を背負って立つようなリーダー人材をぜひとも採用し、育成したいと願っています。

こうした姿が理想ではあるのですが、一方で現実を見ると、新卒採用に関してのボトルネックがいくつかあることも事実です。

まずは財務基盤と収入の安定性です。

これはＴＦＴに限らず、創業期にあるベンチャー組織すべてに言えることでしょう。そしてＴＦＴのようなＮＰＯの場合は、一般の営利ベンチャーにはある「ベンチャー・キャ

ピタルによる融資」や「株式上場」という資金調達手段がないので、創業期の財務基盤は一層不安定です。財務基盤が不安定ということは、収入についても先が見えないリスクがあるということです。現状では、事業をできる限り早く成長させ、事業収入を増やし、財務基盤を安定させることで解消するしかない問題です。

二つめは、人材育成の体制です。これもベンチャー組織全般に言えることでしょうが、ぎりぎりの人数で運営をしているので、入社後の教育、特に社会人としての基礎教育にかけられる人と時間が不足していることは否めません。

大きな組織であれば、入社後には新人研修などが手厚く整備され、名刺の渡し方からビジネス文書の書き方まで、逐一丁寧に教えてくれることでしょう。対して小さな組織の場合は全員が実行部隊なので、実務の指導はできてもこうした基礎的なことまでは手が回らないのが実情です。新卒採用者自身のアルバイトやインターン時代の経験に頼らざるを得ないのです。

三つめは、精神的なケアの面です。大きな組織であれば、新入社員が壁にぶつかったときには先輩や上司、同期など相談にのってくれる仲間がまわりに大勢いることでしょう。僕自身も最初の職場でスランプに陥り、長く暗いトンネルを迷走した経験があります。そこから救い出してくれたのは、先輩や同期といった仲間のアドバイスでした。僕たちのよ

うなベンチャー組織では、そうしたケアを十分にしてあげることができません。誰もが経験するであろうそうした時期のケアをどうするか、というのは大きな課題です。

そして最後はキャリアパスについてです。新卒でＮＰＯに入り、その後キャリアを積んで一般の企業に移る、といったキャリアパスは、日本では残念ながらあまり例がありません。企業側にもＮＰＯでの職務経験を評価する基準はないでしょう。一般の企業とＮＰＯを柔軟に渡り歩いてキャリアを高める、そうしたアメリカのような状況にはまだまだほど遠いのが現状です。

こうしたいくつものボトルネックがあることは事実ですが、やはり、僕は「同志よ、来たれ」と言いたい。

ＴＦＴの事業でできることは無限に広がっていると感じますし、優秀な仲間さえいればそれらは必ずや実現できると確信しています。想像力があり、柔軟性があり、かつ情熱とエネルギーに満ちあふれた若い人材と一緒に世界的な事業をつくっていきたい、強くそう思うのです。

社会事業には、まだまだ手つかずの事業領域がたくさんあります。今からここに飛び込めば、ビル・ゲイツ、スティーブ・ジョブス、そして本田宗一郎のような世界的な経営者になることができるのです。そして、僕はそうした存在になりたいと思うし、できることであれば日本から、もっともっとそうした経営者が育って欲しい。そして、そうした人が育つ環境づくりに、少しでも貢献できればと思っています。

Promotion［宣伝・広報］
――オンリーワンの存在として認知してもらうには

社会貢献のブランド価値は向上中！

企業や商品の価値を高めてマス・セールスに結び付ける、というのがこれまでの一般企業のブランディングでした。商品・サービスの供給者側によって戦略的に行われるこの手法が社会事業にも有効かと言われれば、ちょっと懐疑的な部分があります。というより、

これからはあらゆる世界において、「つくられたブランド」の権威が失墜していく、そんな気がしているのです。

僕たちの世代をはじめ、今の多くの日本人は、生まれたときから物質的な欠乏というものを知らず、まわりにモノが溢れていることに慣れ切ってしまっています。そんな中、モノを売る側は自社の商品・サービスのブランド価値を高め、他社と差別化することに躍起になってきました。売り手側の商業的で一方的な思いが色濃く反映され、買い手側の思いがないがしろにされた結果、僕たちが本当に価値を感じられるブランドが少なくなっているように思うのです。

一方で、「社会に対してよいことをする」ということへの価値は確実に高まっています。これは環境や貧困問題の取り上げられ方からも感じます。その兆候は、「ロハス」や「スローフード」という言葉が浸透したころから見られましたが、そのころはまだ、成熟市場における新たな消費のキーワード、という側面もありました。

ところが、僕が社会起業家であるという点を割り引いても、ここ数年の地球や社会に対する関心の高まりには、ある種の必然性を感じます。もっと言うなら、これが大きなムー

図7

「壁」を越えるということ

組織・会社・国などの「壁」を越えて
人とつながり、世界とつながる

ブメントにつながる気がしてならないのです。このテーマに関心を持つ人も、若者層だけではなく、社会変化に敏感な広範囲の層に広がっていることを感じます。

自分だけが満たされても、自分の働く会社だけが儲かっても、それは結局本当の幸せにはつながらない。組織、会社、国など、これまで多くの人を守り、かつ外界から遮断してきた「壁」は次第にその意義を失いつつあります。この壁を乗り越え、想いを同じくする人たちとつながる方法を、多くの人が模索しはじめているのです。

こうした状況の中、社会とのつながりを強く感じられる社会事業のブランド価

値というのは、これから黙っていても確実に上がっていく。僕は期待を込めてそう予言します。

しかし、だからといって「社会事業に携わる人は、自分たちのブランディングに無関心でいてもいい」というわけではありません。日本では、社会貢献と言うと、奉仕団体や一部の人たちによるボランティア活動と理解されている場合が多くあります。社会問題に関心があっても関わり方がわからなかったり、自分とは関係ないと思ったりする人がとても多いのは残念なことです。

だからこそ、ＴＦＴのように、肩に力を入れず気軽にできる社会貢献活動の存在を積極的に伝えていきたいと思っています。また、そういう活動に参加することは、高級ブランドのバッグを持つのと同じように、あるいはそれ以上に、自分の価値を高めてくれる。そうした合意が社会に形成されれば、さらに参加者は増えることでしょう。そしてその流れは確実にできつつあります。

「この社会をもっとよくしたい」

そうした気持ちを持った人がその想いを形にできる。世の中にはそういうしくみがもっと必要です。そのしくみをつくるのが、まさに社会起業家というわけです。そして、同時にしくみの存在を知らしめ、それに価値を付加し、賛同者と参加者を広く募るということも、社会事業の仕事の一部なのです。

ＴＦＴの戦略的なブランドづくり

ＴＦＴは、かなり戦略的にブランディングに取り組んでいるＮＰＯであると自負しています。ＴＦＴのブランドイメージを固めるのに最重要視しているのが次ページのロゴです。

ベースになっているのはアルファベットのＴ。これはテーブル（Ｔａｂｌｅ）の頭文字です。そして、そのＴが真ん中で二色に分かれているのは、一つのテーブルを先進国と開発途上国が「分かち合っている」というイメージを表すためです。メインカラーは温かみのある赤で、これは「愛情」を意味しています。

ロゴはＴＦＴの象徴ですから、これが浸透すれば、それがそのままＴＦＴの認知につながると考え、資料や配布物などには必ず目立つところにロゴを配置するようにしています。

図8

ロゴ

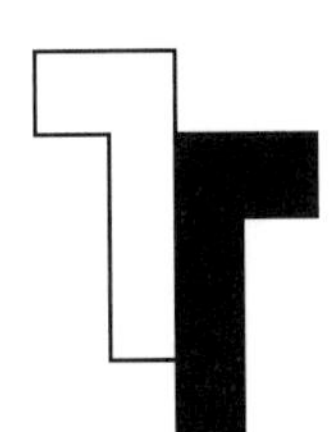

ＴＦＴの導入企業が、社内告知や食堂内の掲示のためにロゴを使うこと自体は大歓迎ですが、その場合、デザインを加工したり、色を変更したりすることは基本的にお断りしています。

ある企業でＴＦＴを導入して頂いたときのことです。

社内告知用にチラシをつくってくれたのはありがたかったのですが、スペースの都合上なのか、ＴＦＴのロゴがかなり引き伸ばされ、色も変更して掲載されていたのです。善意でやってもらったことなのでとても心苦しくはあったのですが、このときもロゴ使用の規定を守るようにお願いしました。

このことをきっかけに、僕たちはポス

ターや食堂に置く卓上ＰＯＰをセットにした「スターターキット」をつくり、導入企業に購入をお願いするようにしたのです。

ロゴの次にはＴＦＴの活動を一言で表わすフレーズをつくり、ロゴと一緒に表示していくことを考えています。今は「ＴＡＢＬＥ　ＦＯＲ　ＴＷＯは、開発途上国の飢餓と先進国の肥満や生活習慣病の解消に同時に取り組む、日本発の社会貢献運動です」というフレーズを使っていますが、ちょっと長くてわかりにくいので、すぐにわかるキャッチフレーズのようなものが欲しいな、と思っているところです。

メディア・個人とどう連携していくか

ブランドイメージ定着のためには、さまざまな手段を駆使して露出の機会を増やすことも重要です。しかし、もちろんＴＦＴにはテレビや新聞の枠を買って広告を出すような資金的余裕はありません。

ＴＦＴでは、リリースなどを配布して番組や記事で取り上げてもらう、いわゆるＰＲ活動を重視しています。メディアから取材の申し込みや番組への出演依頼があれば、どんな

に忙しくても基本的にはすべてお受けするようにしています。視聴率が一〇％の全国ネットのニュース番組に映像が流れれば千三百万人の人が見てくれるのですから、その影響力ははかり知れません。

実際に、メディアで紹介されることのメリットはとても大きいものがありました。僕が紹介された新聞を見た企業の方から「ＴＦＴを導入したい」という連絡が入ったり、個人の方から「寄付をしたい」というお申し出を頂いたり、という効果が出ています。

一緒にメニューを開発する社員食堂の料理長が僕の出たラジオを聞いていたことからスムーズに話が運んだり、労働組合の方が「小暮さんの出ているテレビを見て、導入したいと思っていたんですよ」と言ってくださって一気に導入が進んだりなど、予想外のところでもメディアの効果を感じることもしばしばです。

記者や編集者の方の関心を惹くためには、思わず相手が取り上げたくなるようなリリースを打ち、イベントを企画することも大切です。

ＴＦＴには、「飢餓とメタボを同時に解決」「二十円でできる社会貢献」「日本発の社会事業」など、目を引く切り口がいくつかあるので、メディアにあわせてそういうフックを

あらかじめ用意しておくと、取り上げてもらえるチャンスが広がります。
伝えたいことがあるときは、こちら側から積極的にアプローチすることも大事。ＴＦＴでは、定期的に日々の活動をニューズレターにまとめ、それをメディアに送っています。

また、ＰＲ活動の手段はメディア媒体だけに留まりません。
大規模なイベントを通じて大勢の人たちに対して一気にＰＲを行なうこともしています。アフリカの小学校で子どもたちが食べている給食を提供し、現地の様子をビデオ映像で見せることで、僕たちの活動を全身で理解してもらう、というイベントを開催したこともありました。こうしたイベントを含めたプロモーション活動はすべて自前でやっているので、イベント開催までの数週間は、集客、出欠確認、会場準備、式次第決定など、慣れない作業にてんてこまいになりました。イベント関連の仕事をしている有志者や学生が集まり、無償で手伝ってくれたことでなんとか乗り切ることができました。こうした人たちの善意に支えられ、数百人の参加者に対してＴＦＴのＰＲをすることができたのです。
マスメディアの力は大きいですが、それとあわせて個人の発信力にも大きなものがあります。政治家やアーティストの中には、ＴＦＴ活動の伝道者（エバンジェリスト）の役目

を果たしてくださる人が出てきていますし、ビジネスパーソンや学生、主婦の方たちの中にも、ブログで紹介することなどで応援してくださる方がたくさんいます。

この「個人の発信力」ともうまく連携したいと思い、二〇〇八年の年末には、ブログに食糧問題についてのコメントを二回書くとアフリカに給食を一食届けられる、という「TASTY BLOG キャンペーン」を実施しました。口コミマーケティングの会社と組み、個人ブロガーの方が記事を書くと、そのサイトを運営している企業がTFTに寄付をする、というしくみです。これも予想以上の反響があり、一ヵ月の実施期間中に四千五百食分余りの給食費が集まりました。

TFTブランドの将来

TFTは「食」を現在の事業領域の中心に置いています。将来的には活動する分野は広がるかもしれませんが、その場合もやはり「フォー・ツー」つまり「分かち合う」という言葉がキーワードになる、と思っています。

これまで、「他人より多くを手に入れたい」という自己中心的な欲望は、社会を発達させる促進剤として奨励されてきました。しかし、資源や食糧などは世界全体で配分を考えねばどうにもならない状況にきています。過剰な欲望の対局にある「足るを知る」ということ、そして「分かち合い」という考え方が主流になれば、この社会は誰にとっても、もっと暮らしやすくなるはずです。

「いろいろなものを分かち合って、みんなで幸せになろう」

そのブランドの名前を耳にする、あるいはロゴを目にすると、誰もがそういう精神を思い出す。そして、そこには常に「健康と社会貢献」といったような、二つのことを一度に解決してしまう合理性とユニークさが感じられる。

僕はＴＦＴを、そういうブランドに育てていきたいと思っているのです。

「プロダクト・レッド」というすごいブランド

僕が社会事業のブランディングで注目しているのが、「プロダクト・レッド」というプロジェクトです。

これは、ロックバンドU2のリードボーカルとして有名なボノと、国際的なNPOであるDATAのボビー・シュライバーが発起人となり、二〇〇六年一月の世界経済フォーラムで発表されたプロジェクトです。

このしくみはいたってシンプル。参加する企業が「(PRODUCT) RED」という共通ブランドを冠した商品を開発・販売し、その販売収益の一部が世界基金に寄付され、世界のHIV・結核・マラリア対策に使われる、というものです。

それらの商品・サービスはすべてプロジェクトの名称でもある「RED=赤」がキーカラーとして使われています。

現在、参加企業には、アメリカン・エキスプレス、コンバース、GAP、ジョルジオ・アルマーニ、モトローラ、アップル、ホールマーク、デル、マイクロソフトといった、超有名グローバル企業が名を連ねています。

このプロダクト・レッドが優れているのは、従来の単なる寄付と違って、企業が自分の商品力や販売力をいかし、企業自身も利益を得ることができる「ビジネス」として展開されているために、活動に継続性があるという点です。

たとえば、アメックスは「アメックス・レッド・カード」というサービスをつくり、このカードを選んだ人は会費が優遇され、カード使用金額の一％が自動的に寄付されるしくみにしています（日本では未導入）。アップルは「ｉＰｏｄ　ｎａｎｏ」のラインアップに「ＲＥＤ」を加え、この「ＲＥＤ」を消費者が購入すると、販売価格のうち十ドルが寄付されるようにしています。

アメックスもｉＰｏｄも既に多くのファンを持つブランドですし、どちらの商品・サービスも希少性も手伝ってとてもカッコいい。並んでいたら思わず選びたくなります。そう、プロダクト・レッド・ブランドの商品は、他の商品と同等か、それ以上に魅力的なのです。二〇〇六年にボノが来日した際、当時の安倍晋三首相にプレゼントした、プロダクト・レッド・ブランドのアルマーニ製サングラスは、発売と同時に完売となるくらいのすごい人気でした。

商品自体に魅力があれば、社会問題に関心のある人でもない人でも、プロダクト・レッド・ブランドの商品が購入の選択肢に入ります。加えて社会貢献がその商品・サービスのブランド価値をさらに上げる効果を出しているのです。こういった社会的な問題解決に参加することが「カッコいい」という価値観として認められる時代になっているのです。

ＴＦＴのブランドもこうしたものにしていきたい。ＴＦＴのメニューはヘルシーという他のメニューにはない魅力があります。そこにさらに「アフリカの子どもたちを助けることができる」という価値を加え、「こっちを選ぶのは自分のためにもなるし、他人のためにもなるし、それに、カッコいいよね」、そう思ってもらいたいのです。

Profit［利益・成果］

収益を上げ続け、最適な投資をする

社会事業の収益予測は難しい

「資産やお金の流れを会計原則に則って管理する」という会計の基本は、社会事業も一般の企業も変わりません。特に内閣府の認証を受けたＮＰＯ法人の場合は、期ごとに貸借対照表や損益決算書などの財務諸表を提出することが義務付けられているので、いい加減なことをやっていると認証を取り消されてしまいます。

そして、一般企業と同様に将来の事業計画と収益予測を立てることも必要です。

ただし、僕の実感では、事業開始から数年の収益予測をすることは一般の事業よりも社会事業の方がはるかに難しい、と思います。社会事業はまだ日本での歴史が浅く、通常の新規事業であれば参考になる業界データや近似値というものがほとんどありません。さらにはこの分野に詳しい会計・財務のエキスパートもほとんどいないというのが現状だからです。

ＴＦＴがＮＰＯ法人の認証を受ける際に、向こう三年間の事業計画をつくりましたが、収益予測に関しては、正直あまり自信が持てませんでした。

たとえば、一年間でどれくらいの数の企業がＴＦＴのプログラムを採用してくれるのか、最初はまったく見当がつきませんでした。コンサルタント時代に手掛けてきた一般企業の商品マーケティングプランと違って、需要の規模がまるでわからないのです。

さらには、社員数が一〇〇〇人の会社がＴＦＴを導入したとして、そのうち何パーセントの人がヘルシーメニューを選んでくれるのか、またメニューの内容によってその割合がどのように変化するのか、なども基礎となるデータがないので予想がつきません。

だから、最初は計画通りにいかなくても、その都度修正を施していくより他ない、と考

えました。実際、事業を進めるうちに、「ヘルシーメニューを食べる人の割合はほぼ一〇〜二〇%の間に収まる」というようなデータがだんだんと揃ってきて、翌年度からは収益予測の精度がグンと上がりました。

社会事業の場合、大きなスポンサーが付いているなどの特殊ケースを別にすれば、収入源は不特定多数の寄付に頼る事業モデルになります。組織や運動の名前を認知してもらい、活動の趣旨に賛同して寄付をしてもらえるようになるまでには、ある程度の時間がかかるのが当然です。普通は立ち上げから数年は、資金的な余裕がない状態で活動せざるを得ません。

TFTの場合は、理想的な活動を行おうと思ったら、年間数千万円の運営費が必要です。でも、今の現実としては、それを賄うだけの収入は確保できていません。

寄付のうち運営費に回せる割合も決めていますから、必要なだけの運営費を得るためには、まだまだ提携企業の数が足りないのです。その数に達する見込みのあと三、四年の間は、いろいろな手段を使って運営費を捻出する必要があるのです。

僕たちは、できる限り経費を節約しムダをしないよう気を付けています。

コピーをとるときは必ず紙の両面を使いますし、備品は必要最低限のものでまかないます。ちなみに、今のオフィスで使用している机や椅子などは知人にお願いした手づくりのものです。移動の際には公共交通機関を利用するのが基本ですし、地方に出向くときにも予想される成果を考え、先方から交通費の支給がないときはお断りすることもあります。外部の企業に仕事を発注するときは、複数社から見積りをとって、厳しい値段交渉をさせて頂いています。とはいえ、こうしたムダを省く努力は一般の企業でも同様に取り組んでいることでしょう。当然すべき経営努力の範囲内だと思います。

ムダを徹底的に排除することは大切ですが、「ＮＰＯなのだから、すべてにわたって清貧の状態が当たり前」だとは思ってはいません。たとえば、事業が成長し、十分なお金が集まるようになったら、オフィスはもっと広いところに移して、スタッフも増やしていきたいと思います。給料も一般企業と遜色なく、できればそれ以上にしたいという気持ちもあります。

ＴＦＴが提携関係を結んでいるアメリカの大手ＮＰＯ「ミレニアム・プロミス」はマンハッタンの一等地にオフィスを構えています。それを「経費のムダ」と言う人はいません。

社会変革や寄付集めへの影響力がある人たちへのアクセスやPRのしやすさを考えると立地がよいことは大きなメリットになります。
それに、隙間風の入るようなオフィスでは優秀な人材が集まりませんし、そんな環境に甘んじている人たちの中から、世界の貧困をなくすための画期的なアイデアなど生まれてこない。そのことをみんながわかっているのです。

「お金をかけるべきところ」はどこか

そうは言っても、寄付金の使い道については、日々悩むことばかりです。
今手元にある二十円をそのままアフリカに持っていけば、確実に給食一食分になります。でも、それを事業の投資に回せば、将来的には一〇〇食、一〇〇〇食分になるかもしれません。最も効果的なお金の使い方は何なのか、いつも頭を悩ませています。
「はじめに」のところでも述べましたが、NPOが一般の事業と違うのは、上げた利益の使い道です。一般の事業では、資金を出した株主に還元したり、税金を通じて社会に還元したりします。それがNPOでは、社会を変えるためのNPO自身の事業に還元します。

図9
営利組織と非営利組織での利益の使い道の違い

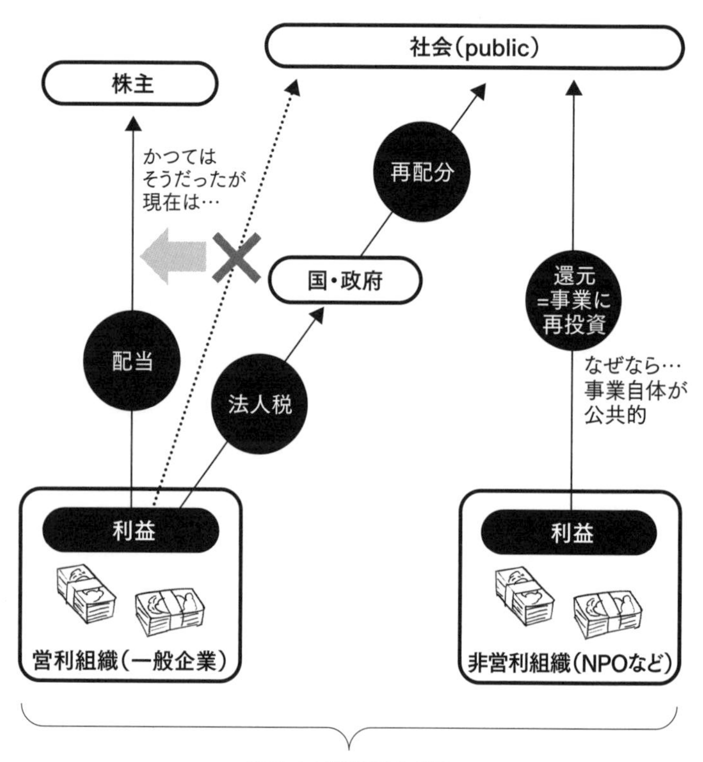

寄付によって支えられているＮＰＯなのですから、集まったお金は一円たりともムダにできないのは当たり前です。一方で、僕たちはこれをビジネスとしてやっています。ビジネスであれば戦略に見合った投資をし、リターンを狙うのは当然のことです。

また、事業をやっていけば当然運営費もかかります。オフィスを借りれば家賃や光熱費が発生しますし、交通費がなければ営業に行くこともできません。電話をかけたり、資料をつくったりするのにもお金がかかります。そうした費用をすべて自己負担していたら、相当なお金持ちでないとＮＰＯの活動に参加できなくなってしまいます。

ＮＰＯ法に「市民が行う自由な社会貢献活動としての特定非営利活動」と明記されているように、社会貢献は誰でもが自由に参加できるものであるべきです。ＴＦＴでは、「寄付金の一部は人件費を含む運営費に充当します」ということをあらかじめ明確にして、企業や個人の方に理解してもらうよう努めています。

ムダを省くべきところとお金をかけるべきところ。

その観点からしばしば議論の対象となるのは、海外に視察に行くときの飛行機やホテルのグレードです。

僕自身は、アフリカまでの長時間フライトであっても飛行機はエコノミークラスを使っ

ています。ただ、アメリカで社会事業に携わる友人からは「マサも早くビジネスクラスに乗れるようになれ」と言われます。僕自身はエコノミークラスでもまったく苦にはならないのですが、アメリカではこうした待遇の差は優秀な人材を惹きつける重要な要素となるのです。

日本でもＴＦＴのようなＮＰＯが社会で認められ、一つの業種として確立した将来は、こうした待遇の問題は個人の嗜好を超えた、人材確保に関わる組織の重要な決定事項になると感じています。小さなことに思われるかもしれませんが、「ＮＰＯに勤めているのだから、二十時間以上のフライトもエコノミークラスで辛抱しなければならない」というのが常識となったら、一般企業の優秀なビジネスパーソンはＮＰＯに転職することに二の足を踏むでしょう。そうしたら、いつまでたっても社会事業には有能な人材が集まらない、ということになるかもしれません。

飛行機はエコノミー派の僕ですが、開発途上国で泊まるホテルに関してはある程度のランクのところを選ぶようにしています。「もう少し安いところでもいいのではないか」という意見がないわけではありませんが、現地を見た結果、ランクが低いホテルでは安全が保証されないと判断してそうしています。

治安のよくないところを移動しながらタイトなスケジュールをこなし、心身ともに疲れ切った状態になり、その上ホテルに戻っても安心して休めないというのでは、体と心がもちません。一度や二度の遊びの旅行であれば、それもスリルがあってよいかもしれませんが、僕たちのようなビジネスの出張では、仕事に集中することを優先すべきだと考えています。一番大切なのは「スタッフがやりがいを持って、仕事に集中して、活動を継続できること」です。お金を節約しようとするあまりに、スタッフが「もう嫌だ」という状態になってしまっては本末転倒です。ある程度の快適さ、そして何よりも安全を確保するためにお金を使うことは、合理的な経営判断だと思うのです。

イベント開催は「投資」である

前にお話ししたイベントを開催するときにも、お金の使い方についてこんな議論がありました。

そのイベントは、日本から地理的に遠く離れたアフリカの食糧事情を知ってもらうこと、そしてＴＦＴの活動内容を理解してもらうことを目的としていました。

会場には都心のイベントスペースを借り、参加者から会費を集める形で開催しました。このとき、周囲から「参加費の一部が会場費や飲食費に使われるのはいかがなものか」という批判が出てきたのです。

しかし、僕はこのイベントを「投資」だと考えていました。

交通の便がよい洗練されたスペースで、アフリカ音楽の演奏を聞いたり、アフリカの子どもたちに届けている給食を食べたり、他にはない魅力的な特徴があるからこそ、多くの人がお金を払ってでも参加したいという気になってくれる。そうして人を集め、ＴＦＴの活動を深く知ってもらい、賛同者になってもらうことに成功すれば、このパーティーへの投資は将来的に一〇〇倍・一〇〇〇倍になって返ってくるはずだ、と。

一般の事業であれば、新商品や新サービスを市場に出すときには、お金をかけて発表会やコンベンションをすることでしょう。そのことに疑問を持つ人はいないはずです。僕たちのやっているイベントなどもそれと同じ位置付けなのです。

ビジネスとして社会事業をやっているのですから、集まった寄付をただ支援先に送っているだけでは、僕たちの存在する意味がありません。「手元のお金を一番効果的に使う方

法を考え尽くす」、それがビジネスをする、ということだと思います。

お金の使い道について、「これが正しい」という絶対的な答えは見付かりませんが、こうした「事業戦略とマッチし、将来のリターンが見込めるものに〝投資〟をする」という考えは、いつも持っていたいと思います。

日本の税制の問題点

ＮＰＯは収入面の大部分を寄付に頼るところがほとんどです。そして、多くの日本のＮＰＯが資金難に苦しむ理由の一つに、ＮＰＯをめぐる寄付税制の問題があります。

現在の法律では、個人や企業が一般のＮＰＯに寄付をしても、税控除の対象にはなりません。ただし、寄付する先が国税庁長官の認定を受けた「認定ＮＰＯ法人」である場合には、税制優遇措置が認められます。

同じような事業を営むＮＰＯ法人が二つあり、片方は寄付金が課税対象になるのに対し、もう片方は税控除の対象となるとしましょう。きっとほとんどの人は税控除の対象となる方に寄付するはずです。つまり、認定ＮＰＯ法人は、寄付金を集める上では圧倒的に有利なのです。

そして、この認定ＮＰＯ法人になるためには、いくつかの条件をクリアしなければなりません。大きな条件の一つは「設立より一年を超える期間が経過し、少なくとも二つの事業年度を終えていなければならない」というものです。

でも、よく考えてみると、「事業開始から二事業年度」というのは、財政的に一番苦しいときです。将来を見据えて事業を育てつつ組織をつくり、安定した経営基盤を固めることを同時に行わなければならず、その活動のためにはまとまった資金が必要になります。それなのに、その時期には認定ＮＰＯ法人になれず寄付金が集めにくい、というのでは、意気に燃える新しいＮＰＯの芽をいたずらに摘んでしまうことにもなりかねません。

外資系のＮＰＯの場合、経営が軌道に乗るまでは本部からの援助でしのぐことができるのでまだ恵まれていると言えますが、そうしたものも望めない場合には状況は深刻です。

もちろん、税制優遇措置を受けるに値するＮＰＯかどうかを見極めるために、ある程度の時間は必要だ、という考え方もわからないではありません。

けれども、国に日本発の社会事業を育てようという意志があるなら、それこそ代表者の人となりや事業計画を見て、もっと短期間で判断してもらいたいと思います。たとえば、

ＮＰＯ法人の格付会社のようなものをつくって、そこが審査するような形も考えられるのではないでしょうか。もしくは、個人や企業からの寄付を集め、立ち上げ期のＮＰＯを目利きして投資をする、いわゆるベンチャー・キャピタルのような存在が出てくれば、素晴らしいことだと思います。

「想い」を仕事にするいくつもの方法

これまでお話ししてきたように、僕はＴＦＴ事務局長に就任する前に、マッキンゼーと松竹という二つの一般企業で働いてきました。

マッキンゼーではコンサルタントとしての論理思考と問題解決のスキルを徹底的に叩きこまれ、松竹では日本の大企業の優れた点と課題点を内部から眺めることができました。どちらでも得難い経験をさせてもらいましたが、「ここに骨を埋めよう」という気持ちにはついになれなかったことも事実です。

世の中のためになる仕事をしたい。

特別道徳的な生き方をしてきた記憶もない——今もそうですが——ので、どうしてそう

いう想いがあるのかよくわからないのですが、僕は物心ついたころから、大人になったら「世のため人のため」になるような仕事をしたい、漠然とながらそう思っていました。

世のため人のためになる仕事をしたい、という想いを実現する社会事業という新しい仕事が日本でも生まれ、認められるようになってきています。地球上で起きているさまざまな矛盾や歪みに対して漠然とした不安を感じながら生きるのではなく、それらの課題解決に積極的に関わっていくことができるようになっているのです。

さまざまな社会課題を解決するのは、決して簡単なことではありません。だから、あえてそれに挑もうという人たちは貴重だし、尊敬と称賛に値するはずです。

僕はTFTの仕事を通じて、社会事業に従事する人たちへの正しい理解と、地位の向上も図っていきたいと思っています。そして、若い世代の人たちは、社会事業に取り組みたいという強い想いがあるなら、ぜひともその思いにフタをしないで欲しい。

「その想いは、仕事にできる」

そのことを知って欲しいと思うのです。

ここまでに述べてきたことで「社会事業にも一般のビジネススキルがほとんどそのまま使える」ことがわかってもらえたと思います。
これは、そのまま僕の実感でもあるのです。コンサルタントとして学んできた問題解決や論理思考の技術、その後の実業の世界で学んだ人や組織を動かすための手法、こういったものは、そのまま社会事業の世界でも有効に使えました。そして、これらのビジネススキルのお陰で、ＴＦＴは短期間でこれだけ多くの支持と賛同者を得ることができたのだと思います。

社会事業はまだ歴史の浅い分野ですし、組織体制や待遇が十分整っていない団体が多いのも事実です。でも、だからこそ、ビジネススキルを世の中のために役立てたいというチャレンジ精神のある人にとっては魅力的な仕事となるはずだと思います。

もう一方で、社会起業家になることや社会事業に就職することだけが、こうした社会活動に関わる方法ではない、ということも強調しておきたいと思います。
これまで、一般のビジネススキルが重要、一般企業との提携が大切、と再三述べてきたのは、社会事業を推進するためには企業で活躍されている方のスキルを借りることが絶対

に必要である、と思っているからに他なりません。

社会課題への想いを共有してくださる方であれば、今の仕事の中で、何らかの連携をしていく方法がきっとあるはずですし、現にそうした方々とご一緒する機会が着実に増えています。そして、そうした方々が企業の中で増えていくことも、社会事業の裾野が広がるための重要な要素だと思うのです。

企業の中からＴＦＴを支える人たち

ある企業でＴＦＴプログラムを導入するにあたり、総務担当の方と給食会社とでヘルシーメニューの試作品をつくっていたときのことです。

最初の試作品を社員一〇人の方に食べて頂きました。しかし、戻ってきたアンケートは「とても食べられたものじゃない」「ボリュームがなさ過ぎる」など惨憺たる結果でした。これを見た総務担当の方はがっかりしつつも、アンケートの内容を給食会社の方に包み隠さず見せて、「悔しいから一緒にいいメニューをつくりましょう」と団結して頑張ってくれたのです。その方が言うには、「社員のメタボ予防だけが目的だったら、きっと給食会

社を説得できなかったと思います。アフリカの子どもを助けるんだから、という大きなゴールがあったから、『それなら頑張ろう』と全員が納得してくれたんです」

また、ある金融機関には、「企業の資金を使わず、かつ社員全員が参加できるCSR活動」を探した結果TFTにたどりついた、という担当者の方がいました。

彼は、新サービス開発部門からCSR担当に異動したばかり。新しい取り組みを設計し、実施することはお手のもので、すぐに社内の承認を得てプログラムを導入することになりました。

実施にあたっては社内のイントラネットやメールでの告知はもちろん、積極的にプレスリリースなどを打つことでメディアにも取り上げてもらいました。

TFTプログラムがスタートする初日には、トップ以下役員全員を社員食堂に連れてきて、TFTメニューを食べてもらいました。これで他の社員にも、「これはトップも支援している取り組みなんだ」と印象付けることができ、何よりの社内広報になりました。

導入後も社員食堂の壁に毎日のTFTメニューの売上額と寄付金額を掲示して社員の意識付けをする、拠点ごとの結果を比較して競争意識を高める、など独自の工夫をされていました。そんな彼の工夫によって「東京には負けられないぞ」「大阪はやっぱりケチなん

じゃないか」などＴＦＴに関する話題が食堂のテーブルで笑顔で交わされるようになりました。

また、彼は社員食堂のレジ係の女性スタッフに働きかけ、ＴＦＴメニューを注文した人だけに「ご協力ありがとうございます」というひと声をかけるようにしてくれました。この小さなお礼がやみつきになって、毎日ＴＦＴメニューを選び続けてくれる人もいるそうです。他にも四季に合わせたメニューを提案したり、健康食品の試供品をＴＦＴメニュー購入者にプレゼントしたりなど、アイデア豊富なプロジェクト・マネジャーとしてＴＦＴの活動に主体的に関わってくれています。

あるとき、こんなこともありました。

ある製薬会社の役員の方が、僕の講演を聞いて、ＴＦＴの理念や活動に興味を持ってくれました。しかし、その企業の本社には社員食堂がないので、ＴＦＴ導入は難しいと思われました。でも、この役員の方はとても情熱的で「何かできる方法はないか」といろいろ考えてくださったのです。

そこから生まれたのが、社内にあるドリンク販売機を使う「カップ・フォー・ツー」というプログラムです。コーヒー代に二十円を上乗せして寄付にあてる、というのがその内

容。「カップ」というネーミングは、コーヒー〝カップ〟とアフリカの子どもたちが朝食のお粥を食べるときに使う〝カップ〟を引っかけて付けました。

新しい試みだったので、新たに専用のロゴや宣伝資材が必要になりましたが、ここでもその役員の方が社内のマーケティング・チームを説き伏せ、素晴らしいものをつくってくださいました。

僕たちの想いを形にするにあたっては、このように一般の企業の中から応援してくれる人たちがいることはとても心強く、企業で仕事をしながらも社会事業に積極的に参加することができる、その好例になっていると思います。

「想い」を持ち続けてもらうための工夫

こんなふうに、TFTの活動は多くの方に支えられています。

TFTのウェブサイトは香港のある会社が無償でつくってくれているものですし、法務面を相談する弁護士さんもボランティアで協力してくれています。他にもイベント会場を無料で貸してくださったり、メディアの方を紹介してくださったり、頂いた好意は枚挙に

いとまがありません。

こうしたたくさんの好意に対して少しでもお礼がしたい、と思ってやっているのが「感謝状」や「名誉会員」というものです。

ＴＦＴに特別に協力してくださった企業の方には感謝状をお送りし、ビジネススキルや専門知識を使ってプロモーション活動や新規プロジェクト推進を支援してくれた方々には「ＴＦＴサポーター」「ＴＦＴファミリー」などの呼び名を使って頂いています。ボランティアで手伝ってくれた学生さんには僕から手書きのカードを送ることもよくしています。

こんなふうに感謝の気持ちを見える形にして伝えられるよう、いろいろ工夫しています。運営費が潤沢でない中でも多くの人の気持ちに報いる方法は、どんどん考えていかねばならないところでしょう。

多くの人に長く支え続けてもらうためには、僕たちの側からの積極的な働きかけも必要です。いっときの高揚ではなく、長く関心を持ち続けてもらうためには、「ＴＦＴに参加することは楽しい」「世の中のためになる活動だ」という実感を持ってもらうことが大切です。そして、そのためには長期的な戦略に基づいた活動が必要になります。ＴＦＴがなるべく多くのメディアに取り上げてもらえるよう努力したり、「かわら版」というポス

ターを定期的につくって配布したりするのはこのために他なりません。

将来的にはＴＦＴを支援してくれる大勢の人が参加できるコミュニティサイトを整備し、食糧問題の情報を集め、発信し、意見を共有できる場づくりも僕たちの手でしていきたいと思っています。

多くの人の気持ちに火を「灯し続ける」ためには、こうしたしかけを、なるべくたくさんつくっていくことが大切だと思うのです。

終章

「しくみ」と「想い」が大きなつながりをつくる

大きな課題解決のための「大きなつながり」

世界には今、地球温暖化、貧困や格差、食糧・水不足、地域紛争など、地球規模の課題が山積みになっています。悲観的にはなりたくありませんが、これら地球規模の課題のなりたちはさまざまな要素が複雑に絡み合っているので、その解決にも相当の労力が必要になります。

これらの課題に対して、僕たち日本人はどう対応したらよいのでしょうか？

「いずれアメリカなどの諸外国がなんとかしてくれる」「国単位ではどうにもならないことだから国連に任せておこう」と傍観することもできるでしょう。でも、世界の中の一員として課題に向き合い、解決策を模索し、問題解決に参加することもできるはずです。

日本人が問題解決の当事者になるといっても、「こんな大きな課題に取り組むのは政府の仕事だ」というのが、普通の人の反応だと思います。政府が決めてＯＤＡや国際外交などの手段を駆使してなんとかすべき問題、そう考えるのが自然です。だって、僕たち一般人は、こうした大きな問題解決に取り組む意志があっても、実際に参加できる方法がない

のですから。あったとしても、その場限りの寄付活動だったり、多くの時間や知識、経験を必要とするものだったりします。
でも、現状を見ると、政府がこうした問題を一手に引き受けるのは、とっくの昔に限界にきていたことがわかります。

地球的な課題の一つである「貧困」を例にとると、ここには「ミレニアム開発目標」というものがあります。
二〇〇〇年九月、ニューヨークにおいて「国連ミレニアム・サミット」が開催され、一五〇人以上の国家元首・首脳が参加しました。ここで採択された宣言と九〇年代にまとめられた国際開発目標を統合し、一つの共通の枠組みとしてまとめたものが「ミレニアム開発目標」です。簡単に言えば、世界が「やりましょう」と約束し合った開発途上国支援に関する目標です。
目標は八つの項目に分かれており、うち一つは「貧困」に関するもので、そこには「二〇一五年までに飢餓に苦しむ人口の割合を半減させる」という内容があります。二〇一五年といったらもうすぐです。それなのに、飢餓に苦しむ人口は減少するどころか、むしろ増加傾向にある、と言われています。

世界の国々が約束した目標を達成するためには、問題解決の大幅なスピードアップを図らなければなりません。そして、この約束をした国々の中には、日本も入っているのです。

地球規模の課題と言うと何だか遠いものに感じてしまいますが、僕たちはこの問題の影響をふだんの生活の中で受けはじめています。夏の異常なまでの暑さや、冬に雪が降らなくなったことを「地球温暖化のせいかなあ」と感じる機会は多いことでしょう。「極東の島国」である日本も、地球上の一つの国である以上、こうした課題から完全に逃れることはできません。

であれば、問題から目を背けて他者や時間に解決を委ねるよりも、ちゃんと向き合って対処した方が気持ちがラクになるのではないでしょうか?

でも、僕たちのような個人が、政府や国際機関だけに頼らず、こうした問題に取り組むためにはどうしたらいいのでしょうか?

僕たち日本人の誰もが地球規模の課題解決に参加して成果を出す方法。僕はそれが「大きなつながり」を生み出すことだと思っています。

地球規模の課題は、問題が複雑に絡み合って解決を難しくしています。解きほぐして解

決するためには、政府や国際機関の知識や力の他に、これまで動員できていなかったパワー、つまりは一般の人や企業などの力を結集する必要があるのです。そして、それを実現するのが「大きなつながり」なのです。

僕の考える「大きなつながり」ができるまでの流れは次のようなものです。

「大きなつながり」を生み出すステップ

①地球規模の課題を解決したいという「想い」を発信する

⬇

②専門機能をつなげて「代表チーム」をつくる（課題解決力が圧倒的に高まる）

⬇

③「しくみ」に高め、価値を生み出す

⬇

④「しくみ」を一般の人に使ってもらい、大きくする

⬇

⑤地球規模の課題解決が進む！

専門機能をつなげて「代表チーム」をつくる

一般企業で大規模なプロジェクトを進めるとき、「クロスファンクショナルチーム（機能横断チーム）」が結成されることがあります。

これは、日産自動車の再建を託されたカルロス・ゴーンCEOが使って業績を復活させたことで一躍有名になった手法です。課題が複雑化、肥大化して、もはや一部門の力ではどうにもならなくなったとき、社内の各部門から優秀な人材を選抜して集め、得意とする機能を結集して課題解決に取り組むのです。生産、営業、マーケティング、研究開発、調達、財務、ITシステムなど、課題解決に必要な知識を持つ人を各部門から選抜して、チームをつくるわけです。

僕のイメージする「大きなつながり」づくりの第一歩は、このクロスファンクショナルチームをつくることです。ただし、クロスファンクショナルチームはあくまで一企業の組織内の活動ですが、これを組織の壁を越え、広くつなげていくのです。

図10

それぞれの「専門機能」

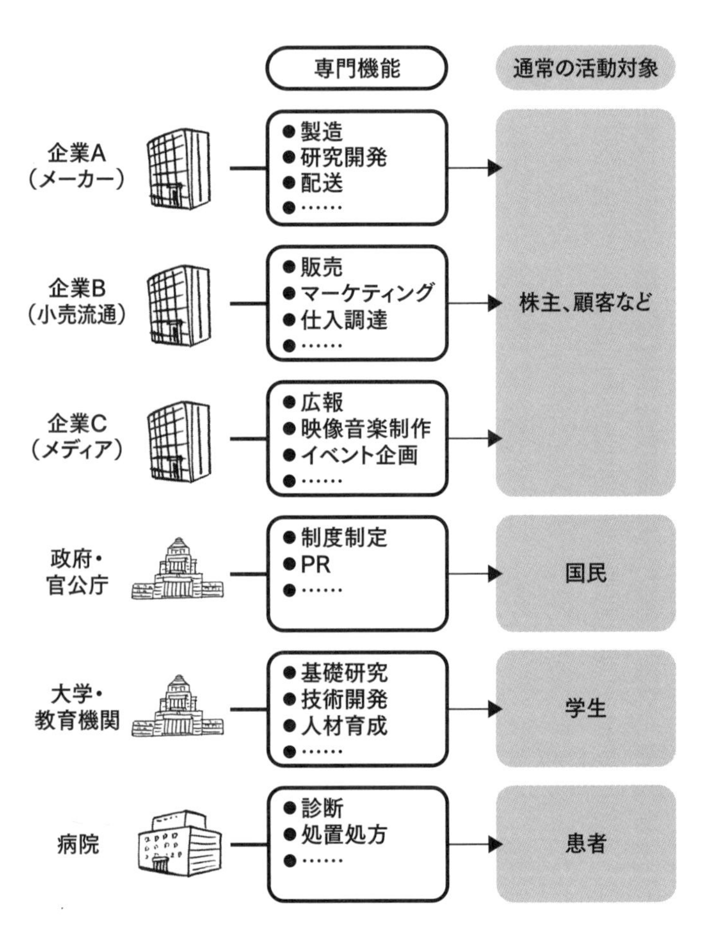

いつもはまったく違う活動をしている組織とそこに属する個人が集まり、各々が持つ専門能力、スキル、知識、経験などの強みとなる機能を結集させます。政府、一般企業、学校、自治体、財団、公益法人、医療機関、ＮＰＯなど集まる組織の種類もさまざまです。一般企業の中にも、製造業、小売流通、金融、ヘルスケア、ＩＴ、メディアなど、業種や職種は数え切れないほどあるでしょう。

ふだん、これらの組織は、株主、顧客、国民、患者など、別の対象に向けて業務を行なっています。それを、このときだけは法人の種類、業界、団体といった壁を越え、地球規模の課題解決という同じ目標のために各々が得意とする機能を提供してもらうのです。

つまりは、オールスターで最強の「日本代表チーム」をつくるといったイメージです。

ここで、ことさら「日本」を強調するのは、アフリカの支援先の人々や貧困問題の専門家と話をしていると、日本への期待がとても大きいことを感じるからです。その理由は日本人や日本企業が持つ技術力にあります。

アフリカの支援先の国で走っている車の大半は日本車です。故障が少なく燃費がよいため、道路や修理環境が整っていないアフリカでは、絶対的な人気があります。

また、アフリカの三大疾病の一つであるマラリアを予防する特殊な蚊帳を開発、提供し

ているのは住友化学です。日本ではあまり知られていないかもしれませんが、この蚊帳のお陰で子どもたちが安心して眠れるようになり、マラリア患者が激減しました。先日訪問したマラウィで農場を視察した際には、現地の人が「ササガワ」と何度も言っているのを耳にしました。聞くと日本の財団が支援して日本で考案された農業技術の一つがマラウィのトウモロコシの生産性を劇的に高めたそうで、その技術を財団の名称である「ササガワ」をとってそう呼んでいるそうです。

このように、技術に関して日本は今も世界のトップクラスにあります。だからこそ、クロスファンクショナルな代表チームを「日本でつくる」ことに、大きな意味があると思うのです。

「想い」を使えば競合同士もつながる

専門機能を持つ組織をつなぎ「代表チーム」をつくるには、「想い」を共有することが必要です。この成功例としては、前にご紹介した「プロダクト・レッド」がわかりやすいでしょう。

プロダクト・レッドにはそうそうたる顔ぶれの企業が参加しています。コンバース、G

ＡＰ、アップル、マイクロソフトなど、金融、ハイテク、通信、飲食、ファッション、流通など業界も多岐にわたる企業が、商品開発、マーケティング、販売など、それぞれが本業とする得意分野で「レッド・ブランド」に関わっています。

これらの企業の顔ぶれを見ると、中には本業では競合関係にある企業も入っていることがわかります。通常のビジネスであれば、決して相容れることのない同士をつないでいるのは、「開発途上国の子どもを感染症から救おう」という想いなのです。

プロダクト・レッドの場合、この想いを発信する核となったのはＵ２のボーカル、ボノでした。彼の想いが社会的な立場やビジネスにおける役割を超え、多様なプレーヤーのつながりを生み出したのです。

ＴＦＴもこうした専門機能を持つ組織とのつながりをつくり、それをさらに広げていきたいと思っています。

ＴＦＴブランドのヘルシー商品を開発する食品飲料メーカー、それを販売するスーパーやコンビニなどの流通企業、世界の食糧事情やＴＦＴの活動を伝える広告代理店とメディア、メタボ予防の効果測定を行う医療機器メーカー、その結果に基づいて指導を行う医療機関、プログラムを制度化して拡大する行政や国会議員、アフリカの子どもや家族に栄養

指導を行う栄養士、現地のニーズに沿った給食室を設計する建築家、日本で集まった寄付金を最適な方法で送金する金融機関など、ＴＦＴを核にした専門機能のつながりは無限に広げることができるでしょう。

そして、このつながりに加わる団体の数と種類が増えれば増えるほど、発揮される課題解決能力は大きくなるはずです。

「しくみ」に高め、価値を生み出す

専門機能が「想い」でつながったら、次はそれが何らかの価値を生み出し、活動を継続させるような「しくみ」に高めなければなりません。

前述のプロダクト・レッドの場合は、そのブランドや想いに価値を感じた消費者がバラエティに富んだ商品を購入します。購入された商品の収益の一部は、世界基金に寄付金として集められ、スペシャリストによってＨＩＶ、結核、マラリアなどの感染症対策に使われる、という「しくみ」ができています。

一般企業の場合、こうしたしくみはビジネスモデルと呼ばれ、そこから生み出されるも

のは利益です。対して、社会事業の場合、しくみから生み出される価値はお金そのものとは限りません。たとえば、「一般の人の声」を集め、それによって世界を変えようとする「アドボカシー（政策提言）・キャンペーン」というものがあります。この場合、しくみによって生み出される価値は「人々の声」そのものです。

社会事業でも利益がなければ活動を継続できない、というのは再三述べてきた通りですが、社会事業には賛助といった、「事業収益以外」のかたちで資金を確保する方法があります。このため、生み出される価値は利益に直結していなくてもよいのです。

専門機能が結集してつくるしくみは、「地球規模の課題解決につながる、何らかの価値」を生み出すことが目的です。TFTの場合、しくみによって生み出される価値は、開発途上国の子どもたちに給食を届けるための「寄付金＝お金」と、世界の食の不均衡を解消しようという「意識変革」の両方があるのです。

「しくみ」を一般の人に使ってもらい、大きくする

価値を生み出すしくみができたら、今度はそれを実際に動かして、一般の人を巻き込み

ながら、大きくしていきます。どんなによくできたしくみでも、利用してくれる人がいなければ意味がありません。専門家が集まって、得意分野を出し合ってつくったしくみを多くの人に知ってもらい、実際に使ってもらうのです。一般の人々の多くの力が結集して、はじめて課題を解決する圧倒的なパワーが生まれます。

アップルの製品・サービスである、iPodやiTunesを例にするとわかりやすいかもしれません。iPodやiTunesは世界中の人たちに愛用され、今では人々の生活の一部になっています。これは技術、IT、マーケティング、デザインなどの専門家が英知を結集し、開発したしくみです。しかし、いくら優れたしくみであっても、実際に多くの人が利用をしなかったら、消えてなくなってしまいます。

これはビジネスの例ですが、「使われなければ意味がない」という点では、社会事業のしくみも同じです。しくみをふだんの生活に融合させ、無理なく使ってもらうようにしなければなりません。食事、運動、ショッピング、読書など、生活の一部にしくみが組み込まれていることで、参加の間口が広がります。

ある食品メーカーでの話です。

CSR担当者の方は、経営層から「うちも社会貢献の実績をつくりたいから何か考えてくれ」と言われました。担当者は「じゃあ、社内で寄付を集めて開発途上国の人たちに食糧支援をしよう」と考えました。

募金箱を設置し、社員に協力を呼びかけましたが、肝心の寄付は当初の予想よりもずっと少ない額しか集まりませんでした。「うちの社員は社会貢献に対する意識が低いのか」、そう思って担当者は頭を抱えたそうです。

でも、そうではないのです。

別の企業で同じことをしても、結果はおそらく似たり寄ったりになるはずです。人を動かし、参加してもらうためには理念だけではなく、「やってみよう」と思わせる無理のないしくみが、生活の一部になっていることが必要です。募金箱にお金を入れてもらうためには、まずは財布を取り出してもらわなければなりません。しかし、簡単そうに見えて、この作業はとてもエネルギーを要します。人前で募金することに慣れておらず、「偽善者に見られるのは嫌」と思って寄付をためらう人も多いのです。そうした人を巻き込むためには考え抜かれたしくみが必要なのです。

ＴＦＴの「大きなつながり」

「地球のみんなが平和に暮らせるような社会にしたい」
「世界の子どもたちに温かい食事を届けたい」
「数年後に水没してしまう島国を救いたい」

今までであれば「何を夢みたいなこと言ってるんだ」と言われそうな、そんな「想い」がたくさんの専門家を束ね、しくみを生み出し、大勢の一般の人たちの参加を経て、大きなつながりを形づくります。

ＴＦＴでも、こうしたつながりの輪が少しずつ広がっています。

これまで、ＴＦＴと一般企業がつながるのは、食堂プログラムが主でした。今後はそこに主軸を置きつつも、それ以外のしくみも増やし、さらに輪を広げたいと考えています。

ここでは、ＴＦＴの活動領域である「食・食事」を本業とする企業とのつながりが大切になってきます。既にいくつかのプロジェクトがはじまりました。

有機野菜などの安心食品を宅配販売する「オイシックス」では、同社が扱うカレーライスやベーグル、フルーツジュースなど、一部商品をＴＦＴ推奨食品として販売してもらっています。健康食品の宅配サイトである「スマイルダイナー」では、冷凍総菜セットや糖尿病予防食などの商品を一食分購入すると、購入者と企業のそれぞれが十円ずつＴＦＴに寄付するしくみをつくってもらいました。

この二つは、経営者の方と想いがつながって、ＴＦＴを彼らの事業に組み入れて展開してもらうことができました。ＮＰＯと食を本業にする一般企業がつながり、適正な利益を見込めるビジネスとして展開しているのです。

これがさらに進化した例が、前にご紹介した三國シェフとコンビニのスリーエフ、そして横浜市とのつながりです。ＮＰＯと一般企業に自治体も加わり、それぞれの強みをいかし、専門機能を結集しています。協力する専門家が増え、しくみが進化し、これまで以上に多くの一般の人が参加してくれることで、ＴＦＴを核とした「大きなつながり」の課題解決能力は確実に高まっていることを感じます。

「想い」が一気につながる瞬間

二年あまり、僕はＴＦＴの事務局長として社会事業に関わってきました。

そこでいつも感じるのは、想いを一つにして、利害関係や組織の壁を乗り越え、人がつながっていくことの素晴らしさです。

僕がこれまで勤めていた一般企業では考えられないレベルで人が動き、組織が動き、一つのものに向かって変化の流れが音を立てて生まれる。そして、予想もしなかったような規模とスピードで社会が変わっていくことを実感する。そんな経験を何度もしてきました。

世界の多くの問題は、既存の組織や役割などの壁の中にいては、到底解決できないところにまで大きく複雑になっています。これをどうにかしたいと思ったら、まずは自分個人の周りの壁を壊すことからはじめなければならないでしょう。

個人を取り巻く壁には、いろいろなものがあります。

長らくやってきた仕事上の価値観や制約条件、会社の組織構成や文化など、毎日を過ごす上で当然だと思っている壁を、一度取り払ってみてください。

もちろん、それはそんなに簡単なことではありません。
ただでさえ忙しい毎日の中で、世界の課題について考えることは大変ですし、会社や組織の中の立場を越えて行動を起こそうとすれば、異を唱える人も出てくることでしょう。
実際、さまざまな団体の人を集めて社会問題を討議する場はたくさんありますが、そうした「〇〇プラットフォーム」「〇〇協議会」などの場は、参加者が所属団体の権益を守ることに終始するなど、あまりうまく働いていないことが多いようです。

でも、僕は今の仕事をしている中で、ランチを食べてアフリカの食事情について話す人たち、アフリカの子どもが給食を食べている写真を見て笑顔になる人たちに出会ってきました。そうした瞬間、その人たちが何かの壁を超えている、そう感じることも事実です。

僕はＴＦＴという日本発のすぐれたしくみを世界に広めたいと思っています。
そして、世界中のすべての人が同じように食事をとれる世の中にしたいと願っています。
その想いに共感してくれる人であれば、ふだん、どんな場所で何をしている人であっても、きっと一緒にやれることがあるはずです。
日本のあらゆる場所で、想いを一つにする人たちとつながりたい。

図11

「大きなつながり」ができるまで

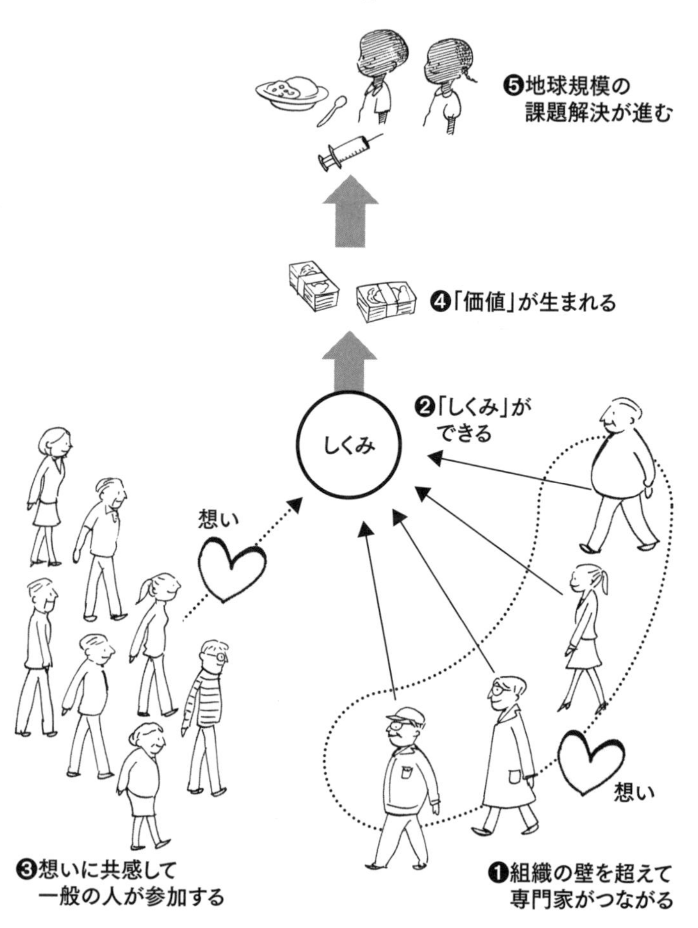
❺地球規模の
課題解決が進む
❹「価値」が生まれる
❷「しくみ」が
できる
しくみ
想い
想い
❸想いに共感して
一般の人が参加する
❶組織の壁を超えて
専門家がつながる

TFTはそれができる存在であり、しくみでもあると信じています。

「想い」の発信源は誰なのか、何なのか。個人なのか、組織なのか。

今の僕はここにはっきりした答えは出せずにいます。

でも、一つ言えるとしたら、大切なのは権威や肩書きではなく、そこで語られる「想いの確かさ」であるはずだ、ということです。

想いを具体的に描き、それを見た人は確かに社会がよりよくなるという実感と実現できる可能性を感じる。そうしたとき、想いに引き寄せられて多くの人が壁を乗り越えて集まってくるようになるのです。やがて、それが大きなつながりをつくり上げ、これまで到底解決できないと思われていた地球規模的な課題に立ち向かうことができる。

それほど「想いによるつながり」はすごいものなのです。

マラウィで芽生えた新しい「想い」

TFTは、現在、ウガンダ・ルワンダ・マラウィというアフリカの三ヵ国に学校給食を

届けています。どの国も最貧国と呼ばれ、食の不均衡の影響を受け、地方の農村地域では日々の食事もままならない状況です。学校給食がなければ、一日ほとんど何も食べられないという子どもたちがほとんどです。僕は事務局長になって以降、この三ヵ国を訪れ、自分たちの送った寄付金が実際にどのようにいかされているのかを見てきました。

この本を書いている最中に、三ヵ国中最後の訪問地となったマラウィに行ってきました。マラウィは三ヵ国の中で一番貧しく、もっと言えば僕が生涯訪れた国の中で最も貧しい、という印象です。

古い教会を借りて教室にしている学校、建物すらなく校庭に椅子を並べて授業をしている学校。そして多くの学校には調理室がなく給食が出せていません。何とか給食を出している学校でも食堂はなく、子どもたちが雨が吹き込み風が叩きつける軒下で濡れながら食事をしている光景を目の当たりにしました。食器も揃わず、学校の先生たちから「お皿とスプーンを何とか支援してもらえないだろうか」と真剣に頼まれるのです。

こうした光景を見て、話を聞くことで、子どもたちの学校給食を届けることに加え、「食」というテーマで僕たちのできることはまだまだある、と改めて実感しました。

もちろん、一方的に与え続けることが支援の理想型ではないと思っています。

僕の考える理想は、現地の人たちが自分たちの力で自分たちの環境を改善し、貧困の悪循環から抜け出すことです。ＴＦＴの活動でも、いずれは支援がなくなることを前提に、現地の学校給食事業の運営の大半を子どもたちの両親や地域の住人に任せるようにしています。薪拾いや水汲み、調理、配膳、片付けまで、親たちが交代制で担っているのです。ＴＦＴを含む外部団体からの支援は、給食室の建設と主食の原料であるトウモロコシの粉を提供することです。それらもすべてを支援するのではなく、たとえば建設に使う資材の一部を両親や村に調達してもらったり、村で農業指導を行ってトウモロコシを栽培してもらったりしています。

どんな事業でもそうですが、一番大変なのは立ち上げ時期です。学校給食事業も同じで、特に、これらのアフリカの国々では事業を立ち上げるための資金や知識が圧倒的に不足しています。僕たちは事業を立ち上げるための資金提供と教育支援をして、ひとたび軌道にのったら、あとは現地の人たちが自分たちの力で給食事業を続けていくことを基本にしたいと思っています。

マラウィの訪問で現地の様子をじっくり観察して確信したのは、この立ち上げ時期の支援を必要としている村や学校がまだまだたくさんある、ということです。外部からの支援によって給食事業が軌道にのりはじめた地域は国全体の一、二割程度といった印象でした。これはきちんとした報告書や専門家の裏付けがあるわけではありませんが、現地を自分の目で見てきた実感としての数字です。給食がない多くの地域では、子どもたちは空腹しのぎに果物をかじる程度で、まともな食事をほとんど食べられていない状況なのです。

マラウィから帰途につくころ。

飲んだ水が原因か、僕はひどい食あたりになってしまいました。七転八倒するような胃の痛みに襲われ、食べものも飲みものもほとんど受け付けません。それでも、長期出張でたまった仕事を放っておけず、よろよろと事務所に足を運びました。

食事をちゃんととらないと、急に元気がなくなります。

そして、笑えなくなります。

仕事柄、笑顔が必要な状況もあるのですが、この数日はかなり無理をしないと笑顔がつくれなくなりました。

そんなとき思い出したのが、マラウィの子どもの笑顔とそのすごさです。いつもお腹を空かせながらもあのきらきら輝く笑顔でいられる、そのことに改めて驚かされました。

校長先生、そして子どもの母親たちが言っていました。「学校給食はマラウィの子どもたちの未来につながる」のだと。給食を食べて一所懸命勉強した子どもたちは、高等教育を受けるために進学し、よい仕事に就き、そして貧困から脱出していく。

子どもたちに、よりよい未来を生きてもらいたい。マラウィの学校で出される給食は、そんな親や先生たちの想いが込められている食事なのです。

「ムワンダマ」という小さな村で、子どもたちや先生と手を取り合った瞬間、僕の中で新たな「想い」が生まれました。それは、「マラウィの国中の子どもたち全員が、温かい給食をお腹いっぱい食べられるようにしたい」ということ。

そして、この「想い」が、TFTの「しくみ」によって、時間と空間を超え、彼らと彼らの国、そして僕と僕の国を確かにつなぐはず。そうした希望と確信に満たされたのです。

おわりに

おわりに

想いはきっと社会を変える

二〇〇八年の北京オリンピック、女子ソフトボールの決勝戦をテレビで観戦していた僕は、アメリカチームの最後のバッターが三塁ゴロに終り、日本の金メダルが確定した瞬間、全身に鳥肌が立つような感動を覚えました。

中でも、驚くべきは日本のエース、上野由岐子投手です。二日間で三試合完投し、投げた球数が四百十三。常識では考えられません。

その常識を超える快投を生み出したのは、なんとしても優勝したいという上野投手の強い想い。そして上野投手をそういう想いにさせるだけの雰囲気がチームにみなぎっていたからだと思います。

そういう状況に置かれると、人は思いもかけない力を発揮する。全身全霊をかけるというのはそういうことです。そして、その姿は必ず周囲の感動を呼び起こします。

逆にどんなに如才なく立ち回っているように見えても、それが義務感や役割意識によるものであったら、そんなものに人は心を打たれないでしょう。同様に、損得勘定で動いている人も多くの人を熱狂させることはできないはずです。

そこで、質問です。
あなたは最近、仕事で何人の人たちを笑顔にしましたか？
あなたの仕事で、誰かが喜んだり、元気になったりしているという実感がありますか？
もし、考え込んだり、答えに窮してしまったなら、あなたは自分の仕事に全身全霊をかけていない、あるいは、そうしたいと思える仕事をしていないのかもしれません。

僕自身がそうでした。いつだってたぎるような情熱で仕事にのぞみたいと心の内では思っているのに、気が付けば、いつもどこかに燃えかすのようなものが残ってしまう。
やがて、それは自分が本当にやりたいことをやっていないからだとわかりました。そして、僕がやりたいことは何だろうと考え抜いて、出した結論が「世のため人のためになること」。何のことはない、答えは子どものころからずっと心の中にあったのです。

そして、ＴＦＴとの出会いという幸運に恵まれ、僕は自分の想いを仕事にする方向に踏み出しました。それは決してラクな道ではなく、苦難の連続の日々であり、それは現在も続いています。でも、後悔はまったくしていません。なぜなら、そこでの仕事には僕が探し求めていた感動があったからです。

ラジオ番組に出演して話をしたら、自分も開発途上国の子どもたちのために役に立ちたいとなけなしのお金を送ってくれた年配の聴取者。大学で僕の講演を聞いて食糧問題に関心を持ったと言い、「とりあえず食事を残さないようにすることからはじめました」と手紙で教えてくれた大学生。ＴＦＴのヘルシーメニューとは別のものを食べるときも、「いいことをすると気持ちがいいから」と必ず二十円の寄付をしてくれる銀行員。

僕たちの想いが伝わって、彼ら、彼女らの心に火が灯ったのです。そういう人たちと出会うたびに、僕は胸がいっぱいになって、本当にこの仕事をやってよかったと心の底から思います。

アフリカで現地の子どもたちの笑顔を目の当たりにしたときもそうです。
日本にいると、世界中の人が自分たちと同じような食生活を送っている気になりがちで

すが、一日三食きちんと食べられることは、決して世界の常識ではありません。
最貧国では、その日の食事が学校の給食だけ、という子どもたちがたくさんいます。彼らにとって給食はまさに命の糧なのです。だから、給食を食べるために学校に来るのです。たとえ食事が目的であっても、学校に来れば子どもたちは授業に出て、先生の話を聞き、勉強します。それはそのまま彼らの将来を明るくすることにつながるのです。
給食を食べている子どもたちの多くは、日本という国がどこにあるのかを知りません。でも、その給食は間違いなく、日本人の寄付によってできている。だから、今こうして彼らを底抜けの笑顔にしているのは日本人の善意なのだ、と感じます。
そして、日本人の善意を開発途上国の子どもたちに届ける役目を担っているのがＴＦＴ。自分の仕事で人の心が動き、笑顔が生まれたのです。こんな気持ちを味わえるのですから、どんな困難にぶち当たっても逃げ出そうなんて思いません。
僕は、「誰もが善意のために働くべきだ」などという気はありません。
ただ、僕自身は同じ働くのであれば、完全燃焼できる働き方をしたいと思っています。
自分の評価や報酬を上げることに生き甲斐を感じる人がその目的のために全力を尽くすこ

とはいいでしょう。でも、今の世の中を見ていると、自分やお金のためよりも、不遇をかこっている人や虐げられている人を救ったり、そういう人が生まれない社会をつくることに貢献したりすることに、より大きな喜びを感じる人が確実に増えている、そんな気がしてなりません。

そして、そういう人たちは、自分の想いに素直に生きて欲しいと思います。

この社会をもっとよくしたいという人たちが、それに真剣に取り組めば、きっと至福の瞬間を味わうことができるはずです。すると、それを見た、同じ想いを持った人が必ず後に続きます。やがて、あたかも湖面に波紋が広がるように、この社会は、大きな想いの輪に包まれていくことでしょう。

何かが劇的に変わるというのは、そういうことなのだと思います。

小さなしくみで革命を起こす

二十円で買えるものというと、何があるでしょうか？

「うまい棒」二本。

日本ではそんなものでしょう。ポケットに入れておいた十円玉二枚は、いつの間にかなくなっても、「まあいいや」で済んでしまう金額です。

でも、世界にはお腹を空かせた子どもがたくさんいて、その子たちは二十円あれば、ちゃんとした食事が一回食べられる、そう知ったらどうでしょうか?

へえ、そうなんだ、と少し二十円の価値を見直すかもしれません。それでもやっぱり、ほとんどの人にとって、二十円はまだ「うまい棒二本」でしかありません。

それが、お腹を空かせた子どもが目の前にいて、誰かに「どなたか二十円寄付して頂ければ、このお皿いっぱいの食事を今ここにいる子どもに食べさせることができます」と言われたらどうでしょう?

わざわざ家に財布を取りに戻るのは面倒だけど、ポケットを探って十円玉が二枚見つかったら寄付してもいいかな、そんなふうに思う人が出てくるのではないでしょうか?

二十円を差し出すと、子どもの前においしそうな料理が運ばれてきて、子どもはそれを嬉しそうに平らげ、あなたに向かって満面の笑みを送る。

その瞬間、「ああ、よかったな」と、なんだか幸せな気分になるのではないでしょうか。そして、「またこういう場面に遭遇したら寄付しよう」と、ふだんから二十円を大事にするようになるかもしれません。

そんな気分を味わえる人を一人でも増やす。僕が仕事でやっているのは、そういうことなのです。

世界には満足に食事ができない子どもたちがいる、そういうことはなんとなく知っているし、気の毒だなとも思う。けれども、自分では助けてあげようもないから、ちょっと目をつぶっておこう……。

僕は、こういう気持ちを責めようと思わないし、また、誰も責められるはずがありません。だって、僕自身も長い間そう思ってきたのです。

遠い国で起こっていることまで「先進国に生きるあなたの責任なんだから、どうにかしろ」と言われても、それは無理な要求でしょう。責任を取るどころか、関わり方もわからない。何もやりようがない、というのが多くの人の本音だと思います。そして、何もできないのであれば、とりあえずなかったことにして無視するより他にない。そうしないと穏やかに日常生活を送ることができなくなってしまいます。

でも、もしその遠い国と今いる場所が、ドラえもんの「どこでもドア」のようなものでつながったらどうでしょう。遠い国の問題が放っておけない現実味のある問題として立ち上がってくるはずです。

そして、ちょっとしたアクションを起こすだけで、その問題を少しだけ解決できるしくみが用意されていたら。そうなったら、今度は無視し続ける方が落ち着かなくなってくるでしょう。しかも、そうすることで精神的な満足が得られるだけでなく、食べ過ぎて肥満気味の我が身も恩恵を受けることができるとなれば、参加したい気持ちがさらに高まるのではないでしょうか。

今、まさにカツ丼の大盛りを食べようとしている人のところに走って行って、その耳元で「あなたはアフリカでお腹を空かしている子どもたちのことを考えないのか!」と大声で言ったところで、言われた人は嫌な気持ちになるだけでしょうし、食べようとしていたカツ丼だっておいしくなくなってしまいます。

こう言って怒る人も、まったくの善意なのでしょう。でも、こんなふうに「いいことをするべきだ!」なんて言われなくたって、誰の心の中にも、「いいことをしたい」という気持ちはあるのです。ただ、皆その方法がわからなかったり、素直に気持ちを出すことが

恥ずかしかったりするだけなのです。

だから、「いいことをするべきだ！」と言うのではなく、「こうすればたいして無理をしないでいいことができますよ」「あなたの気持ちをこういう形で届けますよ」、そう言えるだけのしくみを用意すればいい。そうすれば、みんな喜んでそのしくみを使ってくれるはずです。

社会起業家というのは、そういうしくみをつくる人なのだと、僕は思っています。しくみをつくり、新しい価値を生み出し、上がった利益を最適に配分する。そう、それはまさしくビジネスです。ただ、しくみをつくる目的がちょっと違うだけなのです。

この社会には、人が喜んで、いいことをしたくなるしくみがまだまだ不足しています。だから、社会起業にはやることがいっぱいあるのです。なにしろそこら中が手つかずのフロンティアなのですから、新しいことを考えるのが得意な人や、クリエイティビティに自信のある人にとって、これほどエキサイティングで楽しい業界は他にないでしょう。

社会起業の面白さは他にもあります。

それは、「自分の考えたしくみで社会を変えられる」ということです。
この世界はあまりに不完全なので、いたるところに歪みや偏りがあり、そういうところではいろいろな問題が発生しています。しかし、僕は解決できない問題はない、と信じています。歪みや偏りの原因を探り当て、そこを修正すればいいのです。
もちろん、それは一気にはできません。人類の長い歴史の中で発生した歪みや偏りを力まかせに直そうとすれば、別の場所がまた歪んだり、亀裂ができたりしてしまいます。昔の革命家は、それを知らなかったのでしょう。だからドラスティックに変革を起こそうとして、その結果、多くの血が流されることになったのです。
変革は決して焦ってはいけません。
一ミリずつゆっくりと、望ましい方向に変えていかねばならない。そのために必要なのが、多くの人の小さな力を、継続的に集めていくしくみなのです。
そして、そういうしくみがたくさんできればできるほど、社会が変わる速度は速くなっていくのです。

世の中にたくさんの社会起業家が現れ、彼らがつくるしくみが社会を変える。
そう、社会起業家は、現代の革命家でもあるのです。

［小暮真久プロフィール］

1972年	東京・練馬区に生まれる
1979年	浜松市に転居
1987年	早稲田大学高等学院入学
1990年	早稲田大学理工学部機械工学科入学
1992年	アメリカをはじめて旅行 （カルフォルニア州、フロリダ州など）
1993年	大学在学中にスロバキアのコシチェ工科大学に短期留学
1994年	人工心臓の研究をはじめる
1999年	スインバン工科大学（メルボルン・オーストラリア）にて修士号取得
	マッキンゼー・アンド・カンパニー東京支社入社
2004年	マッキンゼー・アンド・カンパニー ニュージャージー支社に異動
2005年	松竹株式会社入社
2007年	TFTのコンセプトを知る
	ニューヨークで経済学者 ジェフリー・サックスと会う
	TABLE FOR TWO International事務局長に就任
2008年	TFTプログラム導入企業が100社突破

TFTを支える人たちから

ビジネス

高島宏平

［オイシックス株式会社代表取締役社長］

はじめて小暮さんと会ったのは、彼がマッキンゼーに私の一年後輩として入社した一九九九年。二人きりのプロジェクトに配属され、入社したてでわからないことだらけの僕たちで歯を食いしばって乗り切った憶えがあります。二〇〇七年、TFTの立ち上げで再び一緒に仕事をすることになりました。つらいことやトラブルも多く、相変わらず歯を食いしばっていますが、今の小暮さんはとても楽しそうです。私はオイシックスという会社で食材のインターネット販売をしています。地方の安全でおいしい食べ物と都会の人々の食卓とをつなげることが仕事です。TFTの掲げる食というテーマは、これからの地球にとって非常に大切なことであり、その使命は重いものです。小暮さんにはこれからも楽しく歯を食いしばって地球規模の課題に対峙することを期待しています。もちろん私も頑張ります。

ビジネス

松田公太

［タリーズコーヒーインターナショナル会長］

私は幼少時代をアフリカのセネガルで過ごし、餓えに苦しむ人々を身近に見て育ちました。飽食の時代を迎えた先進諸国が多い中、同じ時代を生きながら、一日一食すら食べられない人々が数多く存在するのは非常に悲しいことです。「この世界で苦しんでいる人たちのために少しでもお手伝いする」という気持ちは、社会事業を通じて実現できますが、ビジネスを通じても実現できることだと思います。強い想いは人を動かし、巻き込む力があります。私もそうした気持ちから、創設期からTFTに携わってきました。この本が一人でも多くの方の手に渡り、TFTの活動が世界に広がっていけばと思います。今この時代を共に生きる人々と、これから生まれてくる未来の子どもたちが、毎日食事できるようになることを祈って。

政治

川口順子
［参議院議員］

日本からはじまったTFTの取り組みは、アフリカ諸国などの飢餓・貧困問題を解決すると同時にメタボリック対策など健康増進にも役立つ、という独創的な一石二鳥のビジネス・モデルだと言えましょう。この取り組みの普及加速化を支援すべく、「TABLE FOR TWO推進議員連盟」を立ち上げ、「隗より始めよ」のひそみに倣い、参議院議員会館等の食堂にこの取り組みを導入するように働きかけてきました。さらには、中央省庁の食堂でのTFT導入を呼びかけており、全省庁で実施される日も近いと思っています。いつの日か世界の食の不均衡が解消され、健康的な世界が実現されるまで、この取り組みを推進していくつもりです。

政治

古川元久
［衆議院議員］

私たちが直面しているさまざまなグローバルな課題の解決のためには、国家レベルの取り組みはもちろん、私たちの日々の生活の中での取り組みも必要です。しかも、こうした取り組みが持続可能であるためには、対立関係に陥りがちな先進国と開発途上国が、お互いに歩み寄ることのできるようなW—I—N—W—I—Nのしくみでなければなりません。TFTは、この条件をすべて満たす、日本発のグローバル課題解決のソリューションです。しかも、その精神はお遍路の際の「同行二人」や、他人のことを思いやる気持ち「足るを知る」という言葉にも通じる、日本的なものです。世界的課題を日本的なスピリッツに立った新しい枠組みで解決していく方法として、日本から世界へと発信していきたいと考えています。そして、本書がその発信の第一歩になることを願っています。

学術

石倉洋子

［一橋大学大学院国際企業戦略研究科教授］

二十一世紀は業界や国境などの境界や、官・民・学・消費者などの役割が変わり、社会起業家やNPOなどが登場する中、「世界のオープン化」「力のシフト」が起こっている。本書はTFTという一つの組織の活動とそれに直接携わる個人の実際の体験から、こうした時代に必要な個人と組織の「戦略シフト」――先進国と開発途上国という世界の両極を視野に入れ、従来は二律背反と思われてきた「営利」と「非営利」の両立を実現することを「志」「長期的目標」として、そのためにあらゆる方法を試し、実験すること――を語っている。二十一世紀はこうした戦略シフトを実践する限りない機会を私たちの前に拓いているが、一方、こうした試みはいつの時代も大きな困難を伴う。それをあえて担うのはいつまでも精神的若さを持つ人である。私自身そうした姿勢を持ち続けたいと熱望し、本書を新しい時代を拓こうとする人々にお勧めしたい。

学術

竹中平蔵

［慶應義塾大学教授・グローバルセキュリティ研究所所長］

私の友人でもある経済学者、ジェフリー・サックスの世界の貧困を撲滅するための提言や活動には以前から関心を寄せていました。一方で、こうした貧困撲滅などの社会貢献において日本がリーダーシップをとる機会が少ないことを残念にも思っていました。日本の豊かさをもってすれば、社会貢献はもっと普通に、誰にでもできることになるはずです。TFTの試みは、少しの工夫で日本が世界の課題に対して貢献できる、という証明になるものです。先進工業国では多くの人々が栄養過多による悩みを抱える一方で、世界の他の地域では飢えという長く続く苦痛から依然として逃れられない人々が数多く存在します。こうした不均衡を是正するために、日本発のアイデアが役立っていることは、本当に素晴らしいと思います。

※敬称略

謝辞

この本を書くにあたってご協力頂いた皆さまに御礼を申し上げます。

ＴＦＴのプログラムを導入し、運営くださっている企業とご担当者の方々、そして食堂でＴＦＴメニューを食べて頂いている社員の皆様、ありがとうございます。いろいろな企業の方とＴＦＴを通じてつながっていることの幸せをいつも感じています。

貴重な推薦文を頂いた六名の方々、いつも的確なアドバイスをくださるＴＦＴ理事の皆さん、ありがとうございます。

そして、僕の「想い」の指南役であるジェフリー・サックス氏、梅津光生教授。あなた方のお陰で今の僕があることを、日々感じています。近藤正晃ジェームスさん、松竹芸能㈱の副社長である井上貴弘さん、数々のアドバイスに感謝しています。

ＴＦＴスタッフの安東迪子さん、仲本千津さん、黒松敦さん。皆さんの情熱とたゆまぬ努力によって、ＴＦＴはここまで成長することができました。インターンの学生さん、ボランティアの方々、いつもＴＦＴを支えてくれてありがとう。

僕の「想い」を文字にしてくださった山口雅之さん、イラストにしてくださった小谷松明子さん、写真にしてくださった三井公一さん、デザインにしてくださった遠藤陽一さんとデザインワークショップジンの皆さん、そして僕の「想い」を信じて本にしてくださった杉崎真名さん、ありがとうございます。

僕に「想い」の原形となる名前を授けてくださった梶山智孝上人に感謝します。愛情に包んで育ててくれた両親、心のアドバイスをくれた弟・訓士、そして仕事面でも心強い仲間であり、人生の伴侶である妻・希世、本当にありがとう。

最後に、僕に本を書くエネルギーと情熱をくれたウガンダ、ルワンダ、マラウィの子どもたちに、深く感謝します。

二〇〇九年二月　小暮真久

[著者プロフィール]

小暮真久

（こぐれ・まさひさ）

1972年生まれ。早稲田大学理工学部卒業後、オーストラリアのスインバン工科大で人工心臓の研究を行なう。1999年、同大学修士号取得後、マッキンゼー・アンド・カンパニー東京支社入社。ヘルスケア、メディア、小売流通、製造業など幅広い業界の組織改革・オペレーション改善・営業戦略などのプロジェクトに従事。同社米国ニュージャージー支社勤務を経て、2005年、松竹株式会社入社、事業開発を担当。
経済学者ジェフリー・サックスとの出会いに強い感銘を受け、その後、先進国の肥満と開発途上国の飢餓という2つの問題の同時解決を目指す日本発の社会貢献事業「TABLE FOR TWO」プロジェクトに参画。2007年NPO法人・TABLE FOR TWO Internationalを創設し、理事兼事務局長に就任。社会起業家として日本、アフリカ、米国を拠点に活動中。

私たちと一緒にアフリカの子どもたちに、学校給食と笑顔を届けてください
詳しくは　http://www.tablefor2.org/jp/kojin.html

編集協力――山口雅之
本文イラスト――小谷松明子
カバー・本文写真――佐々木希世
著者写真――三井公一（サスラウ）
撮影協力――三井住友海上火災保険株式会社

「20円」で世界をつなぐ仕事

2009年3月30日 第1刷発行
2009年5月15日 第5刷発行

著　者――小暮真久
©2009 Masahisa Kogure

発行者――吉田元治
発行所――日本能率協会マネジメントセンター
〒105-8520 東京都港区東新橋1-9-2 汐留住友ビル24階
TEL 03(6253)8014［編集］／TEL 03(6253)8012［販売］
FAX 03(3572)3503［編集］／FAX 03(3572)3515［販売］
http://www.jmam.co.jp/

装丁――遠藤陽一
本文デザイン・DTP――DESIGN WORKSHOP JIN,Inc.
印刷所――広研印刷株式会社
製本所――星野製本株式会社

ISBN 978-4-8207-1741-6 C2034
落丁、乱丁本はおとりかえいたします。
PRINTED IN JAPAN

S0-CBX-275

FOREWORD

Will Rogers was my mother's brother, and from my earliest childhood I loved my Uncle Will devotedly.

We lived in the small town of Chelsea, eighteen miles from Claremore, Oklahoma, in a home called "Maplewood." My mother was Will's "Sister Sallie." His other sister, our beloved Aunt Maud (Lane), lived across town at spacious "Sunset Farm." The two sisters were past masters in the art of entertaining, and my own sisters and cousins were trained to help in any kind of social activity. The two hospitable homes were always filled with company—usually kinfolk—but the biggest event in the lives of these sisters was their "Brother Will" coming home to visit.

My first recollection of Uncle Will is his ceaseless working with his ropes in our front yard, with a group of spectators around him. Sometimes he had us children ride by on our ponies so he could practice certain catches of both horse and rider. This game would go on for hours, and it was all business with him.

My happiest memories are of the period shortly after he had married the beautiful and captivating Betty Blake. We all adored her, for she seemed to have a special aura about her. I love to think back to the wonderful evenings when, after a bountiful dinner, we all filed into the parlor for a "program." Aunt Betty, a musician of exceptional ability, would take her place at the piano, and together she and Uncle Will would sing the musical hits of the day. Uncle Will would imitate other actors and their stunts, and tell stories and jokes like the master showman he was.

Often he would break into a buck-and-wing dance while Aunt Betty whistled the song to a banjo or piano accompaniment. Thus they brought Broadway and all its wonders to the well-filled room of relatives and friends. None of us then had the foresight to realize that Will would one day become so famous.

After the Rogerses had established their home in California, I spent a great deal of time with them and was very close to their entire family. Uncle Will and Aunt Betty did not love me any more than they did the other relatives, but because I had been lame since childhood, they tried to compensate for some of the things they felt I had been denied. They—bless them both!—turned my limitations into happy privileges that enabled me to enjoy life to the fullest extent.

When the state of Oklahoma built the impressive Will Rogers Memorial in Claremore in 1938, the Memorial Commission asked my husband, Robert W. Love, to take over the entire management of it. They named me curator. Here we have visited with many of the twelve hundred daily visitors who pass in and out of its doors. Almost without exception they have expressed a desire to read the things Will Rogers said.

It is from them and the requests that have flooded in by mail and telephone for certain Will Rogers "quotes" that the inspiration for this book came. My husband and I began to see the importance of preserving Will Rogers' writings and other related material, and began to build a research library. Rogers' fans contributed a great number of scrapbooks, clippings, letters, and other items. The University of Tulsa lent us their microfilm of the Tulsa *Daily World*, which enabled us to determine the correct dates for Will Rogers' articles and to arrange his works in chronological order. Homer Croy described this collection as being "packed with gold like a crib with yellow dent corn."

Bill and Jim Rogers approved of our making this collection and have given their consent to the use of their father's material.

In this volume I have not tried to write a book about Will Rogers. I have only compiled some of his priceless statements in an effort to preserve them.

PAULA McSPADDEN LOVE

CONTENTS

ILLUSTRATIONS

INTRODUCTION

Will Rogers, The Writer

Cowboy, trick roper, comedian, movie star, humorist, radio commentator, newspaper columnist, citizen of the world, philosopher, humanitarian, ambassador of Good Will, and many more appellations have been applied to Will Rogers, and he filled each one with distinction. But it was as a writer and a speaker that he became America's common-sense philosopher who will be remembered through the ages.

The people who were Will's contemporaries have an entirely different feeling for him from those of a later generation. Since he was able to project his inimitable personality into all kinds and classes of people, he became a part of every family. His insight into human foibles and events, his intolerance of injustice and chicanery, and his sympathy for the unfortunate and suffering were evidenced in the things he said as he played on the heartstrings of America, sensing the truth and tragedy of events and often turning the most tense situation into one of mirth.

All this was voiced by Herbert Hoover not too long ago when he said, "Our country has lost its sense of humor. We need an American humorist. There's been no one since Will Rogers."[1]

Because of his different ways of reaching people, Will Rogers was the most beloved man of his time. He died at the age of fifty-five at the height of his career—America's most popular public speaker; the biggest box-

1 Nanette Kutner, "Herbert Hoover Today," *The American Weekly,* August 10, 1958.

office attraction in the movies; the most widely read of any of the newspaper feature writers.

His witty comments on persons and public issues, his humble, self-effacing manner, and his unfailing good humor were as familiar to the people as the air they breathed. He was not one person on the stage and another in public life. He was always Will Rogers, the spokesman and safety valve for America. He had learned early in his career that it was the way he talked and the things he said that brought the applause, so he remained natural and completely unspoiled as his fame and fortune soared.

"I am just an old country boy," he wrote. "I have been eating pretty regular and the reason I have is, I have stayed an old country boy."[2]

Will did not aspire to be a writer. It was his early ambition to be the best trick roper in America. He achieved that goal, but he also developed into a forceful and much sought-after speaker. He was perhaps more surprised than anyone else when he found out that people wanted to remember the things he said. They liked to discuss them and ponder the wisdom of his funny, often salty quips long after the laughter had subsided.

Will's first book, *The Cowboy's Philosophy on the Peace Conference*, was published in May 1919, and in August of the same year *The Cowboy's Philosophy on Prohibition* appeared. Both of these small books were collections of the jokes, or "gags" as he called them, that he used in his act in the *Ziegfeld Follies* and the *Midnight Frolic*.

His success as a speaker in the years that followed brought him to the attention of editors. They felt that any man who could hold an audience and entertain them as he did would be a very popular writer. V. V. McNitt of the McNaught Syndicate approached him at the *Follies*

[2] Weekly article, August 31, 1924.

to see if he would write for them. As usual Will was reluctant to try anything in this medium. Up to this time he had written only brief and occasional humorous articles for various papers, and he had not yet reached his stride in writing. In the meantime the *New York Times* offered him $150 a week to write his comments on the daily news, which he readily accepted.

On December 31, 1922, he began his series of weekly articles which were released through the McNaught Syndicate. These appeared in the Sunday editions of the papers, expressing his views on current events in true Rogersesque manner. "Slipping the Lariat Over," the *New York Times* called the column; the Los Angeles *Examiner* selected "Roping the News" for its title. Other papers wrote their own headings, such as "Will Rogers Settles the Affairs of the U.S. Without Cost to the Taxpayer." In 1924 a collection of these articles on a diversity of subjects was published under the title *The Illiterate Digest*.

In September 1924 he was engaged by the American Tobacco Company—"to write for us 26 pieces of *Bull Durham* copy, each to be signed by you," the contract read, "and to be approximately 150 words in length and to permit the publication of an illustration of yourself as a part of each advertisement."[3] He began with the following, which was something unusual in the field of advertising:

> I know you people are going to say "What do you think of Will Rogers writing and endorsing 'Bull Durham'?" That's where you're wrong. I am not endorsing it. I never smoked any tobacco in my life, not even Bull Durham.

[3] Letter dated September 29, 1924, from Frank W. Harwood to Will Rogers.

> If you want to know the real truth why I signed up to write a lot of pieces for these people it's because I love animals. Have you ever studied the picture of the Bull carefully? Have you ever seen such a kind looking animal? I thought this: Certainly no one who cares as much about dumb creatures as they do would put out anything but the best smoking tobacco possible. So I said, "All right, I'll write your stuff." Honestly, the money part of it dident have much to do with it. That is, not very much. . . .[4]

Each of the Bull Durham ads was on a different subject, and Will used many of them later for full-length weekly articles

He began writing "The Worst Story I've Heard Today" on May 15, 1925, and continued it until January 15, 1927. This was a daily article and was also released through the McNaught Syndicate. His first story was on the Prince of Wales,[5] who was visiting America at that time. As usual Will wrote about everybody from such leading political figures of the day as Al Smith, Governor Hylan of New York, Barney Baruch, and the mayors of different cities; actors of the theatrical and movie worlds; baseball players; Oscar, the chef of the old Waldorf. Of course, Oklahomans came in for a fair share of stories and even such obscure individuals as his sister's hired man. It was not so much the story he related that pleased his readers as it was the "build up" he gave the person who had told the story. These articles also gave an account of the places he went and some of the people he met, for he

4 Bull Durham advertisement #1 (proof from H. W. Kastor & Sons Advertising, New York, Chicago, St. Louis), Scrap Book #7.
5 The present Duke of Windsor.

had started his lecture tours in October of 1925. These articles were the beginning of what was later to develop into his famous daily telegram.

In the spring of 1926 he went to Europe to do a series of articles for *The Saturday Evening Post.* He called the series "Letters of a Self-Made Diplomat to His President." These were addressed to the then President of the United States, Calvin Coolidge, who, of course, was quite innocent of the matter. Some of the best of Rogers' humor is in this series of vivid accounts of his interviews with the leading figures of foreign countries and his visits to the tourist attractions and resorts. The "Letters" were so popular that they were brought out in book form that year under the same title.

While he was in London, he sent a collect cable to the *New York Times* which read:

> July 29, 1926: Nancy Astor, which is the Non de Plume of Lady Astor, is arriving on your side about now. She is the best friend America has here. Please ask my friend Jimmie Walker to have New York take good care of her. She is the only one over here that don't throw rocks at American tourists.
>
> Yours respectfully,
> Will Rogers[6]

The late Joseph Tebeau, the night managing editor of the *Times*, ordered the piece published on the first page of the second section. With no further arrangement as to space or renumeration, Will continued to send the daily wires to the *Times* from wherever he was in Europe until he returned home in the fall.

6 First daily telegram, July 29, 1926.

The squib was tremendously popular, and the editors of the *New York Times* were delighted to have this exclusive. The McNaught people were well aware of its potentialities. McNitt was also in Europe that summer and made every effort to find Will and sign him up for the article. Whether or not he did so is unknown, but Will did have the following "Worst Story" on McNitt:

September 10, 1926. Worst Story

The Worst Joke I heard today was told me by V. V. McNitt. V. V. is the owner of the McNaught Syndicate of New York. Well, he is over here in London, he and his family, and has been prowling around all over Europe. He has been up to Scotland. I am not sure but I think Mac has a touch of Scotch, and you ever let one of the Scotchmen get over here and he just breaks out for the Heather again like a milk-pen calf to its mother when it gets out. Scotland is having pretty tough sledding now. The Irish since they got freedom are about to come over and take it way from the Scots. Mac had some Scotch yarns to relate. An American who had taken a shooting Lodge in Scotland, got lost one day in the heavy mist and was tramping around and couldn't find his way back. Finally he heard footsteps and looked around and there was a Scotch native of the Moors.

"I'm lost," said the American.

The old Scotch mountaineer answered him. "I know you are lost, but is there any reward for finding you?"[7]

[7] Tulsa *Daily World*, September 10, 1926 (microfilm).

October 14, 1926, Will began his daily telegram captioned "Will Rogers Says," by which he became so well known. This was handled by the McNaught people. It began with ninety-two papers subscribing to the article, a number that increased to over five hundred. The McNaught Syndicate was the only one that ever handled his newspaper articles. He was fond of the men on the staff and appreciated the way they had treated him when he was beginning to write. He always held a warm feeling for the *New York Times*, as shown in the following daily telegram:

> April 9, 1935: My boss is dead. Adolph O. Ochs, owner of the great New York Times is the first man I ever wrote for and it was him personally that got me to try it. Think of being lucky enough to break in at the top, for that paper is tops.[8]

While he was in Europe, he flew to Russia—in August 1926—and as a result of that trip wrote *There's Not a Bathing Suit in Russia*, which was published in 1927. This is one of the best efforts in his field of writing.

After a strenuous lecture tour in 1927 he returned to his California home quite ill. Despite the physical pain and the inconvenience of being unable to do for himself, his thoughts turned to his daily telegram. Summoning Mrs. Rogers to his bedside, he dictated the following wire for release the next day:

> June 16, 1927: Here is where the joke writers and everybody get even with me. I am in the California hospital where they are goint to relieve me of surplus gall, much to the politicians' delight.[9]

8 Daily telegram, Tulsa *Daily World* (microfilm).
9 Daily telegram, Tulsa *Daily World* (microfilm).

Though the operation was a serious one and he was gravely ill, he made good use of the experience later on by recounting it in rollicking detail for *The Saturday Evening Post* and also on the lecture platform. It was issued in book form under the title *Ether and Me*, and is still today a popular book. It was the last of the six books Will published.

He wrote other articles for *The Saturday Evening Post,* which he called "More Letters of a Self-Made Diplomat to His President." These were about his trips to Mexico, and "Letters" to the leading political figures of the day. He wrote articles for the *American Magazine* and introductions to the two Charles Russell books, *Trails Plowed Under* and *Good Medicine*; C. R. Coopers' *Annie Oakley, Woman at Arms*; Chester Byers' *Roping*; and *Around the World in Eight Days* by Wiley Post and Harold Gatty; and even an introduction to a cook book the ladies of Beverly Hills got out.

The old *Life* ran him for President in 1928 when Robert Sherwood was its editor. He wrote some short articles for this magazine, calling his the "Anti-Bunk Party." In them he analyzed the "Political Hooch."

"The greatest name in entertainment is coupled with the greatest name in rubber for your benefit" ran the advertising in the copy Will wrote for the Goodyear Rubber Company in 1929. This was a postal card campaign, and one of Will's ads went like this:

> "The whole business of politics is based on "Expelling Air." Who would have ever thought a giant industry could be built up on "coralling" air. When air goes in a Goodyear tire, it's like going to Sing-Sing for life."[10]

10 #002, Rogers Collection, Will Rogers Memorial.

It did not seem difficult for Will to write, and he could write anything for anybody at any time. He could not answer all the requests that came to him, but he kept up his weekly articles and his daily telegrams to the end of his life.

Wherever he went, he carried a portable typewriter with him and pecked out his articles with his middle fingers at an amazing rate of speed. In the crashed airplane that took his life was found his typewriter with an unfinished weekly article still in the machine. The last word that he had written was "death."[11]

When Will made the transition from monologist to writer, he kept the same personality he had employed on the stage. He wrote as he talked, in an informal intimate manner with no regard for grammar, syntax, or the formal rules of English. He used capital letters at random and a generous supply of commas; occasionally a period would find its way in. He spelled words as they sounded to him, giving them a misshapen, foreign appearance, but this eccentricity only added to the humor of the pieces. He made excessive use of such words as *dident, hadent, aint, 'em* (for *them*), *cuckoo, baloney, hooey,* and *applesauce.*

He had asked the syndicate to print his articles as he wrote them with no editing, and it complied with his wishes. His was a style all his own, set down in his peculiar, homely, often careless but understandable manner. As he explained, "When I write 'em, I'm through with 'em. I'm not being paid reading wages. You can always see too many things you wish you hadent said, and not enought that you ought."[12]

We miss much of the typical Rogers' humor in only the printed word, for Will was primarily a speaker and a show-

[11] Weekly article, Will Rogers Memorial (unpublished manuscript).
[12] Weekly article, September 1, 1929.

man who knew to the split second the timing of a joke or when to bring in the applause line. Some of his statements are classics and timeless; others have to be supplied with background as he wrote on the then present-day situations. However, reading Will Rogers day by day, one gets a very comprehensive history of the United States during the years he wrote.

Will Rogers is one of the most quoted Americans. People love to hear again the things he said. His was an earthy and spontaneous humor that came straight from his own ingenuity and reached the hearts of the American people who were waiting for his interpretation of the events of the day.

THE WILL ROGERS BOOK

~ 1 ~

AMERICA, U.S.A.

The Country

1. There's no other country with as much air, and not knowing where it's going as this country.

2. A Country has got to be based on settlers, not grafters.

3. That's what's the matter with this country. It's been advised to death. An editorial might explain the right course for everyone to pursue, but who wants to pursue it.

4. You can *diplomat* America out of almost everything she has but dont try to bluff her.

5. We are always doing something through the kitchen

door. We like the glory but not the responsibility.

6. It will take America fifteen years steady taking care of our own business and letting everybody else's alone to get us back to where everybody speaks to us again.

7. [At Democratic meeting.] Aint it wonderful to have something come up in a country where you can find out just how many political cowards there are?

8. Now if there is one thing that we do worse than any other nation, it is try and manage somebody else's affairs.

9. America invents everything, but the trouble is we get tired of it the minute the new is wore off.

10. What this country needs is more working men and fewer politicians.

11. The world is with the fellow coming up. Let the fellow that's already up look after himself. Every crowd wants to see a new champion crowned.

12. If you can do anything better than anybody else this old country is so constituted they want to see you get all you can out of it.

13. The trouble with America is we cant even seem to see somebody else only through our eyes. We dont take into consideration their angle or viewpoint. You see, everyone of us in the world have an audience to play to; we study them and we try and do it so it will appeal to what we think is the great majority. So we all have our own particular little line of applesauce for each occasion. So let's be honest with ourselves and not take ourselves too serious, and never condemn the other fellow for doing what we are doing every day, only in a different way.

14. [Luncheon clubs] have to be against something or they wouldent be formed. This old thing of eating at home with the folks is never going to get you anywhere. No real AMERICANISM in that.

15. We got as much [rumors of foreign war] as we've ever had. There is just as much money, as many to eat and as many to feed, as many to buy, but our conditions are uncertain. Because this thing outside our own land is worrying 'em. The whole thing is world wide. We

are effected by it less than anyone. If we keep our nose clean and dont start yapping about somebody else's honor, or what our moral obligations are, we might escape it. But it's going to take better statesmanship than we have been favored with heretofore.

16. We might be the wealthiest nation that ever existed, we might dominate the world in lots of things and because we are richer than all our neighbors or than anybody else, that dont necessarily mean that we are happier or really better off. The difference between our rich and poor grows greater every year. Our distribution of wealth is getting more uneven all the time. We are always reading "How many men paid over a million dollar income tax" but we never read about "how many there are that are not eating regular."

17. But in all it's a great country. It's the best and the worst one I ever lived in, and I been living in countrys for 54 years next November fourth.

The People

18. We are a people that get tired of a thing awful quick and I believe this continual prosperity will begin to get monotonous with us. We cant go through life just eating cake all the time. Of course, we like prosperity but we are having so much of it that we just cant afford it.

19. The American people are generous and will forgive almost any weakness with the exception of stupidity.

20. [American people] like to have you repent; then they are generous.

21. Nobody wants to be called common people, especially common people.

22. They tell you we are living in a fast age. We are . . . if we can live.

23. We do more talking progress than we do progressing.

24. The public dont care how you go to college, it's how you are going to get from the forty yard line to over the goal that they are worrying about. We are a "get the dough" people and our children are born in a commercial age. Why if a babe in arms can cry loud enough to get paid for it we are tickled to death. Make 'em pay for talent whether it's art, music, football, literature, radio announcing or flag pole sitting. Any actors that can draw 88 thousand people in one day is worthy of their hire. Dont let Wall Street get all the gravy.

5'10
645
1875

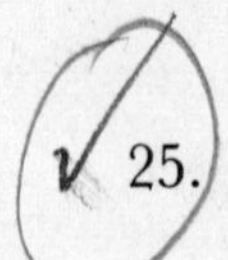

25. People's minds are changed through observation and not through argument.

26. There is still a lot of monkey in us. Throw anything you want into our cage and we will give it serious consideration.

27. The Romans loved blood. What money is to an American, blood was to a Roman. A Roman was never so happy as when he saw someone bleeding. That was his sense of humor, just like ours is. If we see a fellow slip and fall and maybe break his leg, why that's a yell to us, or his hat blow off and he cant get it.

28. There is no country in the world where a person changes from a hero to a goat and a goat to a hero, or visa versa—as they do with us. And all through no change of them, the change is always in us. It's not our public men that you cant put your finger on, it's our public. We are the only fleas weighing over 100 pounds. We dont know what we want, but we are ready to bite somebody to get it.

29. With the human race you may just as well throw your register book in the creek for what mating brings forth. No human can guess much less be certain of.

You are just as liable to bring forth a family of nuts as to produce an amateur Lincoln. Humans, it's just a name and has practically no significance at all.

30. That's what makes us a great country. The little things are serious and the big ones are not.

31. *Re* Senate investigations:

Everybody wants to hear accusations and nobody wants to hear denials.

32. The American people would trade ten investigations for one conviction.

33. We changed with the times, so we cant blame the children for just joining the times without even having to change.

34. Something ought to be done about these "Primitive" people who live in various parts of the world, and dont know a thing but to live off what nature provides. You would think they would get civilized and learn to live off each other like us civilized folks do.

35. [When Queen Marie of Romania visited America] it took two weeks to coach New York politicians how to dress and act to meet the Queen, so they all looked like twins and spoke the same little piece. Americans are getting like a Ford car. They all have the same parts, the same upholstering and make exactly the same noises.

36. A liberal is a man who wants to use his own ideas on things in preference to generations who he knows know more than he does.

37. I'll tell you about temperament—temperament is liable to arrive with a little success especially if you havent been used to success. The best cure for temperament is hunger. I have never seen a poor temperamental person.

38. This country is not where it is today on account of any one man. It is here on account of the real common sense of the Big Normal Majority.

39. Why anybody cant act the same away from home and enjoy just as much freedom as they do there, is more than I will ever know.

40. They have seen the Boragzzi Galleries [Borghese Gallery] and the Louvre, but they think the Smithsonian Institute is a clinic and the Field Museum is a branch of the great department store.

41. All Americans are wired for sound and before they go abroad they ought to detach the wiring.

42. It's always popular when in a foreign country to boost it to the detriment of your own country. You want to be sure that what you say is not going to reach back home, because after, its the home folks that count.

43. It's the Americans, or it's the American in any country that cause the Ambassador or Minister or Consul all the trouble. There is more renegade Americans abroad than there is at home.

The U.S. Government

44. We been staggering along now about 155 years under every conceivable horse-thief that could get into office and yet here we are, still going strong. I doubt if Barnum's circus has housed as many different kinds of species as has been in our government employ during its existence. As bad as they are they can't spoil

it, and as good as they are they can't help it. So as bad as we are, we are better off than any other nation, so what's the use to worry?

45. People dont change under Governments; the Governments change but the people remain the same.

46. If we could just send the same bunch of men to Washington for the good of the nation and not for political reasons, we could have the most perfect government in the world.

47. Why dont we let people alone and quit trying to hold what they call a protectorate over them? Let people do their own way and have their own form of government. We havent got any business in the Phillippines. We are not such a howling success of running our own government.

48. If people had anything to do with nominations personally, instead of it being done by half dozen men in the back rooms of some hotel, America would be a Democracy.

49. The Government has never been accused of being a business man.

50. This running a Government is kinder like our movie business. You are only as good as your last picture. Things over which they have no control comes along and yet if it happens and its bad, why out you go.

51. Course the way we do things, always have done things and will always do things, there just has to be so much graft. We wouldent feel good if there wasent. We just have to get used to charging so much off to graft just like you charge off so much for insurance, taxes or depreciation. It's a part of our national existence that we have just become accustomed to.

52. Nowadays its about as big a crime to be dumb as it is [to be] dishonest.

53. Lord, the money we do spend on Government and it's not one bit better than the government we got for one third the money twenty years ago.

54. As our Government deteriorates our humor increases.

55. If we dident have to stop and play politics any administration could almost make a Garden of Eden

out of us. You could transfer the Senate and Congress over to run the Standard Oil, or General Motors and they would have both things backrupt in two years. They are great guys personally and they know in their own heart that it's all a lot of "baloney" and if they are smart enough to make us feed 'em, why then we are the yaps, not them.

56. The Government has not only hundreds but literally thousands in Washington to see that no man can personally tend to his own business. They go there to do it for him and a mob always gets panicky quicker than an individual.

57. We will never get anywhere with our finances till we pass a law saying that every time we appropriate something we got to pass another bill along with it stating where the money is coming from.

58. Germany has a custom where they allow you to commit suicide in case you have been against the government. Over here we just let you go on making speeches and it amounts to about the same thing in the end.

59. There is no dishonesty in government. If there is,

let's dont dig it up. That's what made our government is our faith in it.

60. No one is going to spoil the country but the people. No one man can do it and all the people are not going to do it, so its going to run in spite of all the mistakes that can happen to it.

61. Always remember this, that as bad as we sometimes think our government is run, it's the best run I ever saw.

62. We have killed more people celebrating our Independence Day than we lost fighting for it.

63. When we got our [Independence] if history aint an awful liar, we sure wasent in much shape to handle it.

64. That liberty that we got 159 years ago Thursday was a great thing, but they ought to pass a law that we could only celebrate it every 100 years, for at the rate of accidents yesterday, we wont have enough people to celebrate it every year. And the speeches! Did

you read them? Never was as much politics indulged in under the guise of freedom and liberty.

They was 5% what George Washington did, and 95% what the speaker intended to do. What this country needs on July the fourth is not more "liberty" or more "Freedom" it's a Roman candle that only shoots out of one end.

65. Certainly lucky for us we got our liberty when we did.

66. What might be one classes "liberty" might be another classes "poison." Course, I guess absolute "Liberty" couldent mean anything but that anybody can do anything they want to do any time they want to. Well any half-wit can tell that wouldent work. So the question rises "How much liberty can you get and get away with it?" *Well, you can get no more than you give.* That's my definition, but you got perfect "Liberty" to work out your own, so get it.

67. Liberty dont work as good in practice as it does in speeches.

Clem Vann Rogers (1839-1911), Will Rogers' father, rancher, cattleman, banker, judge of Cooweescoowee District.

Will Rogers' birthplace near Oologah, Oklahoma, about twelve miles from Claremore.

Will Rogers at about the age of twelve years.

Will (seated) with two school friends.

As a young man, Will liked to dress up and attend social functions.

Will Rogers on furlough from Kemper Military Academy, 1898.

In his early twenties Will could dance the best cake-walk in the Cherokee Nation.

2

POLITICS

Politics was an inexhaustible source of subject matter for Will Rogers. In his early stage career as a rope artist, he began his monologue "I see by the papers," and in a shy, hesitant manner proceeded to comment on the current issues of the day. His deductions were so accurate that he easily earned the title of "Cowboy Philosopher."

When Will began writing for the newspapers in December 1922, he reached a class of people entirely different from theater audiences. These people avidly read his articles on the ever-changing political scene. As he toured the country on his lecture tours, he broadened his own horizon and endeared himself to people all over the United States.

The early 1920's did not have the efficient and rapid news facilities we use today, and there were many people then who did not understand the complexities of national and international politics. What they did read was not always clear to them. But when Will spoke or wrote in his good-natured, rambling style, in a language that all could understand, they welcomed his commonsense philosophy. They laughed over and agreed with his barbs at the absurdities of government policies and legislation. He became a sort of talisman for the American people; their interpreter, their spokesman and their champion.

He turned up at every presidential convention, both Democratic and Republican, to record the events for his public in a style quite unlike any other writer in the press box. He told the people the intimate things they wanted to know, yet beneath the fun he poked at the proceedings, there was a clear understanding of the political situation.

"Washington is really a merry-go-round,"[1] he declared long before Drew Pearson took such a title for his syndicated articles. No one knew this better than Will, who dodged in and out of the nation's capital, visiting the known and unknown politicians and attending functions with Washington's society leaders. He spoke and wrote what was in his mind, regardless of the consequences, though he was careful to point out the fallacies of partisan politics—a trait that made him much loved by the people and much feared by the professional politician.

He explained:

> I generally give the party in power, whether Republican or Democratic, the more digs because they are generally doing the country the most damage, and besides, I don't think it's fair to jump too much on the fellow that is down. He is not working, he is only living in hopes of getting back in on the graft in another four years, while the party in power is drawing a salary to be knocked.[2]

After Will spoke to the newspaper editors and publishers of California at Woodland in January 1933, the editor of the *Woodland Daily Democrat* commented:

> Believe it or not, Will Rogers, the cowboy funster and the man who has probably influenced more

1 Weekly article, May 14, 1933.
2 Weekly article, November 9, 1924.

ballots than any other living individual, has never voted. He told us so last Saturday and we believe he was serious about it. "Nope, if this here country goes to the bow-wows, there ain't no one can blame me for it," he explained. "I keep saying I'm a Democrat, but I ain't. I just pretend to be 'cause Democrats are funny and I'm supposed to be.

"Why, I travel all over the world purposely to get firsthand facts and all the inside information I can. I don't think anyone can joke intelligently unless he has something of fact to back up his humor. I have always maintained that no President can be as bad as the men that advise him."[3]

There was considerable complaint on the Rogers' quips with regard to the election of Franklin D. Roosevelt (versus Hoover) in 1932. Will was quick to defend his position:

> Everybody sure was "jumpy" during this late uprising. They had a vote in their pocket and a chip on their shoulder and any insinuation made against their hero was just too bad for you. If they would just stop to think, I have written on nothing but politics for years. You never heard me on a mother-in-law joke. It was always our national and international affairs. I have been in almost every country in the last few years. I have talked with prominent men of those countries, our ambassadors, or ministers, and I would be pretty dumb not to soak up some information.

3 *Woodland* [California] *Daily Democrat,* January 26, 1933.

Now I read politics, talk politics, know personally almost every prominent politician; like 'em and they are my friends, but I can't help it if I have seen enough of it to know there is some baloney in it. I am going to be like an umpire or referee. I am going to keep on doing the same as I have in the past. I am going to call 'em as I see 'em. If I don't see things your way, well, why should I? I hope I never get so old that I can't peep behind the scenes and see the amount of politics that is mixed in this medicine before it's dished out to the people as pure statesmanship. Politics is the best show in America and I am going to keep on enjoying it.[4]

And that is what Will Rogers did. From the time he established himself as an entertainer, he seldom made a speech without bringing in something of the political situation. In the sixteen or more years he wrote for the press, he devoted much of his space to politics.

Politicians

1. Slogan: "Be a politician; no training necessary."

2. A politician is not as narrow-minded as he forces himself to be.

3. A man's thoughts are naturally on his next term more than his country.

[4] Weekly article, December 18, 1932.

4. Cattlemen made the country, but it takes a politician to spoil it.

5. The more I see of politics, the more I wonder what any man would ever take it up for. Then people wonder why the best men of a community are not office holders.

6. If some efficiency expert would work out a scheme where each would be paid according to his ability, I think we would save a lot of money. Once a man holds a public office he is *absolutely no good for honest work*.

7. A king is sorta like a politician. It's hard to tell when he is making good or bad.

8. Nothing as short-sighted as a politician unless it's a delegation of them. They can ruin you quicker than unseasonable weather.

9. [Politicians] can do more funny things naturally than I can think of to do purposely.

10. Denounced and redenounced. That's what makes politics such a high-class gentlemanly game. Prize-fighters meet and fight.

√11. All legislation is put through by the aid of swaps and trades. They are just a lot of horse-traders.

12. What you say for humanity dont have near the appeal as what you say for political purposes.

13. You cant beat an administration by attacking it. You have to show some plan of improving it.

14. When you are in politics and depending on somebody to keep you in, why you really aint able to act like real life. Politicians will use any means to get their cause launched; a funeral, or a commemoration or a christening, any occasion that looks important, they will decide to launch along with the chaplain's benediction some of the promises the future holds for you.

15. It's awful hard to get people interested in corruption unless they can get some of it. Promise something in return for something whether it is a post office or an oil well.

16. Everybody that is in wants to stay in, and everybody that is out wants to get in. You know that is just what is the trouble with politics . . . there is not enough jobs to go around. You have a good job for every man and that will be the salvation of politics. You will never hear a kick. I am advocating putting into the platform "A job with every vote." If you vote for the government why not work for the government? It's harder to work for the government than it is to vote for it. In fact most jobs is not as hard.

17. Every time we have an election, we get in worse men and the country keeps right on going. Times have proven only one thing and that is you cant ruin this country ever, with politics.

18. It's not the men so much as it is the system. It just looks like they cant get away from it. Every move they take, every step they make, is with some political object in view.

19. Common sense is not an issue in politics; it's an affliction.

20. Abolish salaries and you will abolish politics and taxes.

21. There is no other business in the world that allows a man to work after he is fired except politics.

22. Nobody wants his cause near as bad as he wants to talk about his cause.

23. Everybody figures politics according to what they have accumulated during the last couple of years. Every guy looks in his pockets and then votes.

24. [Truth serum] would ruin the very foundation on which our political government is run. If you ever injected truth into politics, you would have no politics.

25. Politics hits a country like a pestilence. Somebody is going to make some money out of politics this year besides the politicians.

26. You cant believe a thing you read in regard to official's statements. The minute anything happens connected with official life, it's just like a cold night, everybody is trying to cover up.

27. Wherever you find poor soil, you will always find politics.

28. There is no more independence in politics than there is in jail. They are always yapping about "public service." It's public jobs they are looking for.

29. You can't legislate intelligence and common sense into people.

30. When a man goes in for politics over here he has no time to labor, and any man that labors has no time to fool with politics. Over there [England] politics is an obligation; over here it's a business.

31. We got the most thorough training in every line of business but statesmanship, and for that you just decide over night, "I am a statesman."

32. You come in there [as Secretary of State] labeled as a Statesman and limp out headed for the ash-can of political hopes.

33. The funny part about it [the London Conference] is that all those statesmen really thought they were going to "make History." Well, history makes itself, and the statesmen just drag along.

34. No other business in the world could afford to carry such dead wood. But we got 'em and they are going to live off us someway, so we just as well put long-tail coats on 'em and call 'em Statesmen.

35. Lobbyists in Washington are reaping a harvest. A Lobbyist is a person that is supposed to help a politician to make up his mind, not only help him, but pay him.

36. [Party politics] will never be changed because you cant change human nature. You cant broaden a man's vision if he wasent born with one.

37. Party politics is the most narrow-minded occupation in the world. A guy raised in a straight jacket is a corkscrew compared to a thick-headed politician.

38. If we dident have two parties, we would all settle on the best men in the country and things would run fine. But as it is, we settle on the worst ones and then fight over 'em.

39. It ain't much relief to just transfer your debts from

one party to another adding a little more in the bargain.

40. If a man could tell the difference between the two parties he would make a sucker of Solomon for wisdom. This country runs in spite of parties; in fact parties are the biggest handicaps we have to contend with.

Democrats

41. That's one peculiar thing about a Democrat—he would rather be told that he is right, even if he knows the guy is a liar, than he would to know he is wrong but belongs to the Republican party.

42. If the Democrats never split in their lives there would be no such thing as a Republican.

43. A Democrat never adjourns. He is born, becomes of voting age and starts right in arguing over something, and his political adjournment is his date with the undertaker. Politics is business with the Democrat. He don't work at it, but he tells what he would do if he was working at it.

44. When hungry and can't manage to get anything to

eat, [a Democrat] can always satisfy his hunger by dreaming and barking back to "Old Jeffersonian principles." Nobody knows what they were, but they have furnished a topic for the poor "Democrats" to rave about for a couple of generations.

45. Always excitement at a Democratic anything. There is always something that will stir up an argument even if they all agree.

46. A cannibal is a good deal like a Democrat, they are forced to live off each other.

Republicans

47. Republicans . . . take care of the big money, for big money takes care of them.

48. There aint any finer folks living than a Republican that votes the Democratic ticket.

49. Nothing, not even bad food, can ruin a Democratic dinner like some Republican sneaking in.

50. There must be something the matter with a Souther-

ner that would be a Republican as they are naturally in the observation ward at all times.

51. The slaves got their freedom by war and the Republicans got theirs by secession from old Virginia.

52. Prosperity dont divide the two parties, for under either administration, the poor get poorer and the rich get richer. Prosperity is only a question of giving a guy time to get it. So the whole thing, it looks like, goes back to the Civil War. The boys are still fighting it and dont know it. They fought each other in '65 so that made one a Democrat and one a Republican.

53. A flock of Democrats will replace a mess of Republicans. It won't mean a thing. They will go in like all the rest of 'em. Go in on promises and come out on alibis.

54. Split the post office jobs 50-50 and you will have a united Democracy and a united Republicanism.

55. It takes nerve to be a Democrat, but it takes money to be a Republican.

56. I guess the truth can hurt you worse in an election than about anything that could happen to you.

57. Political elections . . . are a good deal like marriages, there's no accounting for anyone's taste.

58. Elections . . . are like *mosquitoes,* you can't very well fight 'em off without cussing 'em.

59. I would rather have two friends in the counting room than a Republican slush fund behind me. More candidates have been defeated after six o'clock in the evening than were ever defeated during election day.

United States Senate and Senators

60. There is nothing in the world as alike as two Senators. No matter how different their politics, how different the parts of the country they come from, they all look alike, think alike and want alike. They are all looking for an appointment for some guy who helped them get theirs.

61. Most all new Senators are earnest and mean well.

Then the air of Washington gets into their bones and they are just as bad as the rest.

62. It must be nice to belong to some legislative body and just pick money out of the air.

63. There is no race of people in the world that can compete with a Senator for talking. If I went to the Senate I couldn't talk fast enough to answer roll call.

64. The United States Senate may not be the most refined and deliberative body in existence but they got the most unique rules. There ought to be one day a year when there is open session on Senators. The Constitution protects aliens, drunks and U. S. Senators.

65. All Senators travel a lot. They all try and keep away from home as much as they can.

66. I like to make little jokes and kid about the Senators. They are a never-ending source of amusement, amazement and discouragement. But the rascals, when you meet 'em they are mighty nice fellows. It must be

something in the office that makes 'em so honery sometimes. When you see what they do officially, you want to shoot 'em, but when one looks at you and grins so innocently, you kinder want to kiss him.

67. When a Gentleman quoted me on the floor the other day, another member took exception and said he objected to the remarks of a Professional Joke-Maker going into the Congressional Record.

Now can you beat that for jealousy among people in the same line? Calling me a Professional Joke Maker! He is right about everything but the Professional. They are the professional Joke Makers. I could study all my life and not think up half the amount of funny things they can think of in one Session of Congress. Besides my jokes don't do anybody any harm. You don't have to pay any attention to them. *But every one of the jokes those birds make is a law and hurts somebody,* generally everybody.

68. Who wants more congressmen? They seem to think the more we have the more loot we will get from the National Treasury in the way of appropriations. There ain't much quality in numbers.

69. I joke about 'em [Congressmen] but at heart I really like the rascals. They are all right. If one wants to

do right, our political system is so arranged that he can't do it. Mighty few retire rich, so there must be a lot more honesty about them than we give 'em credit.

Diplomats

70. Diplomats are just as essential to starting a war as Soldiers are for finishing it.

    You take Diplomacy out of war and the thing would fall flat in a week. Diplomats write notes because they wouldent have the nerve to tell the same thing to each other's face.

    A Diplomatic note is like an anonymous letter. You can call a fellow anything you want, for nobody can find out exactly who's name was signed to it.

71. Even a coward can be diplomatic.

72. There's one thing no nation can ever accuse us of and that's Secret diplomacy. Our foreign dealings are an open book . . . generally a check book.

73. Diplomats have a thing they call diplomatic language. It's just a lot of words and when they are all added

up, they don't mean a thing. On account of the President [Roosevelt] having something to say, and wanting to say it, there is no diplomatic language for that. A diplomatic language has a hundred ways of saying nothing but no way of saying something. Because he has never had anything to say, that's why they call 'em diplomats.

74. England has been the Daddy of the Diplomat, the one with the smooth manners. . . . That's one thing about an Englishman, he can insult you, but he can do it so slick and polite that he will have you guessing till way after he leaves you just whether he was a friend or foe.

75. The higher up our officials get, the less they seem to know about human nature or how to deal square with nations the same as they would with individuals.

76. A diplomat is a fellow to keep you from settling on a thing so everybody can understand it.

77. That's called diplomacy, doing just what you said you wouldent.

3

BUSINESS,
THE LAW AND LAWYERS

Will Rogers loved people. As he traveled over the country he visited with the big and little businessmen "To get their angle, as to how things were going." In this manner he gained an astounding knowledge of the business structure of the nation.

In his own business dealings he had an uncanny insight that he called "hunches." He employed no agent, and he had no adviser; but as calls for the stage, screen, radio and writing came to him, he would deliberate over these opportunities, toss some aside and wait until the prompting hunch presented itself. Fortunately, this led him into the proper channels as he climbed steadily in his craft. He held to the old-fashioned idea that a man's word was his bond; a contract meant nothing to him. "Advice," he said, "can get you in more trouble than a gun can. I don't want somebody telling me how to run my business or my country."[1]

While he numbered among his friends some of the greatest financial men of the time, he was never known

[1] Weekly article, August 20, 1933.

to use this friendship to benefit himself or take advantage of a situation at the expense of another. He took no chances on the stock market, explaining: "I never in my life made a single dollar without having to chew some gum to get it."[2] He played a lone game in the world of business and accepted no binding obligations.

He felt that money was for spending and giving. He bought unlimited happiness and comfort for others. As his fortune increased, so did his giving. No one demonstrated the share-the-wealth plan more bountifully than Will Rogers.

Business

1. A country is known by its strength, and a man by his check book.

2. The old community spirit waves just so long as everybody is collecting.

3. The day of the guy working for himself is past. We are living in an age of "Mergers." When your business is not doing good you combine with something and sell more stock. The poor little fellow, he can't combine with anything but the sheriff in case he is going broke. But "big business" merges with another that's not going good and both do "nothing" together.

2 Weekly article, November 10, 1929.

One of the weaknesses of the American people is that if two things go together they think it must be great.

4. In no business is a man entitled to more than he can draw and every man is entitled to a fair share of every cent he can draw.

5. There is nothing that can break a man quicker than land, unless it's running a grocery store or dealing in second-hand cars.

6. Samuel Gompers has spent his life trying to keep labor from working too hard and he has succeeded beyond his own dreams.

7. I tell you everybody ought to have two or three things they work at; and then when one busts, they got the others.

8. It's not what you pay a man but what he costs you that counts.

9. Half the people in the U.S. are living on interest paid

by people who will never get the last mortgage paid.

10. People that pay for things never complain. It's the guy you give something to that you cant please.

11. A debt is just as hard for a government to pay as an individual. No debt ever came due at a good time. Borrowing is the only thing that is handy all the time.

12. We will never get things really righted in our country till every line of sport, industry, profession or trade have some system of everyone contributing while working to the welfare of the old and unemployed in his own line. I dont mean to put all ball players in an old ball-player's home, I mean a system of help where it's done and they retain their respect and courage and self-esteem.

13. A guy [Saunders] in Memphis that started this Piggly Wiggly business, he figured that if somebody give you a basket and told you to go to it, that you would take more junk than if somebody was digging it out for you. The Woman instinct would naturally make her believe that the fellow looking in the bag at the finish might overlook something.

14. One third of the people in the U.S. promote, while the other two thirds provide.

15. Shrewdness in public life all over the world is always honored while honesty in public men is generally attributed to dumbness and seldom rewarded.

16. There is men in business that don't belong in business any more than the government does and that's why the government has to go in.

17. That's all America is, a business institution.

18. The difference between doing a thing for money and doing it for nothing makes it legal.

19. Our problem is not what is the dollar worth in London, Rome, or Paris, or what even it is worth at home. It's how to get hold of it, whatever its worth.

20. The old dollar might be filthy lucre, but there is

quite a bit of energy and spirit yet in earning one.

21. Big business sure got big, but it got big by selling its stocks and not by selling its products. No scheme was halted by the government as long as somebody would buy the stock.

22. The Stock Market has spoiled more appetites than bad cooking.

23. Wall Street has gone into one tail-spin after another. If it kept on like this it would discourage gambling—that would be bad for the country.

24. They always did say the heart of the American people was sound. In fact, it was sounder than most of the stocks that the sound heart bought.

25. Insurance companies have guys figure the very day you will die. (In fact, they won't insure till they have investigated and find out.) Then you, like a sucker, go bet them you will live longer than that.

26. Lloyds of London . . . will bet with you on anything and let you take either side you want.

27. Fireproofing and insurance have caused more fires than going to bed with a lighted cigarette.

28. The same fellows make them [insurance and political platforms] out. What they say on one page, they can deny on the other.

29. Our country has got so that each one of us has to live by a "racket" of some kind, and none of us must be too critical of the other fellow's racket.

Law and Lawyers

30. Everytime a lawyer writes something, he is not writing for posterity, he is writing so that endless others of his craft can make a living out of trying to figure out what he said. Course perhaps he hadent really said anything, that's what makes it hard to explain.

31. The minute you read something and you cant understand it, you can almost be sure that it was drawn up

by a lawyer. Then if you give it to another lawyer to read and he dont know just what it means, why then you can be sure it was drawn up by a lawyer. If it's in a few words and is plain and understandable only one way, it was written by a non-lawyer.

32. *Re* corruption in politics:

    It's what lawyers call "sharp practice." So it's going to be awful hard to make an issue of corruption.

33. That's one thing about these politicians, when they cant make politics pay, they can always fall back on the honest profession of *Law*.

34. A man dont any more learn where the ice box is in the White House than he has to go back to being a lawyer again.

35. Just addressed the California State Legislature and helped them pass a bill to form a Lawyers' Association to regulate their conduct. Personally, I dont think you can make a lawyer honest by an act of legislature. You've got to work on his conscience and his lack of conscience is what makes him a lawyer.

36. I have always noticed that anytime a man cant come and settle with you without bringing his lawyer, why look out for him.

37. Diplomats are nothing but high class lawyers. Some aint even high class.

38. Here is about the best crime prevention news I have seen. "The California Bar Association is to rid its ranks of any attorney found to have connection with the underworld."

The first thing they do now, if they are taking up crime as a profession (even before they buy the gun) is to engage their lawyer. He works on a percentage. He acts as their advance agent, too. He picks out the banks they are to rob. The Bar Association invented the word "ethics," then forgot it.

39. You almost have to be a lawyer in Washington to hold your own.

40. Some one suggested in case of mis-trial the Judge should hear the evidence and render the decision. What a howl the law profession put up! That was cutting right into their graft. What a justice-seeking bunch of babies they turned out to be.

41. All these laws that they are having so much trouble wondering if they are constitutional, they were all drawn up by lawyers. For almost two-thirds of the membership of the House and Senate are lawyers.

42. America has 110 million population [as of 1924], 90 per cent which are lawyers, yet we can't find two of them who have not worked at sometime or other for an oil company. *There has been at least one lawyer engaged for every barrel of oil that ever came out of the ground.*

43. Thousands of students just gradauted all over the country in Law. Going to take an awful lot of crime to support that bunch. A man naturally pulls for the business that brings him in his living. That's human nature, so look what a new gang we got to assist devilment. All trained to get a guilty man out on a technicality and an innocent one in on their opposing lawyer's mistake. This is the heyday of the shyster lawyer and they defend each other for half rates.

44. Law is complications and complications are Law. If everything was just plain, there wouldn't be any lawyers.

45. We are always saying, "Let the Law take its course."

But what we mean is "Let the Law take *our* course."

46. One level-headed smart man could interpret every law there is. If you commit a crime you did or you dident, without habeas corpus, change of venue, or any other legal shindig. But, lord, if we go into these things that are useless, why two-thirds of the world would have to turn to manual labor. That's really the only essential things there is.

47. *Re* The Legal Record:

"Dedicated to the interests of the legal profession," it's a paper that has nothing to do with news. It tells you right off we take nothing but the lawyers' side. (For there aint any other.)

48. Went down and spoke at some Lawyers' meeting last night. They dident think much of my little squib yesterday about driving the shysters out of their profession. They seemed to kinder doubt just who would have to leave.

49. If it weren't for wills, lawyers would have to work at an essential employment. There is only one way you can beat a lawyer in a death case. That is to die

with nothing. Then you cant get a lawyer within 10 miles of your house.

50. Modern history has proven that there has never yet been a will left that was carried out exactly as the maker of the money intended. So if you are thinking of dying and have any money, I would advise you to leave the following will:

    "Count up the lawyers in the state and divide it among them. If there should by any miracle be any left, let my Relatives, all of them, God bless 'em, fight over it."

51. By all means leave a will. Leave a will so the lawyers can misinterpret what you meant when you knew enough to know what you wanted to do with your money.

Will Rogers about 1905 on his trick pony, "Teddy," named for Theodore Roosevelt.

Betty (Mrs. Will) Rogers and "Teddy," about 1909.

Will Rogers on "Dopey," one of his roping horses, at his Long Island place, about 1916, when he was appearing in the *Follies*.

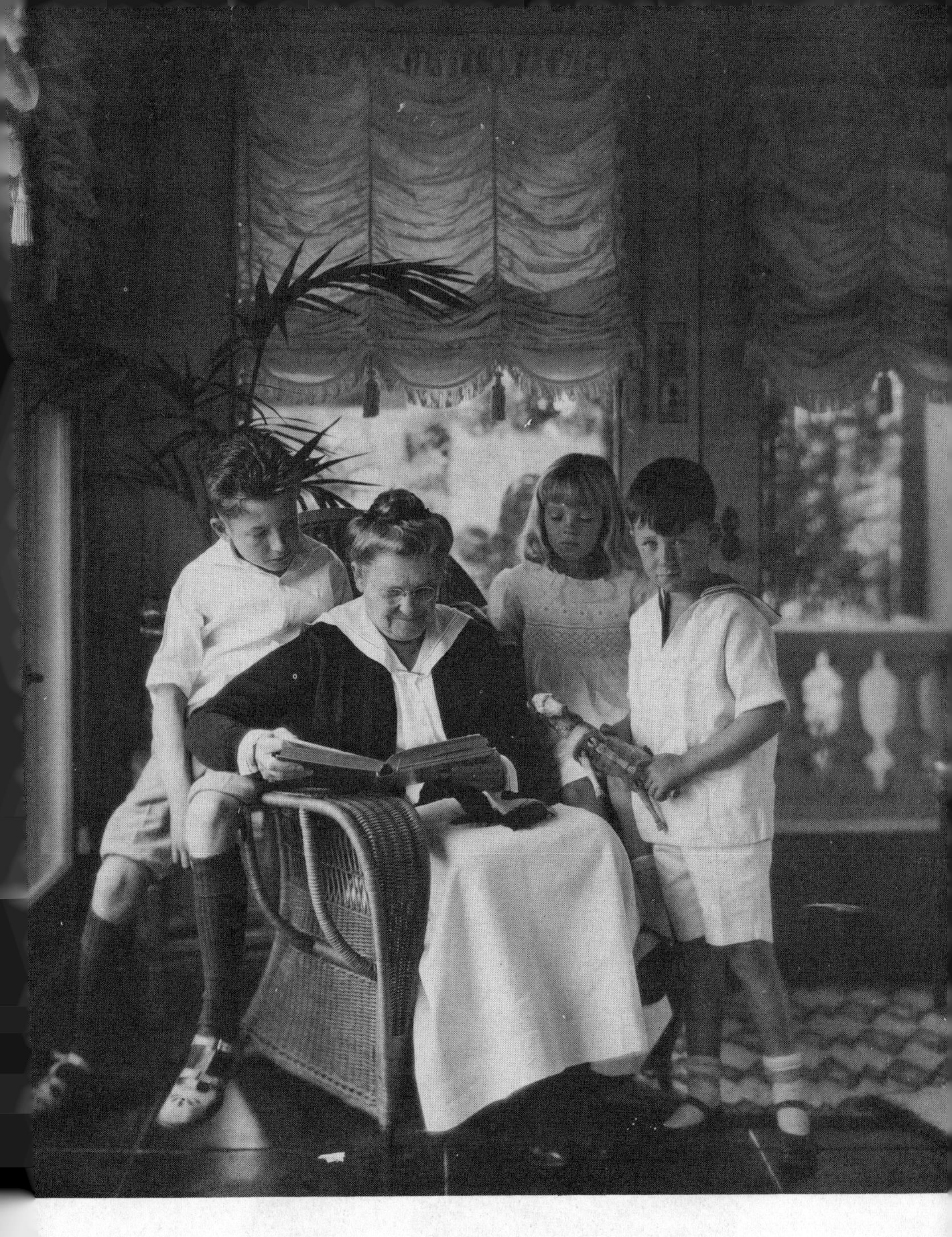

"Mamoo" Blake, mother of Mrs. Will Rogers, with the Rogers' children, Bill, Jim and Mary, at their Beverly Hills home about 1920.

The Rogers family about 1922, when they were living on Long Island, N.Y., and Will was in the *Follies*. Jimmie is in the front seat with his father; Mrs. Rogers is in the back seat with Mary and Will, Jr.

Mr. and Mrs. Rogers returning from a round-the-world trip, Sept. 1934.

Will and Betty Rogers, 1928.

The Rogers family polo team at their Santa Monica, California, ranch,

about 1930. From *left to right*: Jimmie, Mary, Will, Jr., Will Rogers.

4

BANKERS AND TAXES

During the last years of his life in Claremore, Oklahoma, Will's father was a banker. He was a generous-hearted man, affectionately called "Uncle Clem," who helped many of the early-day citizens get started in business and also kept a host of others from financial ruin and the poor house.

Naturally, Will had a great respect for bankers as a whole, but he did not always approve of the way some of them transacted business. Because he was free with his own money and tried to do all he could to help the unfortunates, it was difficult for him to understand why the banker was not more lenient. He had seen the result of the drought in the Southwest when he toured the country on his own relief drive, and felt that some of the most deserving people were entirely overlooked.

The years following the crash of the stock market were some of the most crucial in the banking industry. This was a timely topic for Will, who noted these events in his role as a humorist.

He was a popular speaker at bankers' meetings and conventions and often addressed the bankers as "Loan-Sharks! Shylocks! Skinflints! The greatest bunch of men that ever foreclosed a mortgage on a widow's home."

The bankers laughed spontaneously at his remarks, for each one knew Will was not referring to him, but to the other fellow.

Under the guise of this good-natured banter, Will could drive a point home like a guided missile. As he chose to defend the class of people who were not able to speak for themselves, he usually put himself also on the defensive. In speaking of his holding in this connection he wrote:

> We call 'em ranches in California. It sounds big and dont cost any more on the lien. Mine is called "Rancho Premire y Segundo Mortgages." The literal translation of that is the "Ranch of the First and Second Mortgages," and there would be a third if these old bankers were more liberal minded.[1]

Bankers

1. There are more [bankers] in Ossining[2], N. Y., than any town its size in the United States.

2. Show me ten men that mortgage their land to get money and I will have to get a search warrant to find one that gets the land back again. If you think it aint a sucker game, why is your banker the richest man in your town?

   Let 'em go to work, if there is any job any of them

1 Weekly article, September 17, 1933.
2 Sing Sing Prison is in Ossining.

could earn a living at. Banking and after-dinner speaking are two of the most nonessential industries we have in this country. I am ready to reform if they are.

3. I saw one of their [American Legion] conventions and they act almost half as bad as the American Bankers' Association, who had nothing to celebrate but foreclosed mortgages.

4. All newsboys become politicians and all bootblacks become bankers.

5. An old country boy banker from Colorado slicked the city-slicker bankers out of one-half million bucks and they give him fifteen years so fast that you would have thought he had assassinated a big government official. You let a city bank slick an old country boy out of something and before night he will merge with another bank and finally wind up as a member of the Federal Reserve.

6. There is no such thing as a little bootlegger, no more than there is a little banker. The day of the little banker in a small town is past. He is a member of a chain. He is a subsidiary of some big concern.

7. Is there any way of checking up on a bank president or vice-president to see what he can actually by his own efforts draw into his bank?

8. If a bank fails in China, they behead the men at the the head of it that was responsible. If one fails over here, we write the men up in the magazines, as how they started poor, worked hard, took advantage of their opportunities (and depositors) and today they are rated up in the millions.

9. There is nothing as scary as a banker. He dont wait for the grave yard to whistle, he will do it passing a hearse.

10. Our home bankers, both large and small, are in bad just thru the bad times and an over expansion in good times, but the International one is in bad thru malice aforethought. His devilment was premeditated. He knew he was loaning on no security in Europe, cause there is no security over there. He got his commissions for peddling it out so what does he care.

11. You know, there is nothing as tiring and boring in this country as just a rich man. So my scheme is to bring 'em back to respectability. I am going to start with

the bankers. If I can make Bankers loved by the community again, it is going to be a God-send to their families.

12. The Banker, the Lawyer, and the Politician are still our best bets for a laugh. Audiences havent changed at all, and neither has the three above professions.

Taxes

13. I see a great deal of talk from Washington about lowering the taxes. I hope they get 'em lowered down enough so people can afford to pay 'em.

14. Alexander Hamilton originated the "put and take" system into our national treasury. The tax payers put it in and the politicians take it out.

15. Every statesman wants to vote appropriations but is afraid to vote taxes.

16. Everybody is on a trip somewhere if they work for the Government. I wonder when the taxpayers take their trip.

17. When a party cant think of anything else they always fall back on lower taxes, but no voter has lived to see the day when his taxes were lowered. Presidents have been promising lower taxes since Washington crossed the Delaware by hand in a row boat, but our taxes have gotten bigger and their boats have gotten larger until now the President crosses the Delaware in his private yacht.

18. There is dozens of great humanitarian things that could be done at a very little cost, if the tax was properly applied. It's the waste in government that gets everybody's goat.

19. Every time Congress starts to tax some particular industry it rushes down with its main men and they scare 'em out of it. About the only way I see for 'em to do it so it would be fair to everybody would be for Congress to go into secret session, allow no telephones, no telegrams, no visitors, so no outside lobbyist can get at 'em, then tax everything they should tax, then announce: "Boys, it's all over; there is no use shooting at us now." As it is now, we are taxing everybody without a lobby.

20. If we were run by the Manager form of Government we would be paying so little taxes we would be lonesome.

21. It's a great country but you cant live in it for nothing.

22. Did you ever figure it out, taxes is all there is to politics?

23. Income Tax was another issue of his [William Jennings Bryan] advocated twenty years before it was adopted. If we had started paying it then, we would have been used to it by now and it wouldent seem so hard.

24. The Income Tax has made more liars out of the American people than golf has.

25. The crime of taxation is not in the taking of it, it's in the way it's spent.

26. This is income tax paying day. There is going to be no attempt at humor for it would be mighty forced. No two can agree on what is deductable. When it's made out you dont know if you are a crook or a martyr.

27. Congress knocked the rich in the creek with a [raise

in the] income tax, then somebody must have told 'em: "Yes, Congress, you got 'em while they are living. But what if they die on you to keep from paying it?" Congress says: "Well, never thought of that so we will frame one that will get 'em alive or living, dead or deceased." Now they got such a high inheritance tax on 'em that you wont catch these old rich boys dying promiscuously like they did. This bill makes patriots out of everybody. You sure do die for your country, if you die from now on.

28. I dont see why a man shouldent pay inheritance tax. If a country is good enough to pay taxes to while you are living, it's good enough to pay in after you die. By the time you die, you should be so used to paying taxes that it would be almost second nature.

29. It aint taxes that is hurting the country; it's interest.

30. Nobody has ever invented a slogan to use instead of paying your taxes.

31. A fellow can always get over losing money in a game of chance but he seems so constituted that he can never get over money thrown away to a government in taxes. In other words he will bet on anything but he wont pay it to you in taxes.

32. People dont mind spending their money if they know it isn't going for taxes.

33. Oh, boy—where is all the money coming from that the government is throwing away? Well, it just sorter looks like it might come from the ones that have got it. There is one good thing about our American form of government—the fellow that's got nothing, pays nothing; and too, lots of times the fellow that's got something, but nothing to pay with. But he can at least let 'em have the property and break even. But the big yell comes nowadays from the taxpayers. I guess when the pilgrims landed on Plymouth Rock and they had the whole of American continent, and all they had to do to get an extra 160 acres was to shoot another Indian, I bet you anything they kicked on the price of the ammunition. I bet they said, "What's this country coming to that we have to spend a nickle for powder?" Of course, they got the lead back after they dissected the Indian. No matter what you pay for taxes, high or low, medium, the yell is always the same, 100 per cent.

Course we know our Government is costing us more than it's worth. But do you know of anybody that has a cheaper one? You can try Russia—there is no income tax in Russia, but there's no income.

34. [Baseball] is a skilled game. It's America's game, it and high Taxes.

35. Taxation is about all there is to government. People want just *taxes* more than they want *lower* taxes. They want to know that every man is paying his proportionate share according to his wealth.

36. Incidentally comedians havent improved. Nothing has improved but taxes.

5

PRESIDENTS

Will was considered a great power in the political world, and this fact did not go unnoticed by the Presidents of the United States. His personal acquaintance with Presidents began with Theodore Roosevelt and extended to Franklin D. Roosevelt. A man like Teddy Roosevelt, who lived and typified "the strenuous life," stirred the imagination of the young Will. While he was on the vaudeville circuit in 1905, he wrote home to his sisters from the Chase Opera House, October 30:

> Don't know if I will make the White House this trip as old Teddy aint here and young Teddy is away at school. I don't much care to as I did it once and they might think I wanted to use it for advertising purposes, but I dont know what will show up before the week is over.[1]

Will's clever pony that he used in his roping act was named "Teddy" in honor of the President, but when he played Washington, D. C., at the Gayety Theater the week of February 25, 1907, Teddy was billed as "Arcade" out of respect to the man who held the highest office in the U.S.A.

1 Family letters, October 30, 1905.

Throughout his life Will enjoyed an intimate friendship with the Roosevelts, especially Alice Roosevelt and her husband Nicolas Longworth, U.S. Congressman from 1903 to 1931 and Speaker of the House during the Coolidge and Hoover administrations.

In an undated letter to his sister about 1915, Will tells of appearing before President Woodrow Wilson. He was in the *Follies* at this time. He wrote:

> We played to the President last night. I will write you all about it in a letter in a day or so. I joked all about the Peace Ship [Henry Ford's] going to Europe, he sure enjoyed it. I had lunch today with Mr. and Mrs. Nick Longworth at their home. Their home you could put all Rogers County in it. . . .[2]

Woodrow Wilson was one of the first to call Will Rogers a humorist when he said, "His remarks are not only humorous but illuminating."[3]

In later years Will himself had been mentioned for the Presidency with all seriousness by various groups and individuals, but he always scoffed at the idea. "I would rather tell 'em what I think and retire with satisfaction than be President and be hampered."[4]

Will was always a welcome guest at the White House and each President was glad to laugh at his jokes on the administration, or, in a serious mood, find out how conditions were in certain countries he had visited. He was indeed an unofficial ambassador of good will. His keen analysis of foreign affairs was always sought by the Chief Executive and not thrust on him.

2 Family letters.
3 Michel Mok, newspaper story, 1935.
4 Weekly article, March 4, 1934.

After the bitter campaign of 1932, when Will advised both Roosevelt and Hoover to go fishing and quit the name-calling, he got a number of rebukes from his readers for writing about the President. He answered them in "A Letter to the Times":

> Now I poke my little fun at the Presidents, but I don't care who you are, you havent got any more respect for the man and the office than I have. I think Mr. Hoover knows what I think of him personally and how I admire him as a man. I have never gone to Washington that I havent gone in and had a chat with him and I feel that I can again.
>
> Mr. Coolidge, who I made a living out of for years, had no greater and still has no greater admirer and staunch supporter of his splendid qualities, than I am.
>
> Now this Mr. Roosevelt that's coming in, he is a particular friend of mine for many years standing, he and his whole family, but I have got to start in now pretty soon making a living out of the fool things that he and those Democrats will do, and I am not worried, I know they will do plenty of 'em.
>
> The one thing that I am proud of is the fact that there is not a man in public life today that I dont like. Most of them are my good friends, but that's not going to keep me from taking a dig at him when he does something or says something foolish.[5]

[5] *Los Angeles Times*, November 10, 1932.

Presidents in General

1. Presidents become great, but they have to be made Presidents first.

2. We have lived under over 30 Presidents. They couldn't have all been great. In fact if we told the truth about 'em, maybe some of 'em was pretty punk. But we drug along in spite of 'em.

3. No one of the whole 30 of them that we have had ever did what anyone of the others did. All of the candidates study what to do and who to do it to.

4. It don't make any difference who it is. None of them from any party are going to purposely ruin the country. They will all do the best they can.

5. You can get your name on a button easier than you can get it on the letter box in front of the White House.

6. There just seems to be something about running for President that you can never get out of a fellow's

head. He never seems to figure his chances. It can be on an "off year," or "Leap Year" and just nominate him, and he is perfectly tickled to death. That he will wind up by just being a defeated candidate never seems to enter his head. That "The Time is not ripe for it" is as foreign to his thoughts as the moon.

7. If you eliminate the names of Lincoln, Washington, Roosevelt, Jackson and Wilson, both conventions would get out three days earlier.

8. A good campaign manager can do more than an able candidate. "Trades" makes Presidents, more than ability, but as bad as we are, and as funny as we do things, we are better off than the other countries, so bring on more conventions. No Nation likes "hooey" like we do. We are all cookoo, but we are happy.

9. A guiding hand in any business now needs encouragement and especially in guiding the biggest business in the world. Lord, what a tough time to have a country on your hands.

10. The Congressmen and Senators are not supposed to know anything about the country, and they generally dont, so the President issues his message.

11. Distrust of the Senate by Presidents started with Washington who wanted to have 'em court-martialled. Jefferson proposed life imprisonment for 'em. Old Andy Jackson, said, "To Hell with 'em" and got his wish. Lincoln said, "The Lord must have hated 'em for he made so few of 'em." Roosevelt whittled a big stick and beat on 'em for six years. Taft just laughed at 'em and grew fat. They drove Wilson to an early grave. Coolidge never let 'em know what he wanted, so they never knew how to vote against him, and Mr. Hoover took 'em serious, thereby making his only political mistake.

12. Once a man is President he is just as hard to pry out of there as a Senator, or a town constable or any political office.

13. Sometimes it makes you think we dont need a different man as bad as we need different advisers for the same man.

14. No matter what a President does, he is wrong according to some people, so I couldent even say yes or no if I was him. I would just stall along and if asked I would remark, "I dont choose to answer." But take all in all, it's a tough life. This thing of being President and trying to please everybody—well, not exactly everybody, but enough to re-elect.

15\. Course the President, he is always conceded the nomination at the next election unless he has been notoriously incompetent. But all things being as they usually are, why he of course can have the election if he wants it. And history has never recorded the one that dident. Coolidge dident but he had already had practically two terms. And there is a kind of unwritten law against that. But it wasent a third term bugaboo that kept Calvin out, it was horse sense. He knew just to an inch how much American wind the financial balloon would hold and he got out just two days before it busted. Poor Mr. Hoover dident see the thing any more than poor Rin Tin Tin.

It was set that Mr. Hoover could have it if he chose, and he did choose, and how! They do love to be President. It's the toughest job in the world, but there is always 120 million applicants.

16\. Every party and everybody must have some platform formed even if its in their minds. Mine is that a President should hold office six years with no re-election. Stop this thing of a President having to lower his dignity and go trooping around asking for votes to keep him there another term. He has to do it, naturally, but a six-year term with no re-election will be the remedy. Six years gives him time to do something. It takes him four years to find out who is his friends in the Senate and House. There is a lot of Senators in there for six years. Look at the saving of all the money, all the time, all the uncertainty of another election. It lessens it one-third.

Then pay the man when he goes out one-half of his salary for life. The country should keep an ex-President from bankruptcy if it can keep a railroad or a badly managed bank. Course the Cabinet wouldent have much to do on their last summer in office like they do now, but they could hang around their office and kill time.

George Washington

17. A Virginia planter. A farmer that needs no relief but just wants to clean the British out and figures we can run it ourselves and cut out the overhead.

18. He was the most versatile President we ever had. He was a farmer, civil engineer and a gentleman. He made enough at civil engineering to indulge in both the other luxuries.

19. He was a surveyor. He took the exact measure of the British and surveyed himself out about the most valuable piece of land in America at that time, Mount Vernon. George could not only tell the truth but land values.

20. Of course he was great. He was the Father of our

Country on account of having no children. He was a surveyor and he owned half of Virginia because he surveyed his own lines. He was a General on our side because England wouldent make him one of theirs. He was a politician and a gentleman—that is a rare combination.

21. Washington was elected the first President because he was about the only one who had enough money to give a decent inauguration party. Then every once in a while he would whip England. That wasent an accomplishment. That was a habit. He really took the job so he could locate the capital in Washington.

22. Originally in our country the Government owned all the land there was outside the original 13 colonies and England owned that. Then Washington had a war and took it away from them and annexed most of it personally himself. What he dident get, a Democrat named Jefferson got.

23. [The Capital] was really the first real estate promotion scheme; Washington and Jefferson owned practically all the land down that way, and geographical reasons had nothing to do with locating the capital there. It wasent the center of the country, but it was the center of George's and Tom's land holdings. So while you dident get much money for

being President in those days, it wasent exactly a philanthropic job. George lost no money through the transaction. He and Jefferson landed on two of the best hills in that country, and the Government got the swamps.

24. Even in the beginning when George Washington run against himself there must have been some little issue that the voters could be pro or con over. Even if it was over whether he should bob his wig or just over the white horse he used to have his picture painted on.

25. It's been fairly well established that Washington slept here [Philadelphia] in not only one but various beds. Washington crossed the Delaware (with everybody rowing but him). I don't remember whether he crossed it to get to or away from Philadelphia.

26. Washington . . . fought for his tribe against the invaders [Indians] and wound up with a flock of statutes and a title of Father-of-His-Country. I expect if the truth were known, the old Apache Chiefs went through more and fought harder for their country than George did. But George won, that's the whole answer to history. It's not what did you do, but what did you get away with at the finish.

27. All we seem to celebrate Washington's Birthday for is so we can revive the argument as to "what he had to say about entanglements with Europe." Every speaker makes him say just what that speaker wants him to say. Coolidge says it was Jefferson that made the "wise crack" about not messing with outsiders. So, it looks like added to all his other accomplishments Washington was a diplomat.

Thomas Jefferson

28. He was the most far-sighted Democrat in either his or any other time and they named the Democratic party after him. That is he was for the poor but was himself of the rich.

29. Jefferson sitting up there on that hill believed in equality for all. But he dident divide up that hill with any poor Democrats. (For Democrats were poor in those days as they are today.)

30. Jefferson seemed to be the only Democrat in history with any kind of business ability.

31. They havent had a man that rode a horse to the White House since Jefferson.

32. There's a lad that never missed a shot or a drink while he was in the White House.

33. Course I knew what a great man he had been but at the same time I had heard enough to know that an "Injun" dident exactly rate high with him. I knew he had a lot to do with running the Cherokees out and making them go West, but I knew he had unconsciously favored us in the long run so I forgave him.

34. He is the one that run us Cherokees out of Georgia and North Carolina. I ate the [Jackson Day] dinner on him, but I dident enjoy it. I thought I was eating for Stonewall. Old Andy, every time he couldent find any one to jump on, would come back and pounce onto us Indians. Course he licked the English down in New Orleans, but he dident do it till the war had been over two weeks, so he really just fought them as an encore. Then he would have a row with the Government and they would take his command and his liquor away from him and he would come back and sick himself onto us Cherokees again.

He was the first one to think up the idea to promise everybody that if they will vote for you, you will give them an office when you get it, and the more times they vote for you, the bigger the office. But old Andy made the White House. He got in before the Republicans got their scheme working. The Indians wanted him in there so he would let us alone for awhile. Andy stayed two terms and was the first man that dident "Choose to run" again. He had to get back to his regular business which was shooting at the Indians.

35. He fought duels when duels was duels and not just the inconvenience of getting up before sunrise.

36. About all old Andrew was responsible for was the system that made us all have to sit there and listen to such junk [speeches]. Andrew was the one that said, "If you dont get out and work for the party you don't get in on the gravy after election."

37. [Jackson] brought undying fame to the glorious state of Tennessee. He did it by personal bravery and unmatched intelligence.

Abraham Lincoln

38. Honest Abe wasent hardly a bottle fed baby all through life. Even if he dident split all those rails, just piling up rails after somebody else had split 'em is hardly child's play.

39. I dont know what the particular issue was in Lincoln's election but you can bet as good an axeman as he was he had some kind of a clean cut issue.

40. Is there anybody here [Princeton University] teaches reading or writing or arithmetic or some of the old fashioned things Lincoln struggled along with to Presidency?

41. If Abe Lincoln from Illinois was resurrected and was to fill out this unexpired term and he still insisted he was a Republican, there would be a party vote against him.

42. They dug up another monument or repainted an old one or something over in Illinois. This was to Abraham Lincoln, another Republican. Hoover said: "Get 'em all dedicated on one trip."

43. If it hadent been for Lincoln, the Republicans in N.Y. would sure be short of a cause for celebrating.

44. Some man . . . from Illinois got up to nominate somebody [at the Democratic Convention of 1924] and

we knew we would hear something about Lincoln being born in Illinois. He kept quoting Lincoln's famous remark about "God must have loved the common people because he made so many of them." You are not going to get people's votes nowadays by calling them common. Lincoln might have said it, but I bet it was not until he was elected.

45. The last few days I have read various addresses made on Lincoln's birthday. Every politician always talks about him, but none of them ever imitate him.

46. Lincoln was great. He freed the slaves and put the Southern whites in bondage for the duration of their natural lives. He furnished General Grant with cigars to smoke and poor Lee had no gas mask so he had to surrender. Lincoln tried his best to prevent that war between the Democrats and the Republicans. Since then, they have been settling their difficulties at the polls with about the same results.

47. Papers today say, "What would Lincoln do today?" Well, in the first place, he wouldent chop any wood, he would trade his ax in on a Ford. Being a Republican he would vote the Democratic Ticket. Being in sympathy for the under dog he would be classed as a radical progressive. Having a sense of humor he would be called eccentric.

48. Lincoln made a wonderful speech one time: "That this nation under God, shall have a new birth of freedom, and that Government of the People, by the People, for the People shall not perish from this earth." Now, every time a politician gets in a speech, he digs up this Gettysburg quotation. He recites it every Decoration Day and practices the opposite the other 364 days.

Now Mr. Lincoln meant well, but he only succeeded in supplying an applause line for every political speaker who was stuck for a finish.

49. Another Decoration Day passed and Mr. Abraham Lincoln's 300-word Gettysburg address was not dethroned. I would try to imitate its brevity if nothing else. Of course, Lincoln had the advantage. He had no foreign policy message to put over. He dident even have a foreign policy. That's why he is still Lincoln.

50. No man should ever make a speech after somebody has read or recited Lincoln's Gettysburg Address. It's only about 300 words long and the plainest words. There's not a child or even a comedian that can't understand it. Honest, Lincoln just as well not made his speech as far as it has had any effect on other speakers. He left it as an example but no one ever followed it.

He was not what is always humorously referred to as

the "Principal Speaker." And this little speech of Lincoln's dident go over so big. They all say Lincoln wrote his going up on the train in a day coach, on the back of an envelope. Every speaker that goes to commemorate something or other, should be locked up in a day-coach and if he comes out with over 300 words then he should be put in a cattle car and make it to the stock.

Theodore Roosevelt

51. Teddy Roosevelt was my best bet for a laugh in those days [vaudeville]. He was the best known public man that ever lived, and they kept up with everything that he did. So when you started in talking about something that he had just said or done, you dident have to stop and tell what it was before going ahead with your comment.

52. Teddy was a man that wouldent waste even hatred on nothing.

53. If we can spare men like Roosevelt and Wilson there is no use in any other politician ever taking himself seriously.

54. The reason I advocate electing our officials for life

is that no matter what man is in office, the one that you put in his place is worse. If we had kept our original cast that we had to start with, we would have been better off. We had no business ever letting Washington, (George, not D.C., I mean) go. We ought to have kept him till we got a hold of Lincoln, then been more careful of the protection of his life and preserved him to a ripe old age down to where [Teddy] Roosevelt was say 15 years old. Then we could have turned it over to him. He would have run it as good at that age as most men could at 50.

William Howard Taft

55. In our Decoration Day speechmaking Mr. Taft spoke at some unveiling of a monument in Cincinnati. He made an alibi for the Supreme Court. I don't know what prompted him to tell the dead what the court was doing, unless it was some man who had died of old age waiting for a decision from that august body.

56. *Re* the death of President Taft:

Mr. Taft, what a lovely old soul. Fat and good natured. All of our Presidents that his generation knew, some we felt we dident know, some we admired their ability, some we had great faith in, and all of them symbolized the great office they occupied. But just as a man, and a real honest-to-God fellow, Mr. Taft will go to his grave with more real downright affection and less enemies than any. . . . He always seemed like he was one of us. He was our great human fellow because there was more of him to be human. We are parting with 300 pounds of solid charity to everybody, and love and affection for all his fellowmen.

Calvin Coolidge

57. [Coolidge] got so used as Vice President to have no one pay any attention to what any of them said he cant realize they might listen to him now.

58. He kept his mouth shut. That was such a novelty among politicians that it just swept the country. Originality will be rewarded in any line.

59. My campaign contributions would do credit to Calvin Coolidge as I havent spent a cent.

60. President Coolidge gave a luncheon for visiting Governors where they discussed but dident try prohibition.

61. Being great as President is not a matter of knowledge or far-sightedness. It's just a question of the weather not only in your own country but in a dozen others.

It's the elements that make you great or that break you. So, it's sorter like a World's Series—you got to have the breaks. Bad advice will ruin you just about as a total earthquake would. Every guy just looks in his pockets and then votes. And the funny part of it is it's the last year that is the one that counts. You can have three bad ones and then wind up with everybody having money, and you will win so far you neede nt even stay up to hear the returns. You may think you can out-general Cal, but you look up his record and you are going to have a tough time out-lucking him.

62. He knows . . . a good crop next year will do more for free rent than all the promises he could think of to make now.

63. [Coolidge] came in here with nothing but a valise and a speech on economy. Nobody begrudges him what he has been able to save up during these years and when he is up there [Vermont]. In that town there aint much to look at—only what you bring in with you.

64. Calvin wants to buy something for us but he wants Hoover to pay for it. He is more set on going out of office having his budget balanced than he is going

out with any other thing. We may be in a terrible lot of scrapes, but we wont be in the red.

65. Here comes Coolidge and does nothing and retires a hero, not only because he hadent done anything, but because he had done it better than anyone.

Herbert Clark Hoover

66. In 1914, he was chairman of the American Relief Association and he helped feed Belgians, and a little later it was found we was worse off than the Belgians, so they brought him home to feed us. He is always feeding somebody. Now he is feeding the Republicans. No Armenian that ever lived can eat more than one of them can.

He really won the war for us. Did you ever figure that out? He won the war for us, but he ruined our stomachs. He gave us liberty with indigestion.

67. Hoover is talking about resigning—that shows right there he is not a politician. He seems to think you cant serve two masters.

68. He has seen more of the world, (not only than any

President) but more than any Notre Dame football team. He has no use for politicians, which fact elected him by the largest majority ever recorded. If he will just continue to hate them we are liable to wake up with another Lincoln or Jefferson on our hands.

69. Mr. Hoover hadent been sworne in over three quarters of an hour till the desire to be President on the part of half of Mexico broke out. It looks like his being inaugurated kinder put the same idea into 34 Generals' heads in Mexico. All you had to do to be President was to shoot the one that was and that brought on some pretty fancy marksmanship. The old way of electing Presidents by the bullet instead of the ballot.

70. Mr. Hoover has done all in his power to try and further peace and at the same time leave us a musket loaded in the corner.

71. I always did want to see him elected. I wanted to see how far a competent man could go in politics. It has never been tried before.

72. We ought to have a social President. There just aint any end to what he could relieve Mr. Hoover of.

Get a man and his wife with good digestion, good disposition and a master of Emily Post.

73. [Hoover] reaped the benefits of the arrogance of the party when it was going strong.

Franklin Delano Roosevelt

74. This Roosevelt is a mighty fine human man. Sometimes I think he is too nice a fellow to be mixed up in all this politics.

75. See where the Roosevelts, even down unto the fifth cousins, are straying back into the fold. Nothing will bring back distant kinfolk like the news spreading that you got a job.

76. Say this Roosevelt is a fast worker. Even on Sunday when all a President is supposed to do is put on a silk hat and have his picture taken coming out of church, why this President closed all the banks, and called Congress in extra session. And that's not all he is going to call 'em if they don't get something done.

77. This fellow Roosevelt never gets through surprising us. We just find out now that he speaks French fluently. That's the second linguistic surprise he has handed us. The other was when the banks were closed. We knew he could speak English, but we dident know he could talk "American" till that night. In fact, he has three speaking accomplishments. He is the only guy who can talk turkey to the Senate.

78. Mr. Roosevelt stepped to the microphone last night and knocked another home run. His message was not only a great comfort to the people, but it pointed a lesson to all radio announcers and public speakers what to do with a big vocabulary—leave it at home in the dictionary. Some people spend a lifetime juggling with words, with not an idea in a carload.

79. Mr. Roosevelt made us a mighty fine speech over the radio Sunday night. He spoke our language. Not, "Bally-hoo the Nation to Prosperity"; "Nation in a tailspin"; "Can't make a Hit every time we come to Bat." And in addition to all this, he has the best radio voice in America.

Course he just read the minutes of the last meeting, but he did it so nice that we dident hardly notice that he forgot to mention what might be in his mind for the future.

80. I dont suppose there is any business with as many

unemployed as the "advising" business. What gets these big fellows' goat is Roosevelt listens to 'em all, but they cant tell whether he is paying any attention or not.

81. Yale gives President Roosevelt a degree. But they made him make a speech for it. Degrees are getting higher priced. That's the most anybody has given for one in years. The President kinder held up for his Brain Trust. He said he would take brains anytime in preference to politics. He just as good as admitted you couldent get both in the same body.

82. I wrote a little gag the other day about "appealing to the President for a guarantee," and I bet a lot of you thought it just to be writing. Well, get this in the papers today, "C. L. Bardo, President of the National Association of Manufacturers, asks the President the following:

"Business must have more definite ideas as to the direction in which the government is headed."

I can just see Mr. Roosevelt rushing in with a guarantee reading about as follows: "Nobody guaranteed me anything when I took over this job. No man gambles more than a President of the U.S. So you will pardon me if I am not able to guarantee business that it won't lose."

83. Everybody that is making money has it in for Roosevelt. You will have to explain that one yourself.

84. An awful lot of folks are predicting Roosevelt's downfall, not only predicting but praying. We are a funny people. We elect our Presidents, be they Republican or Democrat, then go home and start daring 'em to make good.

85. The one that I would stake my life on that Mr. Roosevelt has learned since he has been in there, is that people are willing to co-operate, but they are not going to willingly pay to do it. You can bet that his faith in human nature has had quite a jar.

86. This is dispatched just before the President goes on the air tonight. I am anxious to hear the comments in the Press. Even if its good there is plenty of 'em wont like it. He can speak on the Lord's Supper and he will get editorials against it. America is just like an insane asylum, there is not a soul in it will admit they are crazy. Roosevelt being the warden at the present time, us inmates know he is the one that's cuckoo.

Will Rogers (*left*) and a fellow-performer in the Zack Mulhall Wild West Show at the St. Louis Exposition, June 1904.

Will Rogers and Lucille Mulhall, daughter of Colonel Zack Mulhall. Will spent some time on the Mulhall Ranch in Indian Territory (now Oklahoma), perfecting his art of riding and roping.

Will Rogers with his fellow actors during his first days in vaudeville, 1905, probably at Keith's Union Square Theatre, New York, N.Y.

Will Rogers *(left)* in one of his earliest motion pictures, *Cupid the Cowpuncher* (1920), with Gwin "Big Boy" Williams.

Will Rogers during his vaudeville days, 1904-1909.

Will in the *Ziegfeld Follies of 1916.*

Will's parody of Rudolph Valentino (*right*) in Hal Roach's *Uncensored Movies*, 1923.

Will Rogers and Dorothy Stone in *Three Cheers,* 1928-1929, the musical comedy in which he carried on for Fred Stone after that actor was injured in an airplane accident. *Bruce Quisenberry*

Will Rogers parodying Ernest Torrance's performance in *The Covered Wagon* in one of the few pictures Will himself produced, *Two Wagons Both Covered,* 1923.

Will Rogers in one of his greatest roles, David Harum, in the Fox Film motion picture of 1934.

Will Rogers (*far right*) in *The County Chairman,* a Fox Film of 1935.

Three great "western" stars: (*left to right*) Tom Mix, Will Rogers, William S. Hart.

Two of America's greatest humorists: Will Rogers (*left*) and Irvin S. Cobb, in whose "Judge Priest" stories Will starred in motion pictures.

Will Rogers and Irene Rich in *So This Is London,* 1930.

Will Rogers in his last motion picture, *Steamboat Round the Bend,* released in 1935 after his death.

6

EDUCATION

"I am practically world famous for my ignorance,"[1] announced Will Rogers. He liked to appear illiterate, for that tag suited his alter ego and gave him much larger scope for deflating the pompous, the smug and the sophisticated. Although he attended a number of schools in his early years, he did not distinguish himself as a scholar in any of them, a fact he often deplored.

"The fourth reader [McGuffey's] is as far as I ever got in schools," he wrote. "I am not braggin' on it. I am thoroughly ashamed of it for I had every opportunity."[2]

Will did have the best advantages the times afforded, and his parents were determined their son should have a good education, but getting him to embrace it was another matter.

Since there were no schools near the Rogers ranch, his mother taught him at home, but the active and determined lad, who cared only for a rope and a pony, did not have any time to devote to irksome book learning. When he was eight years old, his parents sent him to stay with his sister Sallie and her husband Tom McSpadden, so that he could attend his first school, Drumgoole, an Indian

[1] Weekly article, February 19, 1933.
[2] Weekly article, January 8, 1933.

school supported by taxes from the Cherokee Nation. Years later, he wrote of it:

> Drumgoul [*sic*] was a little one-room log cabin, four miles west of Chelsea. It was all Indians kids when there and I being part Cherokee had enough white in me to make my honesty questionable. There must have been about 30 of us in that room that had rode horseback and walked miles to get there. We graduated when we could print our full name and numerate to the teacher the Nationality of the last Democratic President.[3]

Apparently he must have been able to meet these requirements, for his father thought he had a better plan for him the following year. His sister May was attending Harrell Institute, a girls' school in Muskogee (Indian Territory), so their father made arrangements with its president to permit Will to go to school there and have his lessons with the President's son, Bob Brewer. They felt this experience would have a good influence on the boys. Will spent almost two years in this school for young ladies and did not leave an enviable record.

"I used to go to school here at a girl's school," he wrote after making a relief tour appearance in Muskogee in 1931. "That's a fact. Myself and the President's son were the only boys there. We even roomed in a great big dormatory with the girls. We were ten years old. I better quit before I get too far into this."[4]

After the death of his mother, Will attended a Presbyterian mission school in Tahlequah for one term. His next school was Willie Halsell College, in Vinita, where he

3 Weekly article, September 29, 1929.
4 Weekly article, February 22, 1931.

spent more than three years. He was happy there. Many of the leading families in that area sent their young people to Willie Halsell, where they studied music, elocution, the basic principles of arithmetic, English and history.

In the summer of 1895 Professor J. C. Shelton came into the Cherokee Nation seeking students for Scarrett College, and before he knew it, Will was at school in Neosho, Missouri. His love of roping and playing pranks were not in keeping with the serious curriculum laid down by the Methodist fathers of the institution, so he spent little more than a year there.

> By this time Clem Rogers was quite concerned about his son. He came to the conclusion that a more rigid form of training would be good for the young man, so he took him to Boonville, Missouri, and enrolled him in Kemper Military School, January 13, 1897.[5]

At first military life appealed to Will, for he was proud of his uniform with the brass buttons down the front. His grades fluctuated somewhat as his report card for March 26, 1897, shows: 100 in U.S. history; 65 in algebra; 65 in bookkeeping; and an average grade of 79. His demerits for the month were 50. He soon found that with all the restrictions placed on him he was accumulating more demerits than credits and much of his time was spent walking the "bull ring." He said in one of his articles:

> In 1898 Kemper Military School was not being run in accordance with the standards that I thought befitting a growing intellect. I was spending my third year in the fourth grade and wasn't

[5] *Cadet Days of Will Rogers*, published by Kemper Military School, 1935.

being appreciated, so I not only left them flat during a dark night, but the entire school business for life.[6]

Unknown to his family, he ran away to Texas, where he found a warm welcome and good living on the Ewing ranch at Higgins, and spent some time there as a ranch hand.

Though Will's formal education ended with his sudden departure from Kemper, he had a basic foundation and was much better educated than many of the young men in the Cherokee Nation. The so-called colleges he attended were on a high school level, but they had splendid instruction and would compare favorably with the sophomore year in college in the present-day course of study. In all, he attended school for about ten years.

Will had an amazing memory; he could read anything once and remember it. He was quick to grasp things and did not have to spend long hours over his books. Besides, he preferred to have some fun. He had an inquiring mind that caused him to want to see things for himself and sent him on travels all over the world. His love of people and the exchange of ideas, coupled with his intense reading, made him one of the best informed men of his time.

His many uses of incorrect speech and grammar fitted his character of cowboy-philosopher. Of course, he knew better! When his friend Dr. James Whitcomb Brougher called to his attention that people criticized his syntax, he laughed and said, "Have they put a tax on sin? I am not surprised, as the Government is puting a tax on everything." Then the good minister told him it was his grammar with which the people found fault. Will replied, "Well, I just talk naturally and if there is any bad gram-

[6] Weekly article, March 7, 1926.

mar, it ain't intentional. And I haven't heard that grammars are the best sellers."[7]

His disarming humor made him loved by all classes of people. To the underprivileged and uneducated he symbolized the triumph of the common man. The scholars, purists and educators realized he had an uncommon ability to discover truth and the courage to speak it, clothed in his own whimsical style. They were great admirers of Will Rogers.

At the height of his career several colleges wanted to confer degrees on him, but he always refused, as shown in his reply when Dr. Hamilton Holt, of Rollins College made the proposal: "Now what in the world would I be doing with a degree? A lot of guys that earned 'em dont know what to do with 'em, much less me that wouldent know what one was."[8]

He helped many young people through school by paying their expenses, and to make them feel better he always emphasized that he did not have an education.

If Will had spent more time in the class room in diligent study, conforming to the rules and regulations, the procedure might have stifled that rugged native power of his mind and restrained his effervescent wit. He just would not have been Will Rogers.

Education

1. Everybody is ignorant only on different subjects.

2. When ignorance gets started it knows no bounds.

[7] James Whitcomb Brougher, *Life and Laughter*.
[8] Weekly article, November 18, 1934.

3. Everybody has swimming pools but nobody has got a plain old geography. If a thing is particularly useless it gives you more credits. Most of our work is skilled and requires practice and not education. Like everything else you got to judge it by results. Here we are better educated (according to educational methods) than we ever were, and we are worse off than we ever were, so it's not living up to its billing.

4. An educated man just teaches the thing that he has been taught, and it's the same that everyone else has been taught that has read and studied the same books that he has.

5. When you walk up and ask for a job, you know you know your business, and no man out of a book knows if he knows his or not.

6. I believe the Lord split knowledge up among his subjects about equal after all. The so-called ignorant is happy. Maybe he is happy because he knows enough to be happy. The smart one knows he knows a lot, and that makes him unhappy because he cant impart it to all his friends. Discontent comes in proportion to knowledge. The more you know the more you realize you dont know.

7. There is nothing as stupid as an educated man if you get him off the thing he was educated in.

8. In [the old] days boys wanted an education whether they got a fraternity pin or not. They even had reading, writing and arithmetic, instead of football. Up to then boys had gone there for their heads and not their shoulders.

9. You cant beat education for foolishness. There has always been a problem "Does Education Pay?" Yes, it does, if you got a sense of humor. You got to pay for your laughs at a show, so why not at school?

10. The more you know, the more you think somebody owes you a living.

11. Education never helped morals. The most savage people we have are the most moral. The smarter the guy, the bigger the rascal.

12. Robbing is one profession that certainly has advanced in this country. No schools or anything to learn you to rob. No other line, outside of drinking can show the progress that robbing has in the last five years. We spend billions of dollars on education and we are no smarter today than thirty years ago, and we spend nothing to foster robbing, and here it is one of the most skilled industries we have. So it sometimes

makes you think whats the use of learning people anything anyway. Let 'em alone, and they will progress quicker.

13. You must never tell a thing. You must illustrate it. We learn through the eye and not the noggin.

14. They say children in kindergarten must play in order to get 'em to learn. What do you mean children? Cross word puzzles learned grown folks more words than school teachers. And what arithmetic the women folks know they got at a bridge table. Our splendid English comes from attending the movies. My geography comes from an airplane window. Yes sir, there is 120 million in the American Kindergarten.

15. If nations held 'em [intelligence tests] I dont believe we would be a favorite to win.

16. Naval training will drive millions of Americans to a geography.

17. It's open field running that gets your old college somewhere and not a pack of spectacled orators or a

mess of civil engineers. It's better to turn out one good coach than ten college Presidents. With College Presidents, as far as publicity is concerned, they just as well might have matriculated in Hong-Kong.

18. These baccalaureate addresses dont offer 'em much encouragement outside of advising 'em to vote the straight Republican ticket.

19. Villians are getting as thick as college degrees and sometimes on the same fellow.

20. Professors are just like actors. Actors got press agents that write things about them and they get so they believe it. Professors get to looking at their diploma and get to believing what it says there. And they forget they got that diploma on their *memory* and not on their sense.

21. *Will is offered an honorary degree.*

Degrees have lost prestige enough as it is without handing 'em around to second-hand comedians, and its this handing 'em out too promiscously that has helped to cheapen 'em. Let a guy get in there and battle four years if he wants one, and dont give him one just because he happens to hold a good job in Washington, or manufactures more monkey-wrenches than anybody else or because he might be fool enough to make people laugh.

Keep 'em for those kids that have worked hard for 'em. Keep 'em believing in 'em. They are stepping out in the world with nothing but that sheet of paper. That's all they got. Our civilization dont offer 'em anything else. We offer him nothing. He steps into a world not of his making, so lets at least dont belittle his badge.

22. Actual knowledge of the future was never lower, but hope was never higher. Confidence will beat predictions any time.

23. I think you can learn the same at all schools outside of football.

24. *Re* Smith College:

    It's an awfully common name but a mighty nice college.

25. Harvard is the home of culture and poor football. Everyone in Harvard can speak good English but nobody can make a touchdown.

26. All of our disgustingly rich men are at a loss to know what to do with their money. Funny none of them ever thought of giving it back to the people they got it from. Instead of these men giving money to found colleges to promote learning, why dont they pass a constitutional ammendment prohibiting anybody from learning anything? And if it works as good as the Prohibition one did, in five years we would have the smartest race of people on earth.

27. That's one thing about history, it never has to explain anything. It just gives you the bare facts and there is no way of cross-examining them to find out.

28. History is all we got to go by and history dont record that economy ever won a war.

29. If every history or books on old things was thrown in the river and everybody had nothing to study but the future, we would be about 200 years ahead of what we are.

30. A lot of guys have had a lot of fun joking about [Henry] Ford because he admitted one time that he dident know history. He dont know it, but history will know him. He has made more history than his critics has ever read.

31. [Scientists] can tell you just to the minute when something is going to happen ten million miles away but none of them has ever been smart enough to tell you what day to put on your heavy underwear.

32. A scientist is a man that can find out anything and nobody in the world has any way proving whether he found it out or not, and the more things he can think of that nobody can find out about, the bigger scientist he is.

33. One thing about economics and money theories. Your theory is always right for its never been tried.

34. Some guy invented "Vitamin A" out of a carrot. I'll bet he cant invent a good meal out of one.

35. A man only learns by two things; one is reading and the other is association with smarter people.

36. People could read in [the old] days. They wanted to know what was going on, not what kind of a hat some guy had on. Your looks meant nothing to them. It was what you did that counted.

37. I dont envy the man that cant read because he certainly is not missing anything nowadays, and he is forming his own opinion without having someone else form it for him. The most real, down-to-earth horse sense men in America are the ones that cant read. I'll bet they are more right on any question than the so-called smart fellow.

38. More words aint good for anything in the world only to bring on more argument.

39. I got me a dictionary one time, but goodness it dident last long. It was like looking in the telephone book. I never called up anybody in my life if I had to look up their number. Nobody is worth looking through all those number for and thats the way it was with my dictionary. I could write the article while I was trying to see what the word meant, and thats one good thing about language, there is always a short word for it. Course, the Greeks have a word for it, and the dictionary has a word for it, but I believe in using your own for it.

40. Confucius prespired out more knowledge than the U.S. Senate has vocalized out in the last fifty years.

41. All this exchange of talk [in panel discussions] is a lot of hooey. It changes nobody or effects no opinions, but its kinder like weather-talk. It does no harm. But if one ever travels through your town, go hear it. It's the old cracker-barrel argument over again.

7

TRAVEL

Will loved to travel and absorbed a great deal on his trips because he was interested in everything he saw and everybody he met. Just keeping the date line on his daily telegram as he journeyed from city to city and country to country makes a surprising study in geography. As Mrs. Rogers often remarked, "Will was like a little boy that never grew up. He always wanted to go some place."

He was the greatest booster for aviation our country has ever had and did more than any other private citizen to promote air travel. Because he flew so much when the industry was in its primary stages, he gave confidence and approval to this then new mode of transportation.

Will felt it was essential in his work as a speaker and writer to get first hand information on world events. As he stated, "I crossed and uncrossed about all the oceans we got, but its always been because I wanted to get somewhere. It never was just really for relaxation and pleasure."[1]

Any kind of a trip was fun for Will; by rail, air, car, horse or carriage—just so he was traveling.

Will visited Russia several times, for the country always held deep interest for him. After his trip there in 1926 he wrote a book about it which he called *There's Not a*

[1] Weekly article, February 19, 1933.

Bathing Suit in Russia. Some of the things he said are strangely prophetic; other statements are as true today as the day they were written.

In 1934 Will took Mrs. Rogers and their two sons, Will, Jr., and Jimmie, on an extensive tour into Russia on their trip around the world. He shows a deep understanding of the country and the people in the articles he wrote as well as in the radio broadcasts he made after that trip.

He and Wiley Post had originally planned to fly on to Russia in 1935, but their tragic flight ended at Point Barrow, Alaska, on August 15.

Travel

1. Nothing thickens one like travel.

2. You dont know what a country we have got till you start prowling around it. Personally, I like the small places and sparsely populated states.

3. Never look at a town with one of its prominent citizens. You have just seen what he wants you to see. I always get me a taxi and go prowling.

4. Brigham Young originated mass production, but Henry Ford was the guy that improved on it. He

alone is absolutely responsible for this great era of transportation in which we half-way live.

5. If you want to have a good time, I dont care where you live, just load in your kids and take some congenial friends and start out. You would be surprised what there is to see in this great country within 200 miles of where any of us live. I dont care what state or town.

6. I have never yet seen a man in such a big hurry that a horse or train wouldent have got him there in plenty of time. In fact nine-tenths of the people would be better off if they had stayed where they are, instead of going where they are going. No man in America if he dident get where he is going would be missed. People nowadays are traveling faster, but they are not getting any further, in fact, not as far as our old Dad's did.

7. The present generation doesent know what a milestone is. They go by so fast nowadays that miles mean nothing.

8. Trouble with American transportation is that you get somewhere quicker than you can think of a reason

for going there. What we need now is a new excuse to go somewhere.

9. No wonder American people are filling roads, trains, and air. There is so much to see. What we lack in reading, we make up in looking.

10. America is never in a better humor or feeling better than when moving, so all this traveling (even if it's walking) is a mighty good omen.

11. America has been muscle bound from holding a steering wheel. The only callous place on an American is the bottom of his driving toe.

12. The trouble with America is they are not "running" minded, we are kinder "riding" minded.

13. The manufacturers say [in 1923] in ten years there will be an automobile to every man, woman and child in the U.S. Now all they got to do is control the birth rate.

14. They have the same cars every year, only painted different.

15. Our automobiles dont stay at home long enough to know where homes are even if they could get back.

16. One way to solve the traffic problem would be to keep all the cars that are not paid for off the streets. Children could use the streets for playgrounds then.

17. If we can keep the young happy and the old satisfied, all the middle-aged have to look out for is women automobile drivers.

Foreign Countries

18. If you have never written an autobiography, you havent signed a foreign hotel register.

19. No sir, Europe has nothing to recommend it but its old age, and the Petrified Forest in Arizona would make a sucker out of it for age. Why that forest was there and doing business before Nero took his first violin lesson.

20. [Belgium is] the Gettysburg of Europe. Its really not a Country, but a military highway.

21. Canada is a mighty good neighbor and a mighty good customer. That's a combination that is hard to beat.

22. *Re* Nice:

It's pronounced Neece. Not Nice. They have no word for nice in French.

23. Paris was built just to entertain.

24. Rome has more churches and less preaching in them than any city in the world. Everybody wants to see where St. Peter was buried, but nobody wants to try to live like him.

If you stole from the barbarians you were indexed in your history as a Christian.

I dident know before I got there and they told me all this—that Rome had Senators. Now I know why it declined.

25. When nations in those days had nothing else to do they would take Rome, then sit and pray for somebody to come and take it off their hands.

26. [Switzerland is] the rumor factory of the world. They have neither imports nor exports. It's sole commodities are Conferences and Neutrality.

27. There is nothing that irks a Turk so much as peace.

28. The thing that really makes any two nations a little more sympathic towards each other is the fact they may be able to use each other.

29. Naturally every nation wants to protect themselves according to their own needs.

30. Every nation in Europe goes to bed with a gun under its head.

31. When you have fought each other as much as they have this old trusting each other to never have another war is a lot of beautiful stuff but not what you would want to build our whole mode of defense on. They want peace, but they want a gun to help to get it. Nations are not there so much to protect their little gunboats as they are their national prestige.

32. All those nations over there have been hating each other for years and they cant hate us as bad as they hate each other. They have got it in for each other because every one of them owns land. There is not a piece of land in Europe that every nation over there aint owned it themselves at some particular time, and every one of them is going to try to get it back just as soon as the other bird is not looking.

33. These big babies aint going to give anybody any thing. That's why they are big.

34. A Nation is built on character the same as a person is and no matter what their financial difficulties are that Old Character shows up.

35. I think a country is harder to understand than a woman. It's heart is not at its capital as some think.

36. No Nation has a monopoly on good things. Each one has something that the others could well afford to adopt.

37. Russia is starving her own people to feed propaganda to the rest of the world.

38. Russia has been pretty quiet for the last couple of weeks. They are studying some devilment to pull on the rest of the world. A Russian just loves misery and he wants to get as many in on it as he can.

39. That is one thing about the Russian—he thrives on adversity. He is never as happy in his life as when he is miserable. So he may just be setting pretty, for he is certainly miserable. It may be just the land for a Comarade to want to hibernate in.

40. I have always claimed that that's why they [the Russians] was such great parachute jumpers, was because they was disappointed when it opened.

41. [Russian] marriage and divorce laws are patterned after Hollywood and Park Avenue. Only they eliminate the lawyer. So it gives the poor a chance to get a divorce that over here would only be obtainable by the rich.

42. To get any kind of idea of Russia, everything in the world we do, every viewpoint we have, every matter of fact of looking at anything is entirely different in Russia. I was surprised they dident walk on their hands instead of their feet, just to be different from capitalistic nations.

43. Now the main question everybody asks me is "Are they happy?" That's a tough one to answer. There are millions of people in Russia. I couldent talk their language, so I couldent ask them are you happy. It's awful hard to look at a person and tell just how happy they are. Some of you look awful curious to me. Now we looked at 'em for eight days at hundreds of stations, crossing the Trans-Siberian railway. We'd see the people come down to the trains and just stand there. They'd be standing at the station with a dull, blank expression on their faces—no joy, no smile. They just looked like they dident know what the future held in store for 'em. But I've sat in the gallery of the Senate, and in the gallery of the House of Representatives in Washington and I've seen the same dull, blank expression—not knowing what the next election held in store for 'em.

44. Then too, it's not just what you'd call a good year for happiness in any part of the world anyhow. It's what you might call an off year for happiness. And then too, here's what everybody tells me, the Russians are naturally a sad people. They dont feel good until something's really the matter with them. In other words, a Russian aint happy till he's hurt. He thrives on pain. So to answer the question, "Is Russia happy?" I should answer, "Yes." For they've certainly got enough the matter with 'em to make 'em happy.

45. Russians I dont think would ever be as happy as we

are anyhow, for they havent got as much to laugh at as we have here. Perhaps we're not the most humorous people in the world, but the provocations to humor is greater in this country than anywhere else in the world. There's not a minute that there's not some of us doing something seriously that brings smiles to everybody else over here.

46. It seems the whole idea of Communism, or whatever they want to call it, is based on propaganda and blood. Their whole life and thought is to convince somebody else. It looks to me like if a thing is so good and is working so grand for you, you would kind of want to keep it to yourself. I would be afraid to let anybody in on it, and that generally seems to be about the usual brand of human nature over here. But the Communist has so many good things he just wants you to join in and help him use some of them.

47. One thing that a Communist can do is explain. You can ask him any question in the world, and if you give him long enough he will explain their angle, and it will sound plausible then. Communism to me is one-third practice and two-thirds explanation.

48. A Conservative thinks you ought to divide with him what you have while a real Communist believes that you ought to give it all to him, in exchange you call

him Comrade. It's like Prohibition; it's a good idea but it wont work.

49. It just looks to me like Communism is such a happy family affair that not a communist wants to stay where it is practiced. It's the only thing they want you to have but keep none themselves.

50. The old Communist preaches his doctrines, but he wants to do it where he is enjoying the blessing of capitalistic surroundings. He preaches against the pie, but he sure eats it.

8

PHILOSOPHY AND RELIGION

"My humor is not so hot, my philosophy don't philo and my jokes are pre-war, but my good feeling toward mankind is 100 per cent,"[1] Will Rogers wrote to young Ed Sullivan, who was then a columnist on the New York *Daily News*. That perhaps characterizes the Rogers' philosophy better than anything else, for he could always find the good in people; beyond that, he did not bother.

To understand Will Rogers' deep respect for religion of any kind, his abiding faith in God and an almost Christlike gift of giving and trying to help others, we have only to go back to his forebears to know that these traits were inherent.

His parents, Mary America Schrimsher and Clem Vann Rogers, were descended from a distinguished line. While there was a trace of English and Welsh, it was the Irish and Cherokee Indian blood that predominated in their progeny.

Clem had settled in the Cherokee Nation near the Kansas line until the Civil War interrupted his mercantile and ranching activities. For four years he served the Confederacy under the gallant Indian leader, Brigadier General Stand Watie in the Cherokee Mounted Volunteers, and reached the rank of captain. On his return from

[1] Letter to Ed Sullivan, from the Unclassified Scrapbook, Will Rogers Memorial, 1932.

service, he had to work very hard to recover some of the fortune he had lost during that time. So it was not until 1875 that he selected the picturesque site for their future home near the Verdigris River, about twelve miles from the present town of Claremore, Oklahoma.

The large white house with a central hall and with fireplaces at each gabled end showed definitely the influence of Southern architecture. Native cedars lined the sandstone walk from the front gate to the white portico and made an imposing setting for the yard, which was always a profusion of color and beauty under the capable hands of Mary Rogers.

It was a home of good living and deep affection, of religious and social activity. It was in this home that William Penn Adair Rogers was born on November 4, 1879.

There were few hotels in the rolling country known as Cooweescoowee District—of which Clem was a judge—and the Rogers home was a favorite stopping place for officials of the Cherokee Nation en route to council at Tahlequah, the capital.

"We then had our own government," Will recalled years later, "and the name of Oklahoma was as foreign to us as toothpaste."[2]

Circuit riders made it a point to visit there often, not only because Clem provided well for his family, but also because his wife Mary was deeply religious and any man who carried the Word of God was always welcome. "The only men Papa ever refused meals and lodging were those whose horses had cocklebers in their tails," my own mother[3] told us.

Will's mother died when he was ten years old, and

3 Will's sister Sallie (Mrs. Thomas McSpadden).
2 Weekly article, September 29, 1929.

somehow he always carried the hurt of this parting. Instinctively his heart was touched by anyone who was motherless. His sisters, Sallie, Maud and May, were devoted to him and left nothing undone for their young brother. His father seldom denied him anything. To them he was always someone very special. Neighboring ranchers and all the relatives felt he belonged to them. Their homes were always open to "Uncle Clem's boy." It was this love he prized so much that he never grew apart from the "home folks." In fact, his years of success intensified his love for his people, and it was no wonder everyone in the Southwest claimed kin to him.

In his marriage he was extremely fortunate, for Betty Blake was the perfect companion for the restless trick roper she married in 1908. She was willing to troupe with him on the vaudeville circuit and make a home for him in a hotel room, just as she presided with gracious dignity in their California home when she never knew how many people he would bring to the dining table or ask others to visit indefinitely. She understood his nature perhaps better than anyone else and made him feel free to pursue the things he wanted to do. She helped him see his own potential gifts and skillfully aided in bringing them to fulfillment. Will relied on her judgment, leaving many important decisions up to her. He adored his children to the extent that he could never find it in his heart to correct them—a task he also left up to their mother.

Some of Will's best friends were preachers. They were unconsciously drawn to him and hung on the words he said. They realized he was not merely a wisecracking joker, for beneath his pertness of expression there was a depth of philosophy. Along with others, they knew he was a thinker and were well aware of his keen analysis of any situation.

"I hold the distinction of being the only one that ever preached a sermon in a regular church and dident know it," he wrote after he spoke to a congregation in Canton, Ohio, at the request of the minister, "and I dont even know what denomination the church was."[4]

After his first "lecture" appearance which was made in a church in Elmira, New York, he said, "In making this tremendous leap from the *Follies* to the pulpit, I did not have to change one word of my act. I dont know whether its a compliment to the church audience or the *Follies* audience."[5]

The Reverend James Whitcomb Brougher, a Baptist minister of Glendale, California, was one of his best friends—a very able, charming man and somewhat of a humorist himself. They held several debates on the subject, "*Resolved*, That Cowboys Have Been More Beneficial to Mankind Than Preachers."[6] This was an excellent type of performance as well as thought provoking. "He proved that talking and not preaching is appreciated,"[7] Will wrote. It was Dr. Brougher who spoke the words of consolation at Will's funeral in Forest Lawn Cemetery in 1935. "The greatest honor, yet the most diffcult service I ever conducted," he told us later.

The Rogerses were never a part of the smart Hollywood set of cafe society. They had a world of friends among all the different groups of California artists, but it was the simple, wholesome entertainment they sought. They tried to keep to themselves, but there was always a long line of relatives and friends about them.

"Above all, Rogers' life has been as clean as a whistle," said O. O. McIntyre. "He never wrote or spoke a dirty

[4] Weekly article, October 18, 1925.
[5] Ibid.
[6] Weekly articles, December 16, 1923; April 13, 1924.
[7] Weekly article, November 25, 1923.

line. There is not one tiny black mark against him."[8]

Will had a boyish enthusiasm for anything he undertook, no matter what it was—a trip, a game of polo, the World Series, a new play, helping his friends, roping calves or just talking. He had a deep sense of humility and never realized his own greatness in any line. He did not fret or brood over things that had happened. To him yesterday was gone and done with, but he lived every minute of today. "We are living in a great time. Something to get excited about every minute,"[9] he wrote less than two months before his death.

The complete story of Will Rogers, the humanitarian, will never be told for he seldom revealed what he did, and many who greatly benefited by his bounty were slow to admit it. He felt that he had been lucky and because of that tried to help everyone else who had not been so fortunate. It would be impossible to name even the outstanding things he did to help others, so only a few can be mentioned here.

In World War I, when his salary was a modest one, he gave the Red Cross $100 each week for the duration and sold countless Liberty Bonds. Sunday nights in New York always found him playing some benefit and often two or three the same night. "I don't think any actor of his generation played more benefits than he did; certainly no one played them with more grace and honest enthusiasm," his wife remarked.[10]

Nor were his activities confined to America. While he was in Europe in 1926 a London paper told this story: "Refusing a check that would have amounted to probably $16,000 or more is what Will Rogers did in England

[8] *Tulsa* [Oklahoma] *World*, December 24, 1933 (McNaught Syndicate) (microfilm).
[9] Daily telegram, July 4, 1935.
[10] Betty Rogers, *His Wife's Story*.

last week, and that gracious act was after saving a show from a flop and recouping C. B. Cochran, the producer of the show, to the amount of $60,000 by appearing in the production."[11]

In September of that same year he flew to Dublin to give a benefit for the Drumcollogher Relief Fund, raising more than 2,000 pounds. Nicaraguans will never forget his coming to aid them with financial assistance and good cheer in 1931 after their terrible earthquake and fire. They were the first to issue commemorative stamps honoring him. He flew to New Orleans in 1927 to give a benefit for flood relief, and the city was not lacking in appreciation for the $49,195.68 he raised for them.

In 1931 he arranged a series of benefits for the drought-stricken areas in Texas, Oklahoma and Arkansas under the auspices of the Federation of Women's Clubs, saying, "When you get a group of women behind anything it is always a success." He raised over $300,000 for the cause, and in Tulsa alone made $29,504. This he did by taxing some of his rich oil friends who were in the audience. In each town he always gave something himself besides his services, and that gesture often cost him six performances a day.

Most people know about his taking Fred Stone's place in the musical comedy *Three Cheers* after Stone's airplane accident, but few know of the financial sacrifice he made to do it. One paper stated he canceled $500,000 in engagements to do this.[12] Some of the groups who had booked him had to be paid off for breach of contract, but on the whole most of the organizations were merely disappointed that they would not get to hear him and laugh with him. As Mr. Houston Hart of San Angelo,

[11] *Ibid.*
[12] Los Angeles *Examiner,* August 22, 1928.

Texas, wrote, "I wonder if Fred Stone really needs you half as much as we do?"[13] An American Legion Post in Texas asked $1,000 forfeit, and a wire from Will Rogers shows that he sent them $1,500. But friendship's love outweighed anything else, and in comparison the money meant nothing to Will Rogers.

He supported relatives, cowboys, actors and a varied assortment of friends. On tour he gave programs for the veterans, the crippled children, the hospitals, the jails and anyone who wanted him. He arranged with Helen Keller for several benefits for the blind, and among her wires is this touching one:

> I love you Will Rogers and I don't care who knows it. Your wonderful letter and contribution to the endowment fund for the Blind of America, I am trying so desperately to raise, have given me new courage. . . . Do not fear the scrutiny of the ten eyes in my fingers for they will certainly find the wild flowers of humor in your face.[14]

In 1933 he made a series of broadcasts for the Gulf Oil Company at a salary of $50,000, and he gave the entire amount to the Red Cross and the Salvation Army, the two organizations to which he consistently contributed. Evangeline Booth best describes his generous spirit in her wire to him:

> On behalf of our people toiling from sea to sea to alleviate suffering, and in the name of the hungry and destitute I send a heart of gratitude for your substantial sacrificial contribution. There are some

[13] Letter, 1928, Memorial Files, Rogers Collection.
[14] Telegram, May 21, 1930.

things in this world for which there are neither words nor rewards. This is one. I must leave it to the next. There a multitude in His name will call you blessed.[15]

Manners

1. Customs make manners. Manners are nothing more than common sense.

2. If a man is a gentleman he dont have to announce it. All he has to do is to act like one and let the world decide. No man should have to prove in court what he is or what he comes from.

3. When it comes to a showdown class will tell.

4. Breeding will tell even in a Democratic Convention.

5. If a town has any culture and tourists commence hitting it, your culture is gone. Tourists will rub it out of any town.

6. No one can tell you as much about it [high society] as the one who has just been on the edge.

15 Telegram, Chicago, June 21, 1933.

7. Emily Post tells everything [about opera] but how to enjoy the thing. The fellow that figures out how to enjoy opera in a foreign tongue without kidding himself or four-flushing has a fortune in store for him. . . . I found I was wrong on every line of the whole book. . . . I kept right on learning and from now on I am just mangy with etiquette.

Dress

8. More people should work for their dinner instead of dressing for it. Half the stiff bosom shirts worn nowadays, the laundry is due on them yet.

9. Mink and sable—that's the best financial barometer in the world.

10. Nothing makes people more alike than putting a dress suit on 'em.

11. Any Sunday could be made as popular [as Easter] at Church if you called 'em fashion shows.

Will never wore a dress suit, except in the movie As Young as You Feel. His formal costume was the blue serge suit that became a trade mark with him. He appeared at the most lavish parties, dinners and gatherings in his blue serge suit.

12. I stuck to the old Blue Serge with the mirror effect in the seat and knees. If it was good enough for Ponca City and Muskogee, it was good enough for Uncle Andy's temple of art [Carnegie Hall]. I was the only one that dident attempt to try to have on a dress suit.

13. I got the old Blue Serge double-breasted that has done such valliant service in pinches over in Europe, and my one piece shirt. In fact, I am the only one that ever went through Europe and never lost a shirt stud. She [Mrs. Rogers] had the suit brushed so much that I was afraid to sit down for fear I would slip off the seat.

14. I dident want a dress or Tuxedo, but I did want an old dark blue serge that I could get in the dining room on the boat with, so I found a little place open, not exactly second-hand, but they had been there so long they tasted like it. Then some black shoes, and a black tie, and I was ready to fool the head steward. I was just thinking some people plan for years to go to Europe and wonder what they will wear and all that hooey.

15. I was the only one who did not own a dress suit, so my clothes naturally was the only ones that did not smell of moth balls.

16. The gamest women can keep back tears in sorrow, they cant keep back in happiness.

17. If you let them have their way, you will generally get even with them in the end.

18. Some women are failures, just as well as men.

19. You cant pass a park without seeing a statue of some old Codgar on a horse, it must be his bravery, you can tell it isn't his horsemanship. Women are twice as brave as men, yet they never seem to have reached the statue stage.

20. There is nothing as determined as a woman that carries on, and there is millions of 'em.

21. Money and Women are the most sought after and the least known about of any two things we have.

22. In the old days a woman had to go out and practice

shooting for weeks, perhaps months before she would dare open up on the "better half." But with this marvelous invention, the automatic, the more hysterical she gets, and the more he dodges about, the more direct hits will be scored. If she had been compelled to use the old-time weapon the crime would never have happened, because the present day woman dont wear enough clothes to conceal a real six-gun. Women used to be the alleged "weaker sex" but the automatic and the sentimental jury have been the equalizer. Why divorce him when you can shoot him easier and cheaper?

23. If we can just improve their [women's] marksmanship, we can improve civilization. About every fourth fellow you meet nowadays ought to be shot.

24. If women must insist on having men's privileges they have to take men's chances.

25. The women, poor souls, havent added anything constructive to the art of politics. They take it too serious. I believe they would go further if they kinder ridiculed and kidded the men. They can do that in everything else, so why can't they in politics?

26. The first idea of giving [women] the vote was just

to use the vote. But the women contrary like they are, they wasent satisfied with that. They started to take this equality thing serious. They begin to think they really was somebody.

The women figured that "While we may not be as good as a man, we are at least as good as a politician." So the scamps commenced to want to get in on the loot. As soon as they found out a political job took no experience to hold, that it took only experience to get, why they commenced to making themselves rather embarrassing around the political employment bureau.

27. Of course, the Mother I know the most about is the Mother of our little group. She has been for 22 years trying to raise to maturity, four children, three by birth and one by marriage. While she hasent done a good job, the poor soul has done all that mortal human could do with the material she has had to work with.

28. The best way to get the low-down on women and daughters is to ask your wife.

Philosophy

29. You got to sorter give and take in this old world.

We can get mighty rich, but if we havent got any friends, we will find we are poorer than anybody.

30. Geography dont change human nature. If you are right, people are for you whether its in Africa or Siberia.

31. Rumor travels faster, but it dont stay put as long as truth.

32. Humanity is not yet ready for either real truth or real harmony.

33. What's the matter with the world? There aint nothing but one word wrong with everyone of us, and that's selfishness.

34. The best way to condemn a thing is to know something about it.

35. The best way to judge just how good a man is, is to find out how he stands around his home and among his kind of people.

36. That's all there is to success is satisfaction.

37. We may elevate ourselves but we should never reach so high that we would ever forget those who helped us get there.

38. Be sure you are right and then go ahead, but dont arbitrate.

39. I sometimes wonder if the Lord is going to make the proper distinction between the fellow that means well and the one that does well. I dont believe He will blackball us just because we dont remember.

40. There is nothing as easy as denouncing. It dont take much to see that something is wrong, but it does take some eyesight to see what will put it right again.

41. No man is great if he thinks he is.

42. It's great to be great, but it's greater to be human.

43. A remark generally hurts in proportion to its truth.

44. The older we get the more "standpat" we get. The only change we want as we grow older is a change back to the things of our early life. We dont want a lot of new ones. Just because a thing is new dont mean that it is better.

45. Those were the great old days, but darn it, any old days are great old days. Even the tough ones, after they are over, you can look back on with great memories.

46. [There is] nothing like congenial friends to just sit around with nothing in particular to knock and a good word for all.

47. When there is no malice in your heart there can be none shown in your homes.

48. Everybody has got a scheme to get the world right again. I cant remember when it was ever right. There has been times when it was right for you and you and you, but never all at the same time. The whole thing is a teeter-board even when its supposed to be going good. You are going up and somebody is coming down. You cant make a dollar without taking it from somebody. So everytime you wish for

something for your own personal gain, you are wishing somebody else bad luck, so maybe that's why so few of our wishes come to anything.

49. I would rather be able to criticize a man than to apologize to him.

50. Happiness and contentment is progress. In fact that's all progress is.

Civilization

51. We will never have true civilization until we have learned to recognize the rights of others.

52. There aint no civilization where there aint no satisfaction and that's what's the trouble now. Nobody is satisfied.

53. If we see anything we want, we take it. The more so-called civilized we get the more we kill and take.

54. *When Will Durant asked Rogers to contribute to his "Living Philosophies," Rogers wrote:*

We are just here for a spell and pass on. Any man that thinks civilization has advanced is an egotist. . . . We know a lot of things we used to dident know, but we dont know any way to prevent 'em happening.

We have more tooth paste on the market and more misery in our courts than at any time in our existence. There aint nothing to life but satisfaction.

Indians and primitive races were the highest civilized because they were more satisfied and they depended less on each other and took less from each other. We couldent live a day without depending on everybody. So our civilization has given us no liberty or independence.

So get a few laughs and do the best you can. Take nothing serious for nothing is certainly depending on this generation. Each one lives in spite of the previous one and not because of it.

And dont start "seeking knowledge" for the more you seek the nearer the "booby hatch" you get.

And dont have an ideal to work for. That's like riding towards a mirage of a lake. When you get there, it aint there. Believe in something for another world, but dont be too set on what it is, and then you wont start out that life with a disappointment. Live your life so that whenever you lose you are ahead.

55. Politics is just a custom and has nothing whatsoever to do with civilization.

56. There is nothing that sets a nation back as far in civilization as prosperity.

57. The big [nations] would like to sorter stick together. They say its to protect the little ones, but its to protect themselves. There is no nation laying awake at night worrying about a little nation unless that little nation is one where somebody can march across to get to them. Brotherly love has never crossed a boundry line yet. Yes, sir, geography has more to do with brotherly love than civilization and Christianity combined.

58. I doubt very much if civilization (so called) has helped generosity. I bet the old cave man would divide his raw meat with you as quick as one of us will ask a down-and-out to go in and have a meal with us. Those old boys or girls would rip off a wolf skin breech clout and give you half of it quicker than a Ph.D would slip you his umbrella. Civilization hasent done much but make you wash your teeth, and in those days gnawing on bones and meat made tooth paste unnecessary.

59. Civilization has taught us to eat with a fork, but even now if nobody is around we use our fingers. Civilization is nothing but acquiring comforts for us.

60. That's one trouble with our charities, we are always saving somebody away off, when the fellow next to us aint eating. Something wrong with the Missionaries. They will save anybody if he is far enough away and dont speak our language. This is a time when I dont care where you live, you cant throw a rock without hitting somebody who needs help more than you do.

61. Any nation is a heathen that aint strong enough to punch you in the jaw. Between our Missionaries and our oil men we are just in wrong all over the world.

62. Missionaries are going to reform the world whether it wants it or not.

63. What degree of egotism is it that makes a nation or a religious organization think theirs is the very thing for China or the Zulus? Why, we cant even Christianize our legislators.

64. Now when they [Congress] get the Constitution all fixed up they are going to start in on the Ten Commandments, just as soon as they can find somebody in Washington who has read them.

65. The minute a thing is long and complicated it confuses. Whoever wrote the Ten Commandments made 'em short. They may not always be kept but they are understood. They are the same for all men.

Moses just went up on the mountain with a letter of credit and some instruction from the Lord and he just wrote 'em out and they applied to the steel men, the oil men, the bankers and the farmers and even the U.S. Chamber of Commerce.

I expect there is a lot of lessons in the Bible that we could learn and profit by and help us out, but we are just so busy doing nothing we havent got time to study 'em out. But in Moses time, the rich dident gang up on you and say, "You change that Commandment or we wont play."

66. You cant get far ridiculing a man for upholding the Bible, or even the dictionary if its his sincere belief.

67. That's one wonderful thing about the Bible. There was no censorship in those days. Of course now, some of our churches hold conferences and cut out certain parts they think dont belong in there, or change them to what they think should be said instead of what was said. In other words, we are always improving on the words of the Lord. That's even worse than a scenario writer brightening up Shakespeare.

68. Of course the Bible has always been "the best seller." But unless you are a real seeker of knowledge or of consolation, it sometimes gets hard to read for a dumb fellow, for there is so much that we cant understand. I dont suppose there is two preachers in the world that would absolutely interpret a whole chapter exactly alike, but any interpretation you put on it is good.

Death

69. Nobody wants to know who was born, but everybody is anxious to know who dies, and the better known they are the more anxious they are to read about their deaths.

70. Why is it the good ones are the ones that go? That's one thing about an onery guy, you never hear of him dying. He is into everything else but a coffin.

71. It's only the inspiration of those who die that makes those who live realize what constitutes a useful life.

72. Some honor to be killed by an earthquake. There is a certain amount of dignity to be preserved even in death.

73. You must judge a man's greatness by how much he will be missed.

74. What constitutes a life well spent? Love and admiration from our fellow men is all that anyone can ask.

75. Death knows no demonination; Death draws no color line. If you live right, Death is a joke to you as far as fear is concerned.

76. Us ignorant laugh at Spiritualists but when they die they go mighty peaceful and happy. After all, all there is to living is to go away satisfied.

77. Of course, we are all just hanging on here as long as we can. I dont know why we hate to go, we know it's better there. Maybe it's because we havent done anything that will live after we are gone.

78. *After his gall bladder operation in 1927, Will said:*

People couldent have been nicer to me if I had died.

79. When I die, my epitaph or whatever you call those

signs on gravestones is going to read: "I joked about every prominent man of my time, but I never met a man I dident like." I am so proud of that I can hardly wait to die so it can be carved. And when you come to my grave you will find me sitting there, proudly reading it.*

80. Well, anyhow, we are living in a great time. A fellow cant afford to die now with all this excitement going on.

Religion

81. They were very religious people that come over here from the old country. They were very human. They would shoot a couple of Indians on their way to every Prayer-meeting.

82. I was raised predominantly a Methodist, but I have traveled so much, mixed with so many people in all parts of the world, I dont know just what I am. I know I have never been a non-believer. But I can honestly tell you that I dont think that any *one* religion is *the* religion.

* One of his most famous and quoted remarks. First printed in the *Boston Globe*, June 16, 1930, after he had attended Tremont Temple Baptist Church, where Dr. James W. Brougher was minister. He asked Will to say a few words after the sermon. The papers were quick to pick up the remark, and it stayed with him the rest of his life. He also said it on various other occasions.

If I am broad minded in any way (and I hope I am in many) . . . I am broad-minded in a religious way. Which way you serve your God will never get one word of argument or condemnation out of me. There has been times when I wished there had been as much real religion among some of our creeds as there has been vanity, but that's not in any way a criticism.

83. It's mighty hard for a country or a duly accredited representative of a country to tell or even advise another country how to conduct their religious affairs. That's about the toughest business we got in any man's country to be monkeying with, is religion. It's the one thing, no matter be he Professor, or heathen, they think they have a right to do with it as they see fit, as long as they dont bother with anyone else.

84. These big wars over commerce, they kill more people but one over religion is really the most bitter.

85. There is on argument in the world that carries the hatred that a religious belief does. The more learned a man is the less consideration he has for another man's belief.

86. I have worked at affairs for every denomination in

the world here in New York, because one is just as worthy as the other. Old New York, the so-called heartless city, houses some great people in every denomination in the world, and I cant see any difference in them. I havent been able to see where one has the monopoly on the right course to Heaven.

87. Can you imagine our Savior dying for all of us, yet we have to argue over just whether he dident die for us personally and not for you. Sometimes you wonder if His lessons of sacrifice and devotion was pretty near lost on a lot of us.

88. If some of these birds would follow His example instead of trying to figure out His mode of arrival and departure, they would come nearer getting confidence in their church.

89. If the Lord had wanted us to know exactly how and where we come from he would have let us know in the first place. He dident leave any room for doubt when he told you how you should act when you got here. His example, and the Commandments are plain enough, so just start from there. Never mind going back any farther.

The Lord put all these millions of people over the earth. They dont all agree on how they got here and

90% dont care. But He was pretty wise when He did see to it that they all do agree on one thing (whether Christian, Heathen or Mohammed) and that is the better lives you live the better you will finish. No great religious revival will ever be started from an argument over where we come from. The religious revival of the future, when it comes, if started, will be people's fear over where they are going.

90. It's better to let people die ignorant and poor believing in what they have always believed in, than to die prosperous and smart, half-believing in something new and doubtful.

91. There never was a nation founded and maintained without some kind of belief in something. Nobody knows what the outcome in Russia will be or how long this government will last. But if they do get by for quite a while on everything else, they picked the only one thing I know of to suppress that is absolutely necessary to run a country on, and that is religion. Never mind what kind, but it's got to be something or you will fail at the finish.

92. [For a man] to be allowed to have his spiritual guidance is not an unjust wage to demand for his toil.

93. The trouble with our praying is we just do it as a means of last resort. We just pray for a thing whether we got any dope on it or not.

94. If they are going to argue religion in the church instead of preaching it, no wonder you can see more people at a circus than a church.

95. Any old preacher that is having a time drafting anybody to listen to him, he announces that his sermon next Sunday night will be on "Hell and Damnation," or "I Am Going To Skin the Devil Alive and Show Up Hell." . . . He knew that title would catch 'em. He was looking for something sensational, and that's where the movies got the idea. Both of 'em out to be made to cut it out. A picture that cant draw without "Hell" in the title aint much picture, and a preacher than cant preach without "Hell" in his title is just as weak as the movies.

96. Preaching is one of the few things that folks have never been able to dope out exactly what its worth anyhow. Some preachers ought to pay admission to get into the church themselves, but as a rule preachers do a mighty good job and are underpaid.

Will Rogers and his aunt-by-marriage, Juliette Schrimsher. *International News Photo*

Will Rogers, citizen of the world, goodwill ambassador.

Will on the driveway of his Beverly Hills, California, home, 1927.

One of Will Rogers' last photographs, 1935. *Wide World Photos*

This heroic bronze statue of Will Rogers, by sculptor Jo Davidson, stands in the foyer of the Will Rogers Memorial, Claremore, Oklahoma. A second statue, cast from the same mold, is in Statuary Hall, Washington, D.C.

The Will Rogers Memorial, Claremore, Oklahoma. The tomb is at the lower far right.

Rogers' tomb, Claremore, Oklahoma. Here lie Will, his wife Betty, his infant son Fred.

~9~

MISCELLANEOUS

1. Art aint put-on when you are paying for it out of your own pocket.

2. [Ancestors] dont mean a thing in our tribe. It's as unreliable as a political promise. They no more take after their father and mother than a Congressman will take after a good example.

3. The Camera has made more criminals than bad environment.

4. It's getting so Christmas kills more people than it makes happy.

5. *Re* Congressional Record, mailed free:

Men are gradually realizing that a thing that is free

is of no earthly importance. It lost men more votes than it ever gained for them.

6. *Re* dial telephones:

   You have to cuss yourself instead of some innocent girl.

7. [Divorce] aint so bad I guess when it's only the participants suffer, but it's sure tough on the children. Well, anyhow it's a great industry, and I guess about the only way to stop it is to stop marriage.

8. No man can be condemned for owning a dog. As long as he has a dog he has a friend and the poorer he gets the better friend he has.

9. Heroing is one of the shortest-lifed professions there is.

10. This thing of being a hero, about the main thing to it is to know when to die. Prolonged life has ruined more men than it ever made.

11. Heroes are made every little while, but only one in a million conduct themselves afterwards so that it makes us proud that we honored them at the time.

12. There aint nothing that breaks up homes, countries and nations like somebody publishing their memoirs.

13. I dont know opera but I know common sense and the commoner the better I know it.

14. Oblivion is a one-way ticket town.

15. Popularity is the easiest thing in the world to gain and it is the hardest thing to hold.

16. This is an age of progress. Live fast and die quick. The human side of anything cant compare with so-called progress.

17. Don't miss . . . Boulder Dam. It's the biggest thing that's ever been done with water since Noah made the flood look foolish.

18. There are two things I dont care how smart you are, you will never understand. One is an alienist's testimony and the other is a railroad timetable.

19. Retroactive, means as you were before you got like you are.

20. Like all things you leave to relatives, they get rid of them. You are better off if you leave 'em to outsiders.

21. The Lord so constituted everybody that no matter what color you are you require about the same amount of nourishment.

22. The man with a message is a whole lot harder to listen to.

23. I wonder if it aint just cowardice instead of generosity that makes us give most of our tips.

24. It's always a bird that never does anything that enjoys a vacation. There's nothing in the world as hard as playing when you dont want to.

25. A man should never take a vacation when he don't want one. You can't learn anything the first time, I don't care how smart you are. It takes years to learn how to vacate properly.

REFERENCES

REFERENCES

The following abbreviations are used throughout this list of references:

Bathing Suit—*There's Not a Bathing Suit in Russia*, 1927
Conv. article—From newspaper articles written at the political conventions
D.T.—Daily telegram
Letters—*Letters of a Self-Made Diplomat to His President*, 1926
More Letters—*More Letters of a Self-Made Diplomat to His President*, 1928
W.A.—Weekly newspaper article

CHAPTER 1

The Country

1. Speech at luncheon for Post and Gatty, Tulsa, Oklahoma, *Tulsa World*, July 14, 1931
2. W.A., October 10, 1926
3. W.A., November 30, 1930
4. W.A., May 4, 1924
5. W.A., April 17, 1932
6. *Letters*, 1926

7. W.A., March 22, 1931
8. W.A., May 3, 1931
9. W.A., December 28, 1924
10. W.A., October 5, 1924
11. W.A., September 3, 1933
12. W.A., December 6, 1925
13. *Letters,* 1926
14. W.A., November 13, 1927
15. W.A., October 19, 1930
16. W.A., June 1, 1930
17. W.A., March 12, 1933

The People

18. Squibbs radio talk, May 4, 1930
19. W.A., February 24, 1924
20. W.A., March 2, 1924
21. W.A., June 21, 1925
22. W.A., May 31, 1925
23. *Bathing Suit,* 1927
24. D.T., October 27, 1929
25. D.T., March 16, 1932
26. D.T., July 25, 1935
27. *Letters,* 1926
28. D.T., June 19, 1935
29. W.A., August 4, 1929
30. D.T., October 18, 1933
31. W.A., April 6, 1924
32. W.A., June 15, 1924
33. W.A., June 30, 1929
34. W.A., September 10, 1933
35. D.T., October 21, 1926
36. W.A., February 4, 1923

37. W.A., August 30, 1925
38. W.A., February 22, 1925
39. *Letters,* 1926
40. *Letters,* 1926
41. W.A., July 23, 1933
42. W.A., May 31, 1925
43. W.A., July 9, 1933

The U.S. Government

44. W.A., November 16, 1930
45. *Bathing Suit*, 1927
46. W.A., June 8, 1924
47. W.A., December 14, 1924
48. W.A., November 2, 1924
49. W.A., December 20, 1925
50. W.A., July 21, 1935
51. W.A., November 25, 1934
52. W.A., February 3, 1929
53. W.A., March 27, 1932
54. W.A., June 5, 1932
55. W.A., November 11, 1928
56. W.A., April 17, 1932
57. D.T., February 12, 1932
58. D.T., July 1, 1934
59. W.A., December 26, 1926
60. W.A., October 30, 1932
61. W.A., December 18, 1932
62. W.A., July 22, 1923
63. W.A., December 7, 1930
64. D.T., July 5, 1935
65. W.A., December 18, 1932

66. D.T., September 30, 1934
67. *Bathing Suit*, 1927

CHAPTER 2

Politicians

1. W.A., April 12, 1925
2. W.A., October 14, 1932
3. W.A., June 8, 1924
4. W.A., September 13, 1925
5. W.A., September 27, 1925
6. W.A., March 22, 1925
7. D.T., March 1, 1935
8. W.A., September 12, 1926
9. W.A., January 13, 1924
10. D.T., June 11, 1935
11. W.A., July 1, 1928
12. W.A., December 30, 1923
13. W.A., November 16, 1924
14. W.A., June 28, 1931
15. W.A., April 22, 1928
16. W.A., September 26, 1926
17. W.A., November 4, 1928
18. "A Letter to the *Times*," *Los Angeles Times*, November 10, 1932
19. W.A., October 19, 1924
20. W.A., October 19, 1924
21. W.A., November 16, 1924
22. D.T., September 10, 1934
23. W.A., September 12, 1926
24. W.A., July 15, 1923
25. W.A., September 16, 1928
26. W.A., October 4, 1925

27. W.A., January 1, 1933
28. W.A., November 11, 1928
29. D.T., March 16, 1934
30. D.T., June 5, 1929
31. D.T., November 18, 1934
32. W.A., February 3, 1929
33. D.T., July 14, 1933
34. W.A., November 11, 1928
35. W.A., August 25, 1929
36. W.A., April 22, 1928
37. W.A., March 29, 1925
38. W.A., January 17, 1932
39. W.A., November 27, 1932
40. W.A., November 11, 1928

Democrats

41. W.A., September 29, 1929
42. W.A., August 1, 1925
43. Conv. articles, Democratic Convention, June 20, 1932
44. W.A., October 28, 1928
45. Conv. articles, Democratic Convention, June 24, 1928
46. W.A., April 14, 1929

Republicans

47. W.A., September 27, 1931
48. D.T., November 8, 1934
49. D.T., November 2, 1934
50. W.A., August 17, 1930
51. Squibbs radio talk, May 25, 1930
52. W.A., September 30, 1928
53. W.A., September 14, 1930

54. W.A., October 19, 1924
55. W.A., February 10, 1929

Elections

56. W.A., December 27, 1931
57. W.A., May 10, 1925
58. "A Letter to the *Times*," *Los Angeles Times*, November 10, 1932
59. W.A., November 9, 1924

United States Senate and Senators

60. W.A., January 6, 1929
61. W.A., May 6, 1923
62. D.T., February 28, 1935
63. Conv. articles, Democratic Convention, June 23, 1924
64. D.T., March 6, 1935
65. "The Worst Story I've Heard Today," September 7, 1925
66. W.A., August 4, 1929
67. W.A., March 22, 1925
68. W.A., April 13, 1930
69. W.A., March 15, 1931
70. *More Letters*, 1928
71. W.A., May 17, 1925
72. W.A., October 21, 1923
73. D.T., July 5, 1933
74. W.A., September 8, 1929
75. W.A., March 20, 1927
76. *Letters*, 1926
77. W.A., June 30, 1929

CHAPTER 3

Business

1. W.A., April 7, 1929
2. W.A., May 18, 1924
3. W.A., March 23, 1930
4. W.A., July 15, 1923
5. W.A., September 29, 1929
6. W.A., December 28, 1924
7. W.A., March 12, 1933
8. W.A., March 22, 1925
9. W.A., April 12, 1925
10. W.A., January 3, 1926
11. D.T., March 1, 1931
12. W.A., April 10, 1932
13. W.A., August 24, 1930
14. W.A., October 14, 1923
15. W.A., November 30, 1924
16. D.T., May 14, 1935
17. W.A., October 30, 1927
18. W.A., March 12, 1933
19. W.A., July 23, 1933
20. W.A., December 30, 1934
21. W.A., November 27, 1932
22. W.A., November 10, 1929
23. W.A., December 1, 1929
24. W.A., April 13, 1930
25. W.A., February 24, 1929
26. W.A., June 15, 1924
27. Squibbs radio talk, May 4, 1930
28. W.A., May 6, 1923
29. W.A., May 1, 1933

Law and Lawyers

30. W.A., July 28, 1935
31. W.A., July 28, 1935
32. W.A., April 22, 1928
33. W.A., December 2, 1923
34. W.A., November 11, 1923
35. D.T., March 16, 1927
36. W.A., January 14, 1923
37. W.A., January 14, 1923
38. D.T., December 30, 1934
39. W.A., May 3, 1925
40. W.A., November 20, 1927
41. W.A., July 28, 1935
42. W.A., March 2, 1924
43. D.T., June 15, 1931
44. D.T., February 4, 1935
45. D.T., February 19, 1935
46. W.A., July 28, 1935
47. W.A., August 11, 1935
48. D.T., July 16, 1935
49. W.A., May 31, 1925
50. W.A., May 31, 1925
51. W.A., May 31, 1925

CHAPTER 4

Bankers

1. W.A., March 9, 1924
2. W.A., March 18, 1923
3. W.A., July 24, 1927
4. Squibbs radio talk, May 4, 1930
5. D.T., October 11, 1929

6. W.A., July 6, 1930
7. W.A., March 19, 1933
8. W.A., February 6, 1927
9. W.A., October 25, 1931
10. W.A., April 3, 1932
11. W.A., June 4, 1933
12. W.A., August 11, 1935

Taxes

13. W.A., December 28, 1924
14. W.A., May 19, 1929
15. D.T., February 12, 1932
16. W.A., July 8, 1923
17. W.A., October 19, 1924
18. W.A., November 25, 1934
19. D.T., February 29, 1932
20. W.A., November 11, 1928
21. D.T., February 5, 1935
22. W.A., January 10, 1926
23. W.A., August 9, 1925
24. W.A., November 2, 1924
25. D.T., March 20, 1932
26. D.T., March 15, 1929
27. D.T., March 23, 1932
28. W.A., February 28, 1926
29. W.A., January 6, 1924
30. W.A., April 12, 1925
31. *Letters,* 1926
32. *Letters,* 1926
33. Gulf radio talk, April 7, 1935
34. W.A., February 17, 1935
35. W.A., November 2, 1924
36. W.A., August 11, 1935

CHAPTER 5

Presidents in General

1. D.T., October 22, 1933
2. W.A., March 8, 1931
3. W.A., March 24, 1929
4. W.A., July 8, 1928
5. W.A., October 4, 1931
6. W.A., November 20, 1932
7. W.A., July 1, 1928
8. W.A., July 10, 1932
9. Conv. articles, Republican Convention, June 16, 1932
10. W.A., December 14, 1930
11. D.T., November 1, 1929
12. W.A., May 29, 1932
13. W.A., August 21, 1932
14. W.A., September 22, 1929
15. W.A., October 23, 1932
16. W.A., November 6, 1932

George Washington

17. W.A., April 28, 1929
18. W.A., December 23, 1928
19. W.A., February 13, 1927
20. Squibbs radio talk, June 1, 1930
21. W.A., February 10, 1929
22. W.A., September 22, 1929
23. W.A., February 10, 1929
24. W.A., October 19, 1924
25. W.A., May 19, 1929
26. W.A., March 16, 1930
27. W.A., February 24, 1929

Thomas Jefferson

28. W.A., September 29, 1929
29. W.A., May 23, 1928
30. W.A., February 13, 1927
31. W.A., March 8, 1925

Andrew Jackson

32. W.A., December 18, 1927
33. W.A., October 16, 1927
34. W.A., February 5, 1928
35. W.A., February 5, 1928
36. W.A., July 15, 1928
37. W.A., July 19, 1925

Abraham Lincoln

38. W.A., Demember 23, 1928
39. W.A., October 19, 1924
40. W.A., May 16, 1926
41. W.A., December 26, 1926
42. W.A., June 28, 1931
43. W.A., Febrary 26, 1933
44. W.A., July 6, 1924
45. W.A., February 22, 1925
46. Squibbs radio talk, June 1, 1930
47. D.T., February 12, 1934
48. W.A., June 10, 1923
49. W.A., May 31, 1927
50. W.A., February 26, 1933

Theodore Roosevelt

51. W.A., July 19, 1931
52. W.A., August 9, 1925

53. W.A., February 22, 1925
54. W.A., November 11, 1923

William Howard Taft

55. W.A., June 10, 1923
56. D.T., February 28, 1930

Calvin Coolidge

57. W.A., December 2, 1923
58. W.A., November 16, 1924
59. Conv. articles, Democratic Convention, July 4, 1924
60. W.A., December 31, 1922
61. W.A., September 12, 1926
62. W.A., August 7, 1927
63. W.A., March 3, 1928
64. W.A., February 17, 1929
65. W.A., March 24, 1929

Herbert Clark Hoover

66. Squibbs radio talk, April 20, 1930
67. W.A., February 12, 1928
68. D.T., August 9, 1929
69. W.A., March 24, 1929
70. W.A., December 14, 1930
71. Squibbs radio talk, April 20, 1930
72. W.A., May 31, 1931
73. W.A., November 27, 1932

Franklin Delano Roosevelt

74. W.A., May 22, 1932
75. D.T., January 25, 1933

76. D.T., March 6, 1933
77. D.T., March 31, 1933
78. D.T., March 13, 1933
79. D.T., May 8, 1933
80. D.T., May 23, 1934
81. D.T., June 21, 1934
82. D.T., November 27, 1934
83. D.T., April 2, 1935
84. D.T., April 1, 1935
85. D.T., March 18, 1935
86. D.T., April 28, 1935

CHAPTER 6

Education

1. W.A., August 31, 1924
2. *Letters,* 1926
3. W.A., July 31, 1931
4. W.A., July 5, 1931
5. W.A., September 2, 1934
6. W.A., May 11, 1930
7. W.A., July 5, 1931
8. W.A., August 26, 1928
9. W.A., February 21, 1932
10. D.T., September 4, 1931
11. W.A., January 6, 1929
12. W.A., April 25, 1926
13. W.A., June 25, 1933
14. D.T., April 22, 1935
15. D.T., June 25, 1935
16. D.T., May 9, 1935
17. W.A., September 29, 1929
18. D.T., June 3, 1935

19. W.A., September 11, 1932
20. Newspaper Clipping (a New York paper) of a radio broadcast, January 27, 1935
21. W.A., May 19, 1935
22. D.T., September 19, 1933
23. W.A., May 16, 1926
24. W.A., March 3, 1929
25. Squibbs radio talk, June 15, 1930
26. W.A., January 4, 1925
27. W.A., July 12, 1925
28. W.A., January 16, 1927
29. W.A., January 13, 1929
30. Squibbs radio talk, June 1, 1930
31. W.A., February 1, 1925
32. W.A., January 13, 1929
33. W.A., October 15, 1933
34. D.T., September 19, 1932
35. W.A., October 4, 1925
36. W.A., December 21, 1924
37. W.A., July 26, 1925
38. *Bathing Suit,* 1927
39. W.A., October 29, 1933
40. W.A., July 5, 1931
41. W.A., March 5, 1933

CHAPTER 7

Travel

1. D.T., May 7, 1927
2. W.A., April 3, 1927
3. W.A., January 17, 1926
4. Squibbs radio talk, June 1, 1930
5. W.A., September 7, 1930

6. W.A., November 1, 1925
7. W.A., May 18, 1924
8. D.T., March 12, 1934
9. D.T., July 28, 1935
10. D.T., July 16, 1934
11. D.A., October 25, 1931
12. W.A., July 24, 1932
13. W.A., January 14, 1923
14. W.A., January 18, 1925
15. W.A., September 11, 1932
16. Interview, *Birmingham Post,* November 4, 1925
17. D.T., June 27, 1935

Foreign Countries

18. W.A., July 25, 1926
19. *Letters,* 1926
20. W.A., September 13, 1925
21. W.A., August 28, 1932
22. *Letters,* 1926
23. W.A., July 24, 1927
24. *Letters,* 1926
25. W.A., June 2, 1929
26. W.A., July 11, 1926
27. W.A., December 19, 1930
28. W.A., August 16, 1925
29. W.A., January 12, 1930
30. *Bathing Suit*, 1927
31. W.A., February 9, 1930
32. Squibbs radio talk, April 6, 1930
33. W.A., November 8, 1931
34. W.A., September 20, 1931
35. W.A., December 28, 1930
36. W.A., November 30, 1930

37. D.T., October 16, 1930
38. W.A., December 28, 1930
39. *Bathing Suit*, 1927
40. W.A., June 30, 1935
41. Gulf radio talk, October 7, 1934
42. Gulf radio talk, October 14, 1934
43. Gulf radio talk, October 14, 1934
44. Gulf radio talk, October 14, 1934
45. Gulf radio talk, October 14, 1934
46. *Bathing Suit*, 1927
47. *Bathing Suit*, 1927
48. W.A., November 6, 1927
49. *Bathing Suit*, 1927
50. W.A., January 11, 1931

CHAPTER 8

Manners

1. W.A., August 31, 1924
2. W.A., July 19, 1925
3. W.A., February 25, 1923
4. W.A., July 27, 1924
5. *Letters*, 1926
6. W.A., December 16, 1923
7. W.A., September 9, 1923

Dress

8. W.A., February 25, 1923
9. W.A., November 23, 1924
10. D.T., February 3, 1935
11. D.T., April 22, 1935
12. W.A., May 9, 1926

13. W.A., January 2, 1927
14. W.A., January 26, 1930
15. W.A., May 18, 1924

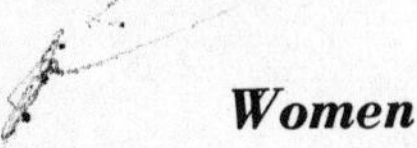

Women

16. W.A., July 27, 1924
17. W.A., February 7, 1926
18. W.A., April 3, 1927
19. D.T., April 2, 1934
20. W.A., June 9, 1935
21. W.A., May 20, 1934
22. W.A., September 20, 1925
23. W.A., April 18, 1926
24. W.A., November 1, 1925
25. W.A., July 8, 1928
26. W.A., March 31, 1929
27. Squibbs radio talk, May 11, 1930
28. W.A., October 24, 1926

Philosophy

29. W.A., June 1, 1930
30. W.A., August 17, 1924
31. W.A., March 9, 1924
32. W.A., July 15, 1923
33. D.T., March 10, 1935
34. W.A., January 1, 1928
35. W.A., November 21, 1926
36. W.A., July 29, 1928
37. Speech on Scribner, January 14, 1925
38. D.T., January 24, 1927
39. W.A., April 14, 1935
40. W.A., July 28, 1935

41. D.T., March 1, 1929
42. D.T., February 28, 1930
43. D.T., March 31, 1925
44. W.A., September 11, 1932
45. W.A., June 2, 1935
46. W.A., August 4, 1935
47. D.T., January 13, 1928
48. W.A., October 2, 1932
49. W.A., March 18, 1923
50. W.A., April 10, 1927

Civilization

51. W.A., November 18, 1923
52. W.A., January 5, 1930
53. W.A., March 16, 1930
54. W.A., July 5, 1931
55. W.A., September 4, 1932
56. D.T., April 2, 1933
57. W.A., July 7, 1935
58. W.A., January 20, 1935
59. W.A., January 20, 1935

Missionaries

60. D.T., March 22, 1932
61. W.A., February 6, 1927
62. W.A., November 8, 1924
63. W.A., April 10, 1927

The Bible

64. W.A., December 31, 1922
65. W.A., March 17, 1935

66. W.A., August 9, 1925
67. W.A., June 22, 1930
68. W.A., March 18, 1934

Death

69. W.A., January 30, 1927
70. W.A., October 25, 1931
71. D.T., March 7, 1933
72. W.A., July 12, 1925
73. W.A., August 9, 1925
74. W.A., August 9, 1925
75. W.A., May 24, 1925
76. D.T., July 7, 1930
77. Introduction to Charles M. Russell's *Trials Plowed Under*, 1926
78. Chapter XVI, *Our Will*, Scott Cunningham newspaper story, 1935
79. *Boston Globe*, June 16, 1930
80. W.A., June 30, 1935

Religion

81. W.A., June 10, 1934
82. W.A., January 8, 1933
83. W.A., January 15, 1928
84. W.A., September 8, 1929
85. W.A., January 20, 1924
86. W.A., May 24, 1925
87. W.A., April 7, 1935
88. W.A., January 20, 1924
89. W.A., July 19, 1925
90. *Bathing Suit*, 1927
91. *Bathing Suit*, 1927

92. W.A., January 15, 1928
93. W.A., May 11, 1930
94. W.A., January 20, 1924
95. W.A., September 11, 1932
96. W.A., January 8, 1933

CHAPTER 9

1. W.A., April 5, 1931
2. W.A., August 4, 1929
3. D.T., December 30, 1927
4. W.A., December 28, 1924
5. W.A., April 27, 1924
6. D.T., March 25, 1935
7. W.A., September 21, 1930
8. W.A., May 8, 1927
9. W.A., February 15, 1925
10. D.T., July 17, 1928
11. W.A., March 20, 1932
12. W.A., December 23, 1934
13. W.A., October 24, 1926
14. W.A., February 5, 1933
15. Squibbs radio talk, May 5, 1930
16. W.A., April 4, 1926
17. D.T., September 6, 1932
18. W.A., August 24, 1925
19. W.A., July 15, 1934
20. W.A., February 13, 1927
21. W.A., May 8, 1927
22. W.A., June 24, 1923
23. W.A., November 25, 1923
24. W.A., February 14, 1929
25. W.A., August 2, 1925